STYLE
CHECK
✔

STYLE
CHECK

✔ ✔ ✔ ✔ ✔

based on

The American Heritage® Dictionary

of the English Language,

Third Edition

Houghton Mifflin Company

Boston   New York

Library of Congress Cataloging-in-Publication Data

Style check : based on The American Heritage dictionary of the English language,
    third edition.
        p.   cm.
    ISBN 0-395-75692-8
    1. English language — Grammar — Handbooks, manuals, etc.   2. English
language — Usage — Handbooks, manuals, etc.   I. American Heritage
dictionary of the English language.
PE1112.S79   1996   96-56
808'.042 — dc20   CIP

Material cited and paraphrased from *THE AMERICAN LIBRARY ASSOCIATION
GUIDE TO INFORMATION ACCESS: A Complete Research Handbook and Directory* by
Sandra Whiteley. Copyright © 1994 by The American Library Association. Used by
permission of Random House, Inc.

For information about this and other Houghton Mifflin trade and reference books
and multimedia products, visit The Bookstore at Houghton Mifflin on the World
Wide Web at http://www.hmco.com/trade/.

Manufactured in the United States of America

BP   10   9   8   7   6   5   4   3   2   1

EDITORIAL AND PRODUCTION STAFF

Editorial Staff

Managing Editor
Marion Severynse

Senior Lexicographer
Joseph P. Pickett

Editor
Ann Marie Menting, *Project Director*

Assistant Editors
Beth Anderson
Susan S. Chicoski

Contributing Editor
Julia Penelope

Production Staff

Production and Manufacturing Manager
Christopher Leonesio

Production Supervisor
Elizabeth Rubè

Senior Art & Production Coordinator
Margaret Anne Miles

Keyboarding
Jane Ellin

Text Design
Melodie Wertelet

CONTENTS

Basic Rules of Standard English Grammar

Sentences

INTRODUCTION

Style Check represents the best current advice on writing clearly. Its concise format and accessible content present the skills necessary for using language effectively in the areas of grammar, usage, research, and composition.

The first part of *Style Check*, "A Guide to Style," analyzes the overall structural aspects of writing. This section provides you with the basic tools for using and styling English correctly. It includes a "Usage Guide" based on the recommendations of *The American Heritage Dictionary*'s celebrated Usage Panel; rules for writing numbers and dividing words; a list of commonly used prepositions; the basic rules of standard English grammar and sentence structure; and a discussion of sentence functions and the ways to correctly construct sentences to make your written material clear and effective.

"A Guide to Writing," the second section of *Style Check*, provides samples of writing used in schools and offices, including résumés, business letters, and reports. This section also explains how to plan, research, write, and index a research paper, as well as how to document sources. Electronic research tools are also discussed. *Style Check* includes both the traditional method of footnoting sources and the newer method of parenthetical documentation within the text. The section concludes with an expanded and updated guide to basic reference works.

Style Check is intended to be a reference work for all who wish to develop the ability to write effectively and to express themselves clearly.

A GUIDE TO
STYLE

✔

PUNCTUATION

Proper punctuation not only makes the structure of your document clear but also guides your reader through the document so that its meaning can be easily and thoroughly understood. Although much of today's writing uses a minimum of punctuation, clarity is often sacrificed when such a minimalist style is adopted. The following rules present a slightly fuller style that is appropriate for most documents.

Apostrophe

Indicates the possessive case of nouns, proper nouns, and indefinite pronouns:

> her friend's car someone's bright idea
> the children's school one's own office
> Sharon Olds's *The Father* the campers' backpacks

Indicates the possessive case of nouns considered as a single unit, especially when possession is shared:

> her sister and brother's store
> Sally and Ted's trip to the museum

> But when possession is separate, each noun takes a possessive form:

> Tom's, Jim's, and Mary's homes
> women's and children's coats

Indicates the plurals of figures, letters, or words used such as:

> 42's and 53's *x*'s, *y*'s, and *z*'s
> in the 1990's an article with too many
> *however*'s

Indicates the omission of letters in contractions:

> isn't   that's
> couldn't   o'clock

Indicates the omission of figures:

> the class of '97   the fiscal year '95-'96

Brackets

Enclose words or passages in quotations to indicate the insertion of material written by someone other than the original writer:

> That's one small step for [a] man, one giant leap for mankind.

> And summer's lease [allotted time] hath all too short a date [duration]; . . .

Enclose material inserted within matter already in parentheses:

> (Washington [D.C.], January 1989)
> (Centers for Disease Control and Prevention [CDC], Atlanta, GA)

Colon

Introduces words, phrases, or clauses that explain, amplify, exemplify, or summarize what has preceded:

> Finally I remembered his name: Samuel.

> The neighborhood was confusing: there were too many one-way streets.

> The lasting influence of Greece's dramatic tradition is indicated by words still in our vocabulary: *chorus, comedy,* and *drama.*

> She has three sources of income: stock dividends, interest from savings accounts, and salary.

Introduces a long quotation:

> In his Gettysburg Address, Lincoln said: "Four score and seven years ago our fathers brought forth on this continent, a new nation, conceived in Liberty, and dedicated to the proposition that all men are created equal. . . ."

Introduces lists:

> Among the conjunctive adverbs are the following: *so, therefore, hence, however, nevertheless, moreover, accordingly,* and *besides.*

> His purchases at the grocery store were to include: coffee, bread, milk, and apples.

Separates chapter and verse number in references to biblical quotations:

> Esther 2:17   Romans 12:6

Separates hour and minute in time designations:

> 1:30 P.M.   a 9:15 class

Follows the salutation in a formal letter:

> Dear Sir or Madam: Members of the Board:

Comma

Separates the clauses of a compound sentence connected by a coordinating conjunction:

> It takes five hours to get to the island, but it is a trip worth taking.

> He didn't know where she got such an idea, but he didn't disagree.

The comma may be omitted in short compound sentences in which the connection between clauses is close:

> She understood the situation and she was furious.
> He got in the car and he drove and drove.

Separates *and* or *or* from the final item in a series of three or more:

> Lights of red, green, and blue wavelengths may be mixed to produce all colors.

> The VCR, television set, and compact disks were arranged on one shelf.

> Would you rather have ice cream, cake, or pie for dessert?

Separates two or more adjectives modifying the same noun if *and* could be used between them without changing the meaning:

>   a short, fast-paced run   a funny, quirky, modern movie

>   Do not add a comma if it would change the meaning:

>   a polished oak desk

Sets off a nonrestrictive clause or phrase (one that if eliminated would not change the meaning of the sentence):

>   The tourists, who had arrived early, filled every seat on the bus.

>   The comma should not be used when the clause or phrase is restrictive (essential to the meaning of the sentence):

>   The tourists who had arrived early filled every seat on the shuttle bus. The latecomers had to stand.

Sets off words or phrases in apposition to a noun or noun phrase:

>   Plato, the famous Greek philosopher, was a pupil of Socrates.

>   The director of *Schindler's List*, Steven Spielberg, won an Academy Award.

>   The novel by Ralph Ellison, *Invisible Man*, was required reading.

>   The comma should not be used if such words or phrases further specify the noun that precedes:

>   The Greek philosopher Plato was a pupil of Socrates.
>   The director Steven Spielberg won an Academy Award.
>   The Ellison novel *Invisible Man* was required reading.

Sets off transitional words and short expressions that require a pause in reading:

>   Unfortunately, the concert was rained out.
>   Did he, after all, accept the job offer?
>   Laura will meet us there, of course.
>   Indeed, I was surprised to see them.

Sets off words used to introduce a sentence:

> No, I haven't seen *Hoop Dreams*.
> Well, why don't you go with us?

Sets off a subordinate clause or a long phrase that precedes the principal clause:

> By the time they finally found the restaurant, they were too tired to be hungry.
>
> After the play ended, the actors were given a standing ovation.
>
> Of all the photographs in the magazine, the most striking were those of Mount Saint Helens.

Sets off short quotations, sayings, and the like:

> Jo told him, "Come tomorrow for dinner."
> The candidate said, "Actions speak louder than words."
> "I don't know if I can," he said, "but I'll try."

Indicates the omission of a word or words:

> To err is human; to forgive, divine.
> Wrong seems right, and right, wrong.

Sets off the year from the day of the month in dates:

> On April 12, 1981, the first U.S. space shuttle was launched.
> Louis XVI of France was guillotined on January 21, 1793.

Sets off the state from the city in geographical names:

> Boston, Massachusetts, is the largest city in New England.
>
> The university in Madison, Wisconsin, is home to many world-renowned researchers.

Separates series of four or more figures into thousands, millions, and so forth:

> 57,395   12,364,903

The comma is not used in years or page numbers:

> the year 1776   page 1617

Sets off words used in direct address:

> Mr. Wadsworth, please submit your report as soon as possible.
> Thank you, Emma, for your help.
> The forum is open to questions, ladies and gentlemen.

Separates a phrase that transforms a statement into a question:

> You did say you had the tickets, didn't you?
> Beethoven's *Eroica* is on the program, isn't it?

Sets off any sentence elements that might be misread if a comma were not used:

> Some time after, the actual date was set.
> To Mary, Anne was just a nuisance.
> Whenever possible, friends provide moral support.

Follows the salutation and complimentary close of informal letters and the complimentary close of formal letters:

> Dear Ken,   Sincerely,

Dash

Indicates a sudden break or abrupt change in continuity:

> Well, you see — I — I've — I'm just not sure.
> He seemed very upset about — I never knew what.
> And then the problem — if it is a problem — can be solved.

Sets apart an explanatory or defining phrase:

> Dairy products — milk, cheese, yogurt — are a good source of calcium.
>
> He suddenly realized what he had forgotten — his overcoat.

Sets apart material that is parenthetical in nature:

> He stares soulfully heavenward — to the great delight of the audience — while he plays Chopin.
>
> Allen — who had a lean face, a long nose, and cold blue eyes — was a stern, authoritarian man.

Marks an unfinished sentence:

> Well, then, I'll simply tell her that —
> "But if the plane is late —" he began.

Sets off a summarizing clause:

> Tuesday, Thursday, and Saturday — these are the days I go to the gym.
>
> The real measure of employee satisfaction is intangible — it can't be calculated in dollars and cents.

Sets off the name of an author or a source, as at the end of a quotation:

> There never was a good war or a bad peace.
>> — *Benjamin Franklin*

Ellipses

Indicate the omission of words or sentences in quoted material:

> This ended the trial . . . and the defendant was free to go.
>
> Because the treaty has not been approved by the Senate . . . it is not embodied in law.

Indicate a pause in speech or an unfinished sentence:

> "Yes . . . I mean . . . what . . ." she stammered.
> I thought I had better not . . .

Indicate the omission of a line or lines of poetry:

> I do not know which to prefer,
> . . . .
> The blackbird whistling
> Or just after.
>> — *Wallace Stevens*

Exclamation point

Indicates a command, an expression of strong emotion, or an emphatic phrase or sentence:

Be quiet!	What a game!
Go home immediately!	You can't be serious!

Indicates an emphatic interjection:

Great!	Ugh!	Bravo!

Hyphen

Joins the elements of some compounds:

great-grandfather   ne'er-do-well
cure-all

Joins the elements of compound modifiers preceding a noun:

a well-traveled road   ten fifth-grade students
built-in bookcases   a two-thirds share
a four-hour seminar

Indicates that two or more compounds share a single base:

three- and four-volume sets   six- and seven-year-olds

Separates the prefix and root in some combinations:

anti-Semite, pro-American (prefix + proper noun or adjective)

re-form, reform; re-creation, recreation (to distinguish between
   similar words of different meanings)

Substitutes for the word *to* between two figures or words:

pages 6-20   the Milwaukee-Cleveland
the years 1920-29   shuttle

At the end of a line, indicates that part of a word of more than
one syllable has been carried over to another line:

The library charges a small fine for over-
due books.

Parentheses

Enclose material that is not an essential part of the sentence
(material that if eliminated would not change the meaning of
the sentence):

> In an hour's time (some say less) the firemen had extinguished the flames.

> It was a dream (although a hazy one) of an ideal state, one in which poverty did not exist.

> Marion doesn't feel (and why should she?) that she should pay a higher rent.

Often enclose letters or numerals to indicate subdivisions of a series:

> Some of the letter styles most often used in business correspondence are (1) the full-block letter, (2) the modified-block letter, and (3) the simplified letter.

Period

Indicates the end of a complete declarative or mild imperative sentence:

> The style of the uniform dates back to the turn of the century.
> Come home when you can.

Follows the abbreviation of a word or words:

Jan.	Ave.	Mr.
pp.	Ms.	Co.
Rev.	Ph.D.	

Question mark

Indicates the end of a direct question:

> What kind of work would you like to do?
> Who was that odd-looking stranger?

> But:

> I wonder who said "Speak softly and carry a big stick."
> He asked when Harold would leave.

Indicates uncertainty:

> Ferdinand Magellan (1480?–1521)
> OK?

Quotation marks

Enclose direct quotations that are whole or partial, such as those used in paraphrasing :

> "Are there any questions?" the speaker asked.
>
> "I think," the tour guide announced, "we will soon arrive at the museum."
>
> Will Rogers said: "Things in our country run in spite of government. Not by aid of it."
>
> According to one commentator, the pitcher's fastball was "overpowering."

Enclose words or phrases to clarify their meaning or to indicate that they are being used in a special way:

> "Ms." is a title many women prefer to "Miss" or "Mrs."
>
> By "faster" I didn't mean 90 miles per hour!
>
> "The Big Apple," a name for New York City, is a phrase that originated with jazz musicians.
>
> Supervisors are urged to "prioritize" their responsibilities.

Set off the translation of a foreign word or phrase:

> de facto, "in fact or reality"   déjà vu, "already seen"
> la dolce vita, "the sweet life"

Set off the titles of series of books; of articles; of chapters in publications; of essays; of short poems; of individual radio and television programs; of songs and short musical pieces:

> "The Peterson Field Guide Series"
> "Some Notes on Case Grammar in English"
> Chapter 2, "Romancing the Shadow"
> Frank O'Hara's "Ode on Causality"
> "65th Academy Awards"
> Mary-Chapin Carpenter's "Down at the Twist and Shout"

Single quotation marks. Enclose quoted material within a quotation:

> "To me, the only word for this weather is 'perfect,'" Hunter declared. "I don't understand your discomfort."

Use with other punctuation marks. Put commas and periods inside closing quotation marks; put semicolons and colons outside. Other punctuation, such as question marks and exclamation points, should be put inside the closing quotation marks only when it is actually part of the material being quoted.

Semicolon

Separates the clauses of a compound sentence not connected by a coordinating conjunction:

> The questions are provided by the analyst; the answers come from the data.

> Many industries were paralyzed by the strike; factory owners left the district, taking their money with them.

Separates the clauses of a compound sentence in which the clauses contain internal punctuation, even when the clauses are joined by a conjunction:

> Picnic baskets in hand, we walked to the beach, chose a sunny spot, and spread out the blankets; and the rest of the group followed us in a jeep.

Separates elements of a series in which items already contain commas:

> Among the guests were Katherine Ericson; her daughter, Alice; Henry Faulkner, formerly of the Redding Institute; and two couples whom I could not identify.

Separates the clauses of a compound sentence joined by a conjunctive adverb, such as *nonetheless, therefore,* and *hence:*

> Downtown was in ruins after the hurricane; indeed, it looked as if it had been bombed.

> We demanded a refund; otherwise we would get in touch with the Better Business Bureau.

Virgule

Separates the numerator of a fraction from the denominator:

c/d   1/2

Represents the word *per:*

miles/hour   ml/kg

Means "or" between the words *and* and *or:*

articles of linguistic and/or sociological importance
Take skates and/or skis.

Separates two or more lines of poetry quoted in text:

Some students laughed when he read the lines "I am tired of words /
and literature is an old couch stuffed with fleas."

CAPITALIZATION

The tendency in contemporary writing is to use fewer capital letters. In all written works, though, it is most important to establish a logical style for capitalization and to be consistent in applying that style. The following guidelines will help you apply a system of capitalization that is appropriate for most documents. Capitalize

The first word of a sentence:

> Some diseases are acute; others are chronic.
> Are you the next person in line?
> Great! Let's go!

The first word of a direct quotation unless it is closely woven into the sentence or is the first word of a split quotation:

> Helen asked, "Do you think the meeting was useful?"
>
> "No," I responded, "we left the important questions unanswered."
>
> Do you agree with G.B. Shaw that "assassination is the extreme form of censorship"?

The first word of the salutation and of the complimentary close of a letter:

> My dear Katherine,   Best wishes,
> Sincerely yours,   Dear Mr. Atkins:

All words except articles, prepositions, and conjunctions in the titles of works such as books, poems, articles, plays, movies, serial radio and television programs, and musical compositions:

> *Waiting to Exhale*
> "A Good Man Is Hard to Find"

"The Finiteness of Natural Language"
Cat on a Hot Tin Roof
From Here to Eternity
Picket Fences
Appalachian Spring

Proper nouns and adjectives:

Martina Navratilova	China, Chinese
Jesse Jackson	Bohemia, Bohemian
Helen Mirren	Morocco, Moroccan
Albert Einstein	Hegel, Hegelian

But do not capitalize words derived from proper nouns and adjectives and having distinct special meanings:

china plates	roman type
a bohemian lifestyle	plaster of paris
moroccan leather	french fries

The standard names of geographic divisions, districts, regions, and localities:

Arctic Circle	Gulf Coast
Western Hemisphere	the North
South Pole	the West
Middle East	the Midwest
Continental Divide	Great Plains
Mountain States	

But do not capitalize words designating points of the compass unless they refer to specific regions:

Holyoke, Massachusetts, is eight miles north of Springfield.

We traveled south for ten miles before finding a route that went west.

The popular names of districts, regions, and localities:

Bible Belt	East End
Windy City	Bay Area
Lake District	Upper West Side

The names of rivers, lakes, mountains, oceans, and other topo-
graphical features:

Rio Grande	Pacific Ocean
Cascade Mountains	Mount Shasta
Lake Erie	Long Island Sound

Names for a deity, for sacred designations, and for sacred books:

God	the Messiah
the Almighty	the Bible
Allah	the Koran
Jehovah	the Talmud
the Buddha	

The names of religious denominations:

Catholicism	the Orthodox Church
Judaism	Islam
Protestantism	Society of Friends
Buddhism	the Church of Jesus Christ of
the Roman Catholic Church	Latter-day Saints

The names of periods, events, and documents of historical significance:

Middle Ages	Battle of Shiloh
Reformation	Declaration of Independence
Civil War	Magna Carta
World War II	Constitution

The names of entities, divisions, and parties associated with
politics:

Byzantine Empire	Democratic Party
Holy Roman Empire	Republican Party
French Republic	Social Democrats
Green Party	

The names of legislative and judical bodies:

Congress	United States Supreme Court
United Nations	Parliament

| the U.S. Senate | Diet |
| the U.S. House of Representatives | Knesset |

The names of departments, bureaus, and other administrative divisions of the federal government:

the Department of Agriculture
the United States Geological Survey
State Department
Central Intelligence Agency
the Department of Health and Human Services

The names of treaties, acts, laws, and similar agreements:

the Treaty of Versailles	Americans with Disabilities Act
Sherman Antitrust Law	Medicare
Fourteenth Amendment	

Titles — such as civil, military, noble, and honorary — when they precede a name:

Justice Ginsburg	Queen Elizabeth II
General Powell	Pope John XXIII
Mayor White	Professor Kittredge

But all references to the President and Vice President of the United States should be capitalized:

| President Carter | the President |
| Vice President Gore | the Vice President |

Epithets used as a substitute for a name:

| Eric the Red | the Great Emancipator |
| Ivan the Terrible | the Iron Chancellor |

The names of groups of people, such as nationalities, races, and religious groups:

Irish	Hispanic
Asian-American	Muslim
Maori	

The names of languages and of periods in the history of languages:

German   English
Old High German   Middle English

The names of eras, periods, and other geological terms:

the Paleozoic Era   the Bronze Age
the Precambrian Period   the early Pliocene

The names of constellations, planets, and stars:

the Milky Way   Mars
the Southern Cross   Venus
Jupiter   Polaris

Genus — but not species — names in binomial nomenclature:

Chrysanthemum leucanthemum   *Rana pipiens*
Macaca mulatta   *Canis familiaris*

The names of holidays, holy days, months of the year, and days of the month:

Independence Day   Passover   Thanksgiving
Labor Day   Ramadan   Christmas
January   Monday

Personifications:

Marvelous Truth, confront us
at every turn,
in every guise.
— *Denise Levertov*

Trademarks:

Prozac   Xerox   Kleenex
Grammy   Polaroid   Coca-Cola

The names of buildings, streets, parks, organizations, and similar civic entities:

the State House   Benefit Street Route 91
Golden Gate Park   Dulles Airport the Girl Scouts

ITALICS

Italics distinguish letters, words, or groups of words from the rest of a sentence. Use italics to

Indicate titles of books, plays, and poems of book length:

> *The Joy Luck Club*   *Spring and All*
> *The Piano Lesson*

Indicate words, letters, or numbers used as such:

> The word *buzz* is onomatopoeic; that is, it sounds like what it stands for.
>
> *Can't* often means *won't*.
>
> She formed her *n*'s like *u*'s.
>
> A *6* looks like an inverted *9*.

Emphasize a word or phrase. This device should be used sparingly:

> I *never* should have let you talk me into whitewater rafting.
> We're *exceedingly* upset over the outcome of the election.

Indicate foreign words and phrases that have not been assimilated into English:

> *C'est la vie* was the response to my complaint.
> Abu Ammar is Yasser Arafat's *nom de guerre*.

Indicate names of the plaintiff and defendant in legal citations:

> *Marbury* v. *Madison*
> *Brown* v. *Board of Education of Topeka*

Indicate titles of long musical compositions:

> *The Messiah*   Bartok's *Concerto for Orchestra*
> *Porgy and Bess*   Ellington's *The New Orleans Suite*

Indicate titles of magazines and newspapers:

Gourmet magazine   the New York *Daily News*
Atlantic Monthly magazine   *New York Times*

Set off titles of motion pictures and television series:

The Silence of the Lambs   *Murphy Brown*
Straight out of Brooklyn   *Masterpiece Theater*

Distinguish names of genera and species in scientific names:

Homo sapiens   *Sciurus carolinensis*

Set off names of ships, planes, trains, and spacecraft:

Queen Elizabeth II   *The Wolverine*
The Spirit of St. Louis   *Viking I*

Set off names of paintings and sculpture:

Mona Lisa   *Pietà*
Thinker   *Starry Night*

WORD DIVISION

The rules that follow are intended as a guide to traditional practice in word division. The general principles stated here reflect conservative practices followed by printers and publishers and not the comprehensive syllabication indicated in *The American Heritage® Dictionary of the English Language, Third Edition* or *Word Check*, which reflects the phonetic structure of the word. The word breaks indicated here, however, will always coincide with one or more syllable divisions as shown in these books, so if you are in doubt about the syllabication of a word, do consult your dictionary. It will provide you syllabication points for words having more than one syllable. The rules that follow will help you choose which word breaks, among those permissible, you should use.

Never divide a word of one syllable:

breadth	point	horde
mashed	cough	types

Never divide words beginning or ending with a single-letter syllable in a manner that would isolate the single-letter syllable:

ane-mia (not a-nemia or anemi-a)
uto-pia (not u-topia or utopi-a)

Words like *area, Ohio, ego,* and *ogre* should not be divided at all, because no matter how the word is divided there will be a single vowel either at the end of a line or the beginning of the next line.

Never divide a word after an internal single-syllable vowel:

visi-tation (not vis-itation)   oxy-gen (not ox-ygen)
maxi-mum (not max-imum)

This rule does not usually apply to words with the suffixes *–able* and *–ible*. In such words the division is before the lead vowel of the suffix, not after it.

account-able   collaps-ible
answer-able   divis-ible
prob-able

However, there are many words ending in *–able* and *–ible* where the *a* and *i* do not stand alone as a single syllable. They are divided after the vowel:

ca-pa-ble   char-i-ta-ble
hor-ri-ble   in-el-i-gi-ble

Divide between doubled consonants when the doubling occurs to the final consonant, usually when adding a suffix to produce an inflected form:

red-der   dim-mer
control-ling   bar-ring
thin-nest   regret-ted

If the root word ends in a double or single consonant, division is after the consonants or consonant:

fall-en   coerc-ing
confess-ing   confid-ing

When there are double interior consonants the division is between them:

foun-tain   hin-drance
ter-res-trial   con-fes-sion
recom-mend   bat-tlement
expres-sive, but express-way

When *–ing, –ed,* or *–er* are added to a verb ending in *–le*, the division comes before one or more of the consonants, as in the preceding rule:

| gig-gled | whis-tler | fiz-zling |
| daw-dled | crum-bling | |

Divide hyphenated words at the hyphen:

all-fired	window-dressing
self-control	public-spirited
strait-laced	wash-and-wear (divide at either
make-believe	hyphen)
ready-made	

Compound words, if possible, are divided between their elements:

| steel-worker | under-cover | wing-span |
| barn-yard | over-estimate | hail-fellow |

Many words are made up of a prefix plus a base word. Division is usually after the whole prefix:

| anti-body | micro-scope |
| bi-annual | sub-way |

Never divide abbreviations or acronyms:

UNESCO	D.A.R.	D.D.S.
WAVES	FAA	NATO
OCS	OSHA	

Never divide numbers having fewer than five digits. If a number has five or more digits, divide after a comma:

346,-422,898 or 346,422,-898   10,-000

In business and legal documents, numbers should never be divided.

Never divide dates between the month and the day. Instead divide dates between the day and year.

| August 26, | *not* August |
| 1920 | 26, 1920 |

In business and legal documents, dates should never be divided.

Divide proper nouns according to the rules for division of common nouns. In business and legal documents, however, the division of proper nouns should not be necessary and well might result in confusion or error.

Divide a proper name formed of initials and a last name after the initials:

T. S.	e. e.
Eliot	cummings
not T.	*not* e.
S. Eliot	e. cummings

Try to avoid separating a name from a title:

John Martin, M.D.	Ms. Jones
not John Martin,	*not* Ms.
M.D.	Jones

In business and legal documents, these should not be divided.

Avoid dividing contractions whenever possible. If it is necessary to divide a contraction, it should be done according to the syllabication:

| should-n't | have-n't | Hallow-e'en |

If contractions must be used in business or legal documents, they should never be divided.

Never divide years, time, temperatures, latitudes, longitudes, compass directions, and similar units:

| A.D. 19 | NNW | 4:30 p.m. |
| 28°C | 40°28' | |

NUMBERS

When should a number be spelled out and when should it be written in figures? In cases in which the following rules do not apply, the choice is determined by the kind of document you are writing; numbers are customarily written out in formal writing and figures employed in informal writing and business writing. As with many areas covered in this book, consistency of style is paramount. Whatever method you use, stick with it throughout.

Numbers from one to ten are spelled out, and numbers over ten are written in figures:

> There are five candidates running for the council seat in this ward.
>
> We received 17 letters inquiring about the job.

Indefinite and round numbers are spelled out:

> The college president received dozens of angry calls denouncing the faculty layoffs.
>
> They drove five hundred miles yesterday and plan to drive six hundred today.
>
> Management and staff agreed to a sixty-forty split of the profits.

Definite amounts and long numbers are written in figures:

> They paid $83,000 for the house.
> She won the election by 759,323 votes.
> The pistachio nuts are $12.95 a pound.

Numbers in the millions and above, however, are written in either figures or words and followed by *million* or *billion*:

The population of the island nation is nearly 47 million.

The house and stables cost four and a half million dollars to build.

The budget included a proposal for a three-billion dollar space-craft.

Two or more related numbers in the same sentence should be expressed in the same style; if one of the numbers is greater than ten, all should be expressed in figures:

Today he typed 4 reports, 11 memos, and 7 letters.

There were 25 players trying out for 10 spots on the team.

Spell out numbers at the beginning of a sentence:

Three shipments arrived today.

Seventy-five percent of the inventory was damaged by the flood-waters.

If this produces too great an inconsistency within the sentence or produces too unwieldly a sentence, you can either break the related numbers rule or rewrite the sentence so that the number does not come first:

Five people applied for the 12 positions.

We received 5 applications for the 12 positions.

Forty-five hundred acres were planted in corn.

Corn was planted in 4,500 acres.

Unrelated numbers in the same sentence should be distinguished for clarity. Figures and words can be used to differentiate them:

In three days, we sold 24 cars, 6 campers, and 11 trucks.

State records for the second quarter indicate 0.7 inches of rainfall, 25 sunny days, and temperatures ranging from 45-98°F.

Unrelated numbers should not be placed next to each other when written as figures. You can spell out one of the numbers, use a comma to separate them, or rewrite the sentence:

The show consisted of 3 one-act plays.
There are 35 twenty-nine-cent stamps left on this roll.
In 1982, sixteen incumbent senators were defeated.
There were 16 incumbent senators defeated in 1982.

Specific amounts of money are written in figures. The dollar sign is placed before the figure, and the decimal point and zeroes are usually omitted for even dollar amounts:

$10.90	$357,928
$35	$5 a pair

Remember that indefinite numbers are spelled out; it is only in such cases that *dollar(s)* is used after the number (rather than the dollar sign before):

He spent about twenty dollars at the market.
It is estimated to be a forty- to fifty-dollar repair job.

Sums under a dollar are usually expressed in figures, but they may be spelled out in formal writing:

35 cents   thirty-five cents

Remember, however, that consistency would demand:

One item cost $1.25 and the other is $.69.

In legal documents, sums are given in both words and figures:

The collection of baseball cards has been appraised at five hundred dollars ($500).

The necklace was appraised at two million dollars ($2 million).

Fractions standing alone are spelled out. If they are used as adjectives they must be hyphenated; if they are used as nouns, they are not hyphenated:

The court awarded them a two-thirds share of the profits earned in the past 20 years.

She bought one third of a pound of basmati rice.

Fractions in mixed numbers are expressed in figures; a space separates the whole number from the fraction, and a diagonal line separates the parts of the fraction:

3 1/2   20 7/8   9 2/3

When writing dates in which the day precedes the month, the date should be expressed in spelled-out ordinal numbers:

I met with her on the sixth of May.
We will see them again on the twelfth of July.

When the date follows the month, figures are used:

They are arriving on August 21.
She was born on January 14, 1950.

In formal writing, numbers applying to years, decades, and centuries are spelled out:

Nineteen hundred and eighty-three was a banner year for the team.

He often reminisced about what it was like growing up in the sixties.

Putting an astronaut on the Moon before the end of the twentieth century was a goal of the Kennedy administration.

In informal writing, figures are often used. If the date is abbreviated, an apostrophe is used to show the part that has been left out:

Jimmy Carter was elected President in 1976.

The popularity of this novel remains as strong today as when it was first published in the 1920s.

I haven't seen him since '73.

Street names above ten are expressed in ordinal figures (in this case two numbers can be placed next to one another):

My address is 60 31st Street.

You only need to use *st, nd, rd,* or *th* if a numbered street is not preceded by either East or West:

Her office is at 105 West 12 Street.

In formal writing, the time of day is spelled out and, if a whole hour, is used with *o'clock:*

> Orders will be taken beginning at ten o'clock.
> She arrived at the theatre at quarter to eight.

For exact time, figures are used with A.M. and P.M. and occasionally with *o'clock.* Whole hours include zeroes:

> The wedding reception will be held from 11:00 A.M. to 2:30 P.M.
> Business hours are from 9:30 A.M. to 5:00 P.M.

Figures are used to express exact dimensions, sizes, measurements, and temperatures:

> The painting measures 2 by 4 feet.

> (In technical writing, *x* is used to indicate *by* and " and '
> to indicate *inches* and *feet* respectively.)

> A mile equals 1,760 yards or 5,280 feet.
> At birth the baby weighed 6 pounds 7 ounces.
> The high today was 82°F.

Percentages in text are expressed in figures and are most often followed by the word *percent:*

> All plan members received a 10 percent discount.

Numbers that appear with abbreviations or symbols are written as figures regardless of the size of the number:

> 3%   32°F   5 mm

BASIC RULES OF STANDARD ENGLISH GRAMMAR

Grammar is a system of basic rules by which the words in a language are structured and arranged in sentences. It is a system that can be a challenge to understand, in part because the term itself can be used in more than one way.

At its most fundamental, grammar refers to the system of rules that allows speakers of a language to create sentences. Its rules govern word order, the formation of words, and the use of inflections, such as *–s* to make plurals or *–ed* to form the past tense. This type of grammar is unconsciously learned by nearly every child who has heard a particular language spoken since birth.

Grammar is also used to refer to a set of rules that establish a standard for usage and govern what is sometimes called "good" or "correct" grammar, especially in written communication. This kind of grammar must be consciously taught, even to native speakers of a language, and can be hard to remember. The following section deals with the often difficult-to-remember rules that are included in the grammar of the English language.

Parts of Speech

Traditionally, words are classified by the ways in which they function in a sentence. These classifications are called *parts of speech*. Knowing what parts of speech do will help you understand how words are used in sentences. This in turn will help you to avoid making mistakes in sentence construction. The parts of speech that are described here are the noun, pronoun, verb, adjective, adverb, preposition, and conjunction.

Nouns

A *noun* is a word that names a person (*Joe, editor*), place (*Dallas, town*), thing (*book*), or abstraction (*faithfulness*). Nouns can be either *proper* or *common*. Proper nouns name specific persons, places, or things (*Joe, Dallas, Internet*) and are usually capitalized. Common nouns are sometimes classified as *abstract nouns* that name ideas, beliefs, or qualities (*freedom, biology, capitalism*) or *concrete nouns* that name tangible things (*chair, computer*).

A noun can function in a sentence in a number of ways. It can serve as the *subject* of a sentence or a clause:

> The *children* are playing outside.

It can function as the *direct object* of a verb:

> The teacher watched the *children*.

It can be the *object* of a preposition:

> The photographer took a picture of the *children*.

It can serve as the *indirect object* of a verb:

> We gave the *children* a new ball.

As these examples show, the form of the noun is the same regardless of its function.

Most nouns form their plurals by adding *–s*, or in some cases, *–es*, to the singular form (*frogs, potatoes, telephones*). These are called *regular plurals*. Other nouns have *irregular plurals*, indicated by a change in the base form or vowel (*mouse, mice*). A few words, such as *ox* and *child*, have plurals that end in *–en* (*oxen, children*). Some nouns have more than one acceptable plural form (*phenomena, phenomenons*) while others undergo no change to indicate number (*deer, sheep*). Finally, certain nouns may be used as both singular and plural nouns (*physics, politics*), depending on what meaning is intended.

Regardless of whether the plural is regular or irregular, though, a plural noun takes the plural form of a verb:

> The boys hit the girls.
> The oxen pull the wagon.
> The phenomena have yet to be explained.

Collective nouns are nouns that refer to a collection of persons or things that is regarded as a unit (*committee, jury, flock, congress*). Such a noun takes a singular verb when it refers to the collection as a whole and a plural verb when it refers to the members of the collection as separate persons or things:

> The *committee was* in executive session.
> The *committee have* all left for the day.
> The *jury* is sequestered in the hotel.

Pronouns that refer to collective nouns used must agree in number with the noun:

> The *company is* determined to press *its* [not *their*] claim.
> The *jury* are fighting about their verdict.

Possessive forms of a noun are generally formed by adding *'s* to the singular and an apostrophe (*'*) to plural nouns that end in *s*.

> The *dog's* toys were strewn about the yard.
> The *lady's* clothes are packed in this suitcase.
> The *man's* suit is made of wool flannel.

If the plural is irregular and does not end in *s*, then *'s* is added to the plural form:

> The *dogs'* toys were strewn about the yard.
> The *ladies'* clothes are packed in these suitcases.
> The *men's* suits are made of wool flannel.

The same possessive forms are used when the possessives are in the predicate:

> These are the *dog's*.   These are the *dogs'*.

Pronouns

A *pronoun* is a word that functions as a substitute for a noun. A pronoun refers to a person or thing that has been named or understood in a particular context. There are several kinds of pronouns, and one pronoun may serve a variety of functions.

Personal pronouns have different forms for first, second, and third person. *I* and *we* are first-person pronouns, *you* is the second-person pronoun, and *he, she, it, we,* and *they* are third-person pronouns:

> *We* will produce the program, and *they* will distribute it.
> *I* am glad that *she* was willing to help.

Relative pronouns introduce a dependent clause. The pronouns *who, that,* and *which* are relative pronouns. *Who* is used with persons; *that* is used with persons, animals, or inanimate objects; and *which* is used with animals or inanimate objects:

> She is a leader *who* is destined for greatness.
> The house *that* has green shutters is for sale.
> The new restaurant, *which* opened yesterday, features Italian food.

Interrogative pronouns are pronouns, such as *who, which,* and *what,* that introduce a direct question:

> *What* do you want us to do?
> *Which* of these sweaters are you going to wear?

Demonstrative pronouns, such as *this, that, these,* and *those,* refer to specific persons or things:

> *That* is the latest policy directive.
> *This* is the best book I have read in years.

Indefinite pronouns refer to persons and things that are not specified or identified. Some examples are *all, any, anybody, anyone, anything, each, either, everybody, everything, few, neither, nobody, none, one, several,* and *some:*

> *Anybody* with any luck can win at this game.

We brought *everything* except the silverware.
Some will no doubt drop out at the last minute.

Reflexive pronouns end in *–self* or *–selves* and are used as the direct or indirect object of a verb or as the object of a preposition:

He bought *himself* a new computer.
We treated *ourselves* to an ice cream.

Reflexive pronouns usually refer to the subject of the sentence. They can also be used as an appositive to a noun or pronoun for emphasis:

I *myself* prefer a less crowded office.
The book was signed by the author *herself.*

Personal and reflexive pronouns can be further classified by grammatical *case* (nominative, possessive, or objective), *number* (singular or plural), *person* (first, second, or third), and *gender* (masculine, feminine, or neuter).

The *case* of a pronoun is determined by its function in the sentence. The *nominative case,* which includes the pronouns *I, we, you, he, she, it, they,* and *who,* is required when the pronoun is the subject of a sentence or clause:

We are ready to go.
Tennis is a sport that *he* plays very well.

A traditional grammatical rule also requires that the nominative case be used after forms of the verb *be:*

This is *he.*   It is *I.*

These constructions can sound pompous and stilted, however, and should probably be avoided.

Another grammatical rule requires the nominative case in formal writing after the conjunctions *as* and *than:*

She is a faster skater than *I.*   She skates as fast as *he.*

These constructions can sound needlessly formal, unless you include a verb to follow the pronoun:

She skates as fast as *he* does.
We are even more upset than *they* are.

The *possessive case* includes the pronouns *my, mine, our, ours, your, yours, his, her, hers, its, their, theirs,* and *whose.* This case is required to show relationships such as possession and origin:

Our house was just painted.
Their work is outstanding.
His paintings are on display in the museum.

A traditional grammatical rule also requires the possessive case before a gerund:

Susan could understand *his* [not *him*] wanting to go.

The *objective case* includes the pronouns *me, us, you, him, her, it, them,* and *whom.* This case is required when the pronoun serves any of several functions in the sentence:

The object of a verb:

The good news delighted *him.*
The fall in sales disturbs *us.*

The object of a participle or gerund:

He spoke rapidly, urging *her* to be on time.
Meeting *him* was an interesting experience.

The object of a preposition:

Between *you* and *me,* the new policy won't work.

The object of a verb that has been omitted from a clause following *as* or *than:*

He likes Melissa more than [he likes] *me.*
The boss praised Anne as much as [he praised] *them.*

An appositive to a noun that is an object:

The company promoted two sales representatives — Jennifer Black and *me* — last week.

Pronouns used as subjects should agree with their verbs in

number; that is, singular pronouns take singular verbs and plural pronouns take plural verbs:

> *He has* a good job.   *They have* good jobs.

Problems in number agreement are often caused by indefinite pronouns such as *anyone* and *everybody*. It is often difficult to know which pronoun to choose in sentences such as this one:

> *Everyone* thinks (*he is/she is/they are*) entitled to a raise.

This problem also occurs in sentences with personal pronouns that refer to nouns of indefinite gender:

> A good judge must never indulge (*his/her/their*) personal prejudices.

The traditional solution has been to use *he, him,* and *his* in these cases to stand as the representative member of the group being discussed. But this usage has been attacked as sexist. To avoid gender bias, many people sometimes use compound pronouns such as *his or her.* These constructions can be cumbersome when used on a sustained basis, however. Other people choose to override the standard grammatical rule of number agreement and use *their* to refer to a singular noun of indefinite gender:

> Everyone must take *their* assignment home.

Perhaps the best solution to this problem is to write in the plural:

> All students must take their assignments home.

Personal pronouns are classified as *first, second,* or *third person*, and must agree with their verbs accordingly. First person refers to the speaker or speakers:

> *I* am happy.   *We* are not worried.

Second person refers to the person or persons being addressed:

> *You* will never change.

Third person refers to the person or thing being talked about:

> *He* looks like his grandmother.
> *She* is very wealthy.
> *It* is a very big sandwich.
> *They* are buying a house.

When using any type of pronoun, it is important that you construct the sentence so that your reader clearly understands which noun the pronoun refers to. Unclear antecedents occur when more than one noun can logically be the antecedent to any given pronoun:

> Marie told Lucy that she had won the prize.

In this example, it is unclear whether *she* refers to Marie or Lucy. Technically, a pronoun is supposed to refer to the nearest antecedent, but this rule is not always strictly followed. Sentences containing unclear antecedents cannot be corrected by a simple repositioning of words; they must be rewritten:

> Marie had won the prize, and she told Lucy about it.
> Lucy had won the prize, and Marie told her about it.

Verbs

A *verb* is a word that expresses action (*jump, open, speak*) or a state of being (*is, exist*). Verbs are usually classified as *main* or *auxiliary, transitive* or *intransitive,* and *regular* or *irregular.*

Most verbs are *main* verbs. Main verbs change their form by adding suffixes to agree with their subject, such as *he goes* or *she runs,* and to form participles, such as *sleeping* and *slept.* Main verbs also follow *not* and require a form of the verb *do* to form the negatives:

> I do not *enjoy* bowling.

In questions main verbs must use a form of *do* and always follow the subject:

> Do you *live* in this building?

Main verbs also take an infinitive with *to:*

> I *promised* to call him tonight.

Auxiliary verbs are sometimes called *helping* verbs because they help complete the form and meaning of main verbs. There are several features that distinguish auxiliary verbs:

Auxiliary verbs do not take word endings to form participles or to agree in number with their subject:

> She *may* [not *mays*] go to the store.

Auxiliary verbs come before *not* and do not use *do* to form the negative:

> You *might* not like that.

Auxiliary verbs come before the subject in a question and do not use *do:*

> *Would* you like to go to the movies?

Auxiliary verbs take the infinitive without *to:*

> I *will* call you tomorrow.

A *transitive* verb is a verb that has an object:

> She *worked* the keyboard with nimble fingers.

An *intransitive* verb is a verb that does not have an object:

> She *worked* hard.

Regular verbs form the past tense and the past participle by adding *–d* or *–ed* to the base form:

> He *called* this morning.

Irregular verbs do not follow the *–ed* pattern of regular verbs. Irregular verbs form the past tense and the past participle by changing their base form, often by changing their vowel:

> He *did* the work.   He *has done* the work.

Examples of irregular verbs include the verbs *begin* (begin, began, begun), *draw* (draw, drew, drawn), *meet* (meet, met, met), *stand* (stand, stood, stood), and *think* (think, thought, thought).

Transitive verbs have a property, known as *voice,* that can express the relation between the subject and the verb in one of two ways. Verbs in the *active* voice have the performer of the action as the subject:

> Linda *found* the ring.   Bob *signed* the contract.

In the *passive* voice, the situation is reversed. The person or thing that is acted upon becomes the subject, and the performer of the action is put in a phrase beginning with *by* or is left out of the sentence:

> The ring *was found* by Linda.   The contract *was signed.*

Passive verb phrases consist of a form of the verb *be* and a past participle. Passive verbs may occur in any tense and may use an auxiliary verb:

> The contract *has been signed.*   The ring *may have been lost.*

As the name implies, the passive voice tends to be weaker than the active voice. Passive verbs also require more words than their active counterparts. For these reasons, writers often avoid the passive unless they do not want to be direct.

A *mood* is a set of verb forms that convey the attitude of the speaker about the likelihood or factuality of what is said. English has three moods: *indicative, subjunctive,* and *imperative:*

The indicative mood of a verb states a fact or asks a question:

> You *know* the procedure.   *Does* he ever get up early?

The *subjunctive* mood of a verb expresses wishes, commands, or conditions that are contrary to fact. The subjunctive is usually used after a conjunction such as *if, though, lest, that, till,* or *unless:*

> If I *were* you, I would recommend a change in that policy.

For most verbs the subjunctive is identical to the base form of the verb, and is only noticeable in the third person:

> I insist that the chairman *resign*!

Note that *resign* does not end in *–s* to agree in number with *chairman*, as it would if it were in the indicative mood.

In general, the subjunctive has limited use in English, its functions largely being performed by auxiliary verbs like *might, should,* and *would.*

The imperative mood of a verb expresses a request or command, often with the subject omitted:

> *Hand* me the new manual, please.

The *tense* of a verb specifies the time or nature of the action that occurs and is designated as past, present, or future:

> I *walked* to work this morning.   I *enjoy* walking to work.
> I *will walk* to work tomorrow.

When past, present, or future action is described as completed, or *perfected,* it is in the *past perfect, present perfect,* or *future perfect* tense:

> I *had walked* to work by the time you got up.
> I *have walked* to work.
> I *will have walked* to work by the time you get up.

When past, present, or future action is expressed as being in progress, or *progressive,* it is in the *past progressive, present progressive,* or *future progressive* tense:

> I *am walking* to work this morning.
> I *was walking* to work yesterday when the thunderstorm began.
> I *will be walking* to work until my car is repaired.

A verb must agree with its subject in *person* (first, second, third) and *number* (singular, plural), as described in the following table. This rule means, for example, that a first-person singular verb is used with the simple subject *I* or that a third-person singular verb is used with any singular noun or third-person singular pronoun.

	singular	*plural*
first person	I send	we send
second person	you send	you send
third person	he/she/it sends	they send

It can be difficult to apply this rule. Here are some special cases of the rule:

The conjunction *and* joins two simple subjects in a compound plural subject and demands a plural verb:

> John and Jane *walk* out on the boardwalk. (third-person plural verb)

> Jane and I *walk* out on the boardwalk. (first-person plural verb)

The conjunction *or* does not form a plural subject from two singular nouns or pronouns and therefore takes a singular rather than a plural verb:

> Either John or Jane *gets* a paper each day. (third-person singular verb)

The true subject of the sentence may be hard to identify:

> A deck of cards *sits* on the shelf. (third-person singular verb, subject is *deck, cards* is the object of the preposition *of*)

In addition, certain words and expressions sometimes pose problems in connection with *subject-verb agreement.* For example, a verb must agree with the subject even when a singular or plural prepositional phrase intervenes:

> The manager is *one* of those people who *has* always maintained a positive attitude.

A verb must agree with its singular subject, not with a plural phrase that follows the verb:

> The *topic* of my memo *is* the many different types of procedural errors that have occurred during this trial.

A verb must agree with its subject even when expressions intervene between that verb and its subject:

> The *executive*, along with a receptionist and two secretaries, *is* in charge of registrations.

A verb having a singular subject preceded by *each, every, many a, such a,* or *no* must be singular in number even when two or more of such subjects are linked by *and:*

> *Each* manager and *each* division chief *has urged* the employees to invest in the thrift plan.

A verb should agree with the subject closest to it even when *either-or* and *neither-nor* are used:

> Neither the supervisor nor the union *members are* willing to negotiate.

Participles are *verbal adjectives.* Although the present participle of a regular verb is also formed by adding *–ing,* it is used as an adjective modifying a noun rather than as a noun:

> He shouted over the *roaring* engine.

Past participles are also used in this way:

> He fixed the *broken* vase.
> *Tired* workers tend to make mistakes.

Adjectives

Adjectives modify words, phrases, and clauses that serve as nouns and pronouns. An adjective describes, qualifies, limits, or otherwise makes a word distinct and separate from something else:

> a *tall* building   a *reasonable* offer
> a *beautiful* garden

Adjectives may occur in the *positive, comparative,* or *superlative* degree. The regular forms of comparison are made by adding *-er* (comparative) or *-est* (superlative) to the positive form of the adjective:

The *easy* method   The *easier* method
The *easiest* method

Most adjectives with two or more syllables require *more* or *most,* rather than *-er* or *-est,* to form the comparative and superlative:

The *reliable* source   The *more reliable* source
The *most reliable* source

Irregular adjectives have comparative and superlative forms that are not derived from the positive, or uncompared, form of the adjective:

A *good* suggestion   A *better* suggestion
The *best* suggestion

Adjectives can also be compared in a decreasing way using less and least, as in *less* skillful and *least* skillful. Some adjectives (*asleep, disastrous*) cannot be compared. Many technical terms (*biological, hydrodynamic, linguistic*) fall into this category.

Adverbs

An *adverb* may modify a verb (She reads *fast*), an adjective (She is a *very* fast reader), or another adverb (She can read *very* fast). There are several types of adverbs. For example, a *sentence* adverb modifies an entire clause or sentence:

Unfortunately, the advertisement did not get the desired results.

An *interrogative* adverb is used in asking or stating a direct or indirect question:

How are you feeling?   *Where* did you go?

A *conjunctive* adverb connects sentences:

The conference is over; *however,* there is still work to be done.

Some adverbs can be identified by determining whether they express time (*already, finally, lately, never, now, then*), place (*above, far, here, near, there, upstairs*), manner (*easily, otherwise, surely, well*), degree (*equally, fully, less, much, too*), cause or purpose (*consequently, therefore, wherefore, why*), or number (*first/firstly, second/secondly, third/thirdly*).

Like adjectives, regular and irregular adverbs can be compared by using the *comparative* or *superlative* form of the *positive* adverb. Regular adverbs commonly add the words *more* and *most* or *less* and *least* to form the comparative or superlative forms of the adverb, although a few can add the word endings *–er* (*sooner*) and *–est* (*soonest*):

> He is *often* available on Fridays.
> He is *more often* available on Fridays.
> He is *most often* available on Fridays.

Also like adjectives, some adverbs use different forms to indicate comparison rather than adding a word ending such as *–er* or requiring a word such as *more*:

> He did *badly* on the test.
> He did *worse* on the test than she did.
> Of all the students in the class, he did *worst* on the test.

Prepositions

A preposition connects and shows the relationship between a noun or pronoun and other words in a sentence. The noun or pronoun is the *object* of the preposition. The preposition together with the noun or pronoun is a *prepositional phrase*:

> in the room   out of paper   under the desk

Prepositional phrases can indicate a variety of situations or conditions including the following:

> Joe attended the meeting *with several colleagues*. (accompaniment)
> The trip was cancelled *because of bad weather*. (cause)

Those who are not *for us* are *against us.* (support or opposition)

We drove *to the city.* (destination)

I have everything *but a private office.* (exception)

The arrogance *of that official* defies description. (possession)

I want a desk *of polished mahogany.* (composition or makeup)

I worked out the problem *with my personal computer.* (means or instrument)

Treat all visitors *with courtesy.* (manner)

I ran *across the hall* to find you. (direction)

John is *in the study.* (location)

They'll do anything *for a quick profit.* (purpose or intention)

The new manager is *from Chicago.* (origin)

Call me *at noon.* (time)

Many familiar words that are used as prepositions, such as *in, to,* and *with,* can also function as other parts of speech, particularly as adverbs. *Above,* for example, can be used as an adverb (The balloon floated *above*), adjective (The *above* figures are correct), and noun (Read the *above* for information about verbs) as well as a preposition.

Conjunctions

A *conjunction* links words, phrases, clauses, or sentences and is used to show how one element is related to another. The three principal types of conjunctions are *coordinate, subordinate,* and *correlative.* Conjunctive adverbs, such as *besides, however,* and *nevertheless,* also connect sentences and words.

Coordinate conjunctions, such as *and, but, for, or, nor,* and *yet,* connect elements of equal value:

He is the president of the company, *and* he is our boss.
She is successful *but* modest.
Jim had to act as coach, *for* Bill was sick.

Subordinate conjunctions, such as *as if, because, in case, inasmuch as, provided that, since, when,* and *where,* connect a subordinate element to another element in a sentence:

> *Because* the report is late, the meeting will have to be postponed.
> Andrew is a skilled writer, *although* he has difficulty researching complex subjects.

Correlative conjunctions, such as *as . . . so, both . . . and, either . . . or, not only . . . but also,* and *whether . . . or,* are used in pairs or a series. Correlatives connect elements of equal value and must be positioned correctly in the sentence to avoid confusion:

> Overpopulation has been a problem *both* in India *and* in China.
> We are having pot roast, *whether* you like it *or* not.
> *Either* the executive *or* the assistant is coming.

SENTENCES

Subject and predicate

A *sentence* is an independent grammatical unit that has at least one *subject* and one *predicate*. In some sentences, such as imperative sentences, the subject is understood. The simplest standard sentence has a noun or pronoun that serves as the subject of the sentence (underlined in the following examples) and a verb (italicized in the following examples):

<u>I</u> *sleep*.   <u>Kittens</u> *play*.
<u>He</u> *eats*.   <u>You</u> *fell*.

A written sentence ends in a period, question mark, or exclamation point. There are several types of sentences, including those discussed in the "Sentence Functions" section.

The predicate of a sentence consists of the verb and any words that are governed by or that modify the verb, and it tells what action the subject is performing or what action is being performed on the subject. The simplest predicate possible consists of only a verb:

The clown *danced*.

A simple subject-and-verb sentence has an *intransitive* verb, one that does not require or cannot take an object:

The cat *purred*.   The bell *rang*.

Direct object

If the verb takes a *direct object,* it is called a *transitive* verb. The direct object is part of the predicate of a sentence.

The basic sentence pattern for a transitive verb consists of a subject, verb, and direct object (italicized in these examples):

I like *you*.	We played *checkers*.
He eats *strawberries*.	Henry outran *Charlie*.

Notice that in most cases the word order indicates which is the subject and which is the direct object. The form of the word does not change; only its position changes. In the following examples the direct object is highlighted in italics, the verb is underlined, and the subject is unmarked:

Henry <u>hit</u> *the ball*.	Lisa <u>likes</u> *someone*.
The ball <u>hit</u> *Henry*.	Someone <u>likes</u> *Lisa*.

Sentences can be lengthened by modifying the subject, the predicate, or both. These modifications usually add information to the sentences. Each detail makes a sentence more specific.

Modifying the subject

The subject of a sentence is usually modified by adding articles, demonstrative adjectives (such as *this* or *that*), adjectives, and noun-modifiers. Adjectives can themselves be modified by *adverbs*.

Notice the ways details can be given to the subject of the simple sentence "The cat eats fish":

The *striped* cat eats fish.

The *striped tawny* cat eats fish.

My striped tawny cat eats fish.

That pathetically skinny alley cat eats fish.

Modifying the predicate

In the predicate of a sentence, the verb or one of its objects may be modified. Articles, pronouns, and adjectives may modify the direct object. Adverbs may modify the verb itself. Adverbs or adverbial phrases may also modify the adjectives that modify direct objects. Below, the simple sentence "The dog jumps fences" is made more specific as details are added to the predicate:

> The dog jumps *picket* fences.
> The dog jumps *our neighbor's picket* fence.
> The dog jumps *that* fence *quickly*.
> The dog jumps *our neighbor's freshly-painted picket* fence *quickly*.

Notice the different functions of the adverbs, *freshly* and *quickly*. The adverb *freshly* modifies *painted* — an adjective. The adverb *quickly* modifies *jumps* — the verb.

Indirect object

An *indirect object* is a noun or pronoun that identifies the person *to whom* or *for whom* an action is performed or the thing *to which* or *for which* an action is done. The indirect object follows a verb in the active voice and precedes the direct object. The best way to identify an indirect object is to imagine the word *to* or *for* precedes it as you read the sentence. The following examples show the indirect object in italics and the direct object underlined:

> Tom gave *Jenny* <u>a gift</u>.   They built *themselves* <u>a house</u>.
> He told *Sarah* <u>the news</u>.   Ellen cooked *the family* <u>a meal</u>.

If, however, the word *to* or *for* is actually part of the sentence, the noun or pronoun that follows it will be the object of the preposition *to* or *for,* rather than an indirect object. The examples above can be rewritten to make the indirect object in each the object of a *prepositional phrase*. In the following examples the direct object is underlined and the prepositional phrase is in italics:

> Tom gave <u>a gift</u> *to Jenny*.
> They built <u>a house</u> *for themselves*.
> He told <u>the news</u> *to Sarah*.
> Ellen cooked <u>a meal</u> *for the family*.

Be and other linking verbs

A few verbs take as complements nouns or adjectives that refer to the subject. These verbs are called *linking verbs* and form the predicate by linking the subject to a noun or adjective. The most common linking verb is the verb *be* and all its forms. Certain other verbs such as *appear, seem, look, taste,* or *smell* may follow the same pattern when they function as linking verbs.

The important point to note is that the adjective that occurs in the predicate part of the sentence modifies the subject. Such adjectives are known as *predicate adjectives* or *predicate complements.* The following examples show the predicate adjectives in italics:

> Joan is *clever.*   The mouse seems *frightened.*
> John appears *tall.*   The soup tastes *delicious.*

Sometimes the verb *be* links two nouns. In these cases, the noun that follows *be* is not an object. It is known as a *predicate nominative.* The following examples show the predicate nominative in italics:

> I am *a person.*   The sign had been *a beacon.*
> Eddie was *a tenor.*   They were *the leaders.*

There used to begin a sentence

Sentences can begin with the pronoun *there:*

> *There* are ten people in the room.
> *There* is hope.
> *There* does not seem to be any chance.
> *There* may be some left.

In such sentences, *there* is not the subject. In fact, when *there* begins a sentence, it usually signals that the verb comes before the subject. Thus the verb must agree with the noun or pronoun that follows it, especially in sentences containing a verb such as *be, seem,* or *appear.* In the following examples, the subject has been underlined:

> *There* is a great <u>deli</u> across the street.
>
> In this direction, though, *there* seem to be <u>trees</u> obscuring the view.

Passive voice sentences

All the sentences discussed so far have been in the *active voice.* In the active voice, the subject performs the action expressed by the verb, and the direct object, when there is one, receives the action.

In the *passive voice,* the subject receives the action of the verb. Passive constructions are formed by making the direct object of a transitive verb into the grammatical subject of a passive verb. The first two examples below are sentences in the active voice. They are rewritten in the passive voice for the following two examples. Notice that the verb (under-lined) agrees with the subject (italicized). Notice also that a form of the verb *be* (underlined and italicized) is needed to form the passive:

> *Amy* <u>found</u> the treasure. *The treasure* <u>*was* found</u> by Amy.
> *Paul* <u>hears</u> the bells. *The bells* <u>*are* heard</u> by Paul.

The use of the passive voice places the emphasis on the re-ceiver of the action. This kind of emphasis is important in many kinds of writing. It is useful when the persons or things performing the action are unknown, unimportant, or uniden-tified. For instance, it is important in news reporting when sources may not be named. The passive voice is also found in scientific and technical writing, where it is often the preferred style. In general, you can use the passive voice to focus atten-tion on the object of the verb's action.

Although many composition books warn against excessive use of the passive, you need not avoid it completely — just use it wisely. Even in writing about movement, the passive has its place:

> Slugger *was hit* by the pitch.

The writer could have written the sentence in the active voice:

> The pitch *hit* Slugger.

But this construction would place the emphasis on *the pitch* instead of *Slugger* and would change the intended meaning of the sentence.

Coordinate elements

Most of the sentences examined so far have been fairly simple in structure. In each example there is generally only one subject, one verb, and one of each kind of object, so it is fairly easy to identify these parts of the sentence.

Sentences can, however, grow far more complex. A sentence may have several subjects, verbs, or objects; it may have many phrases and clauses. The more complicated a sentence becomes, the more difficult it may be to identify the subject and predicate.

One of the simplest ways to enlarge a simple sentence is to use more than one subject, verb, or object. When there are multiple elements, it is important to keep them parallel in form. The multiple elements may be subjects:

> *Dogs and cats* run wild in the street.
> *Men and women* played tennis.
> *Wisdom and learning* are not the same.
> *Sheep, horses, and pigs* live on the farm.

Avoid ill-matched combinations, such as "Wisdom, learning, and to know are not the same." "To know" is an infinitive and does not fit the same pattern established by "wisdom, learning . . . ." "Wisdom, learning, and knowledge . . ." would be better.

The multiple subject may be a series of phrases instead of individual words:

> *Going to school, keeping house, and maintaining a job* complicate her life.

> *Antique tapestries from France, handwoven Navaho blankets, and Early American samplers* cover the walls.

There should be no comma between the last subject and the verb. And, of course, the verb must agree with the subject.

It is acceptable either to repeat the preposition or to allow one preposition to govern the various elements: "Dreams *of* wealth, (*of*) fame, and (*of*) happiness kept her going." (When *of* appears only once "Wealth, fame, and happiness" are all understood to be objects of the preposition *of*.) Good style would be to use the preposition once and allow it to work for all applicable elements or to repeat it with each element. Avoid a mixture: "Dreams *of* wealth, fame, and *of* happiness kept her going."

The same preposition may not work for all the elements in a series. It is then necessary to give the appropriate preposition for each element.

The multiple elements may be verbs:

> He *cut, fit, and sewed* the clothes in one day.
> She *tried, failed, and tried* again.
> The children *dried* their tears *and began* to sing.

Note that two or more verbs may accompany a single subject. Sometimes the verbs are simple. Sometimes, as in the third example, there may be more than one predicate.

In these cases, each verb may have its own objects or modifiers. A comma should not separate the subject from either verb:

> We *ate* our sandwiches and *drank* our milk.
> Jimmy *waved* good-by to his friends and *drove* home slowly.

When using auxiliary and main verbs, it is important to make sure that the tenses are consistent. It is easy to forget that the auxiliary verb governs all the verbs in the series. In this example, "He has *come* and *gone*," the verb *gone* is correct. *Went* would not be correct because the auxiliary verb *has* governs both past participles.

In this example, "The time machine *has not been*, perhaps never *will be*, invented," two different auxiliary verbs are needed. *Has been* establishes the present perfect tense and *will be* serves for the future. The past participle works with both auxiliaries.

The multiple elements in a coordinate construction may be objects, either direct objects, as in the first three examples, or indirect objects, as in the final two examples:

> We ate *fish* and *chips.*
> Felicia bought *books, clothes,* and *CDs.*
> I enjoy *going to movies, riding a motorcycle,* and *building birdhouses.*
> Give *Tom, Dick,* and *Lyle* the tickets.
> Did you throw *him* or *her* the ball?

In each example given thus far there has been one subject and several verbs, one verb and several subjects, or one verb and several objects. There may also be multiple verbs, subjects, and objects in one sentence:

> Dick and Jane walked or ran all the way. (two subjects, two verbs)
>
> The cat and the kitten sniffed and ate the fish and chicken. (two subjects, two verbs, two direct objects)
>
> The cat and the kitten ate the fish and drank the milk. (two subjects, two verbs, two direct objects; both subjects govern both verbs but each verb has its own direct object)

Clauses

A *clause* is a group of words that has a subject and a predicate. A clause may be *independent* or *subordinate.*

An independent clause can be a sentence in itself. It can also be the main clause of a larger sentence. The main clause is sometimes called the basic sentence.

A subordinate clause also has a subject and a predicate, but it cannot stand by itself as a complete sentence. It depends on the main clause. The subordinate clause is sometimes called a dependent clause:

> If it rains, we'll go home.

We'll go home can stand as a separate sentence. It is an independent clause. *If it rains*, on the other hand, cannot stand alone as a sentence. It is a subordinate clause.

Compound sentences

Two or more independent clauses can be connected to make a *compound sentence*. There are several ways to join the independent clauses of compound sentences. A comma and a *coordinate conjunction* such as *and, and so, but, or nor, for, yet,* or *so* may be used:

> I tried to buy sugar, but the store was out of it.
>
> He will pick up the package tomorrow, or you will have to mail it.
>
> Henry will prepare the dessert, Molly will make the salad, and I'll cook the main course.

Notice that the last example has more than two independent clauses. In a series of three or more independent clauses, use a comma alone between all but the last two clauses.

A semicolon may be used if there is no coordinate conjunction:

> John didn't win the match; he didn't even try.

A comma may be used instead of a semicolon, but only in very short sentences:

> Sometimes you win, sometimes you lose.

A coordinate conjunction alone may be used, especially if the two clauses are very short:

> We tried and we failed.

Each of the above examples can be rewritten as two or more separate sentences:

> I tried to buy sugar. The store was out of it.
>
> He will pick up the package tomorrow. You will have to mail it.
>
> Henry will prepare the dessert. Molly will make the salad. I'll cook the main course.
>
> John didn't win the match. He didn't even try.
>
> Sometimes you win. Sometimes you lose.
>
> We tried. We failed.

The subjects of the independent clauses in a sentence may be identical, or they may be different. But the subject must be stated in each clause. If it is not, the sentence is not a compound sentence:

> He ran, and he jumped.   He ran and jumped.

The first sentence is a compound sentence because it can be separated into two sentences: "He ran. He jumped." The second sentence is not a compound sentence because its subject is stated only once. It is a simple sentence with a compound predicate.

It is important to recognize the difference between these two kinds of sentences so you can punctuate them correctly. The first sentence should have a comma before *and*, but the second should not.

Because independent clauses can be combined into a single sentence, some writers have a tendency to overdo the combining or to use incorrect punctuation. Some common errors that arise from this tendency are *run-on sentences*, *comma splices*, and *fused sentences*.

Run-on sentences. Sentences in which too many independent clauses have been combined are called *run-on sentences*. They are difficult to read. Run-on sentences can usually be corrected by separating the clauses into individual sentences. The conjunctions that connect the clauses of a run-on sentence can then be eliminated. The following example is a run-on sentence; the second example is its corrected version:

> The wicked witch cast a spell *so* the prince fell asleep, *and* the princess didn't know what to do, *but* the queen sent the knight to fight the dragon, *then* the prince awoke.

> The wicked witch cast a spell. The prince fell asleep, and the princess didn't know what to do. The queen sent the knight to fight the dragon. Then the prince awoke.

Comma splices. A *comma splice* occurs when a comma separates the main clauses of a compound sentence:

> The moon hid behind a cloud, all the world turned dark.

This type of writing error can be corrected in one of four ways. You can correct it by inserting a coordinating conjunction:

> The moon hid behind a cloud, *and* all the world turned dark.

You can correct it by replacing the comma with a semicolon:

> The moon hid behind a cloud; all the world turned dark.

You can correct it by rewriting the clauses to make separate sentences:

> The moon hid behind a cloud. All the world turned dark.

You can correct it by turning one clause into a subordinate clause:

> *When* the moon hid behind a cloud, all the world turned dark.

Fused sentences. When two or more sentences are joined without punctuation, they are said to be *fused sentences*:

He didn't ask me he just did it.

John said he was going to enter the big race then his mother said
that she would not allow it.

Correct fused sentences by separating them into individual
sentences:

He didn't ask me. He just did it.

John said he was going to enter the big race. Then his mother said
that she would not allow it.

Complex sentences

A *complex sentence* has one independent clause and at least one
subordinate clause. The subordinate clause is introduced by a
subordinate conjunction such as *if, because, although, when, as
soon as, whenever, even though, before, since, unless,* or *until.*

The subordinate clause may come before or after the main
clause. When it comes before the main clause, a comma usually separates the clauses. The following examples show the
subordinate clauses in italics:

I'll go to the dance *if mother lets me.*
Because I laughed, the teacher asked me to leave the room.
He will return *as soon as he has train fare.*
Do you know the man *who sat next to you?*
We enjoyed the party *that you gave.*

Compound-complex sentences

Compound-complex sentences are sentences that have two or
more independent clauses and at least one subordinate clause.
The following examples highlight the subordinate clause in
italics; the independent clauses are underlined:

After the war ended, <u>prices continued to rise, and the black market
thrived</u>.

<u>Everybody stopped speaking, and the ticking clock was all that
could be heard</u> *when the president took the stage.*

> The bell rang, the children filed out of the school, and the teach-
> ers checked the classrooms *because they wanted to lock them.*

Subordinate clauses as subjects, objects, modifiers

When subordinate clauses occur in sentences, they often fill
the job of a particular part of speech. The entire clause may
serve as a noun, an adjective, or an adverb.

When a subordinate clause fills the role of a noun, it may
serve a number of functions in the sentence. It may serve as a
subject:

> *How the pyramids were built* remains a mystery.
> *That she is an impostor* cannot be proven.

It may function as an *object of a verb:*

> The archeologist discovered *how the pyramids were built.*
> Can you prove *that she is an impostor?*

It may serve as an *object of a preposition:*

> John learned about *what had been said.*
> She will go to *whatever school she chooses.*

It may function as a *predicate nominative:*

> The story is *that he disappeared.*
> It seems *that he did run away.*

When a subordinate clause, underlined in the following examples, fills the role of an adverb, it can modify a *verb:*

> He will *return* as soon as he has train fare.
> Sally will *dance* if you ask her.

It can modify an *adjective:*

> The movie was *funnier* than I expected.
> Simon is as *tall* as I am.

It can modify another *adverb:*

> She ran *quickly* as a gazelle might.
> He gossiped more *indiscreetly* than I expected.

When a subordinate clause fills the role of an adjective, underlined in the examples below, it generally modifies a *noun:*

> I like the *dress* <u>that you bought</u>.
> I find myself on the *street* <u>where you live</u>.
> The *man* <u>who is wise</u> avoids trouble.

In summary, clauses are classified by their function in a sentence and not by the part of speech with which they begin. Thus a noun clause functions as a noun in a sentence but does not begin with a noun, an adverbial clause functions as an adverb in a sentence but does not begin with an adverb, and an adjectival clause functions as an adjective in a sentence but does not start out with an adjective.

Periodic sentences

In a *periodic sentence,* the main clause or its predicate is at the end of the sentence and is preceded by two or more clauses or phrases that are often parallel in construction. The periodic sentence can have a very dramatic effect if it is used well and infrequently, so it is important that the main clause justify the lead-up. The following example of a periodic sentence shows main clauses, highlighted in italics, preceded by subordinate clauses and by phrases:

> Working long hours, saving every penny she could, denying herself luxuries, using every resource she had, *she managed to save enough for an education.*

Phrases and verb forms

A *phrase* is a group of words that together have meaning. Broadly speaking, clauses are phrases that have a subject and a verb, but the term *phrase* usually is applied to meaningful groups of words that do not have a subject and verb.

Phrases may be used to modify nouns, adjectives, verbs, and

even complete sentences. Phrases may be used in the same way that single words may be used in a sentence.

Apposition. A noun or pronoun may have a noun or a phrase in *apposition*. That is, a noun or phrase (italicized in the following examples) may appear next to the noun or pronoun and extend its meaning:

> We, *the committee*, are responsible for the decision.
> My brother *Seamus* has red hair.
> The book *under the counter* is rare.
> We thanked our teacher, *Ms. Grimby*.

Notice that either the subject or the object may have a word or phrase in apposition. It is the first noun or pronoun — not the one in apposition — that determines the form of the verb. (For example, "We, the committee, *are*," not "We, the committee, *is*," and "You, the organizer, *deserve*," not "You, the organizer, *deserves*.")

Object complement. Some verbs seem to have two objects. The second object is not really in apposition to the first; it is instead an *object complement:*

> The council elected Jane *president*.
> We appointed Sara *leader*.

An *adjective* can also be an object complement:

> The heat made the plant *brown*.
> Opposition turned the deal *sour*.

Verb forms in noun positions. *Verbals* are words derived from verbs that are used as nouns or adjectives. *Infinitives* and *gerunds* are *verbal nouns*.

The *subject* of a sentence may be the infinitive of a verb:

> *To travel* requires money.
> *To speak* honestly is sometimes difficult.

Even though the infinitive (*to speak*) may take the place of a noun, its verbal nature is maintained. It is modified by an adverb (*honestly*) as a verb would be modified.

The infinitive can also serve as an *object:*

He likes *to knit.*   He wants *to play* hockey.

The object (*to play*) resembles a verb in that it has its own object (*hockey*), but it also functions as a noun.

A *gerund* is the *–ing* form of a verb that functions as a noun. A gerund may serve as a subject or as an object:

Traveling requires money.
His *going* relieves us of a problem.
Good *singing* gives us pleasure.
Singing well gives us pleasure.

Note that a gerund (*singing*) may be modified by an adjective (*good*) or an adverb (*well*). When the gerund has more of a noun sense, an adjective modifies it; when it has more of a verb sense, an adverb modifies it.

Gerunds have more noun functions than infinitives do. Gerunds may be used in apposition, as object complements, and as object of prepositions, where infinitives may not.

Modifiers. A *modifier* is a word, a phrase, a clause, or a whole sentence that specifies or limits the meaning of a word, a phrase, a clause, or a whole sentence.

Since a clause or a phrase may function as an adjective, an adverb, or a noun, the phrase or clause that acts as a modifier must be placed in the correct relationship to the word it modifies:

Having seen the house, she left.
Thinking he would be given a raise, he went to work.

Although these examples are grammatically acceptable, the sentences could also be rewritten:

She left *having seen the house.*
He went to work *thinking he would be given a raise.*

The sentences still make sense because the modifying phrase logically applies to the pronouns (*she* and *he*).

Dangling modifiers. A *dangling modifier* occurs when a modifier does not modify the subject of the main clause. It most often appears at the beginning of a sentence. Sentences that have a dangling modifier must be rewritten. The following sentences contain dangling modifiers, shown in italics:

> *Though sick,* I saw him at work.
> *After running the race,* we saw him faint.

Rewriting can eliminate such modifiers:

> Though he was sick, I saw him at work.
> We saw him faint after running the race.

Notice that the problem with a dangling modifier occurs because the modifier has no subject of its own. The subject of the main clause is usually taken to be the subject of the modifier. This can create some ridiculous images:

> *On returning home,* the door slammed shut. (The door was not returning home.)
> *Falling from the tree,* the girl caught the apple. (In this case, the apple was falling from the tree, not the girl.)

Absolute construction. Some modifiers modify an entire sentence. This kind of modifier is an *absolute construction:*

> *The moment having arrived,* we went inside the courthouse.
> *The primary lost,* we abandoned our headquarters.

Such constructions are acceptable in English and should not be confused with dangling modifiers. Whereas sentence modifiers modify an entire sentence, dangling modifiers modify the wrong elements in a sentence.

Parenthetical remarks. Occasionally you may want to insert a comment or explanation within a sentence. Such insertions are known as *parenthetical remarks,* and they may be punctuated with commas, parentheses, brackets, or dashes.

Commas are used only when the parenthetical remark is not a complete sentence, is very short, and flows well within the sentence:

> My friend, *the one who moved to Chicago,* just got married.
> John, *old and infirm though he is,* walked all the way home.

Commas are used in these sentences only for *nonrestrictive* phrases or clauses:

> My son, *the doctor,* sent me a letter. (The writer has one son who happens to be a doctor.)

When a sentence contains a *restrictive* clause or phrase, commas are not used:

> My son *the doctor* sent me a letter. (The writer has more than one son. The one who is a doctor sent her the letter.)

Parentheses are used for longer material, full sentences, further explanation, and side comments:

> The whole group (*except for those who had resigned*) agreed to settle the debt.

> The article on cryogenics (*see page 38*) suggests that the future may hold great appeal for some sufferers.

Note that parentheses may be used for whole sentences as well as for words or phrases.

Brackets may be used also in place of parentheses but are usually reserved for more formal situations:

> . . . life, liberty, and the <u>pursuit</u> [*underline added*] of happiness.

> The women live in purdah [*social seclusion as required by religion and custom*] and few men ever come in contact with them.

Dashes may be substituted for parentheses to set off a parenthetical remark:

> The medium spoke of spirits — *poltergeists, ghosts, ghouls* — as if she thought we all believed in them.

A two-week camping trip — *whenever the weather allows us to leave* — will be the high point of our planned vacation.

The use of parentheses, brackets, or dashes is often a matter of personal choice. The important point is to be sure that the sentence written around the parenthetical remark makes sense in its own right. If you remove the parenthetical remark, the sentence should remain grammatically correct.

Sentence functions

Declarative sentences. A *declarative* sentence is a sentence that makes a statement. It ends with a period. In the following examples, the subject has been underlined and the verb has been italicized:

> The <u>horse</u> *was led* to the winner's circle.

> The <u>horse</u> *was led* to the winner's circle and a <u>blanket</u> of red roses *was draped* across its withers.

> The <u>horse</u>, which was named The Princes' Revenge, *was led* to the winner's circle and a <u>blanket</u> of red roses *was draped* across its withers.

Interrogative sentences. An *interrogative* sentence is a sentence that asks a question. It ends with a question mark.

There are a limited number of words that can be used to begin an interrogative sentence. Some interrogative sentences begin with auxiliary verbs such as *is, do, are, can, may, have,* or *has.* The auxiliary verb comes before the subject. Often this means splitting the verb, with the auxiliary before the subject and the rest of the verb after the subject. The following examples show the auxiliary verb in italics and the main verb underlined:

> *Must* Ted and I <u>go</u> to the store right now?

> *Must* Ted and I <u>go</u> to the store right now or *may* we <u>go</u> in about an hour after we have finished rollerblading?

The main verbs *have* or *be* may be used without a second verb to begin an interrogative sentence. In such cases, the verb (italicized in the following sentences) comes before the subject:

> *Are* they at home?   *Have* you any wool?
> *Is* she a singer?   *Has* he a home?

Interrogative sentences may also begin with the words *who, what, where, when, how, why, which,* or *whose*:

> *Who* is coming to dinner?   *How* did they learn of it?
> *What* did he do?   *Why* hasn't Kerry written?
> *Where* are my socks?   *Which* house is yours?
> *When* will you leave?   *Whose* mess is that?

Indirect questions. An *indirect question* is not an interrogative sentence. Indirect questions are clauses that mention or suggest a question. Usually indirect questions are a part of declarative sentences and therefore end in periods. The examples below present three interrogative sentences followed by three declarative sentences containing indirect questions in italics:

> Where do they live?
> How much does it cost?
> Where did he find it?
> He asked me to find out *where they live.*
> Please find out *how much it costs.*
> She wondered *where he found it.*

The word order of an indirect question is not the normal word order used for an interrogative sentence. For example, "He asked me to find out where do they live" is not correct word order for an indirect question.

Exclamatory sentences. An *exclamatory* sentence is a sentence that expresses surprise, anger, or other strong emotion. It ends with an exclamation point:

> You did it!   What a change!   Stop!
> How good you are!   Don't hit me!

Some words — *interjections* — are used chiefly in this type of sentence:

Wow!   Phooey!

Note that exclamatory sentences do not need to have subjects and verbs. The word order may be the same as or different from that of a declarative sentence.

Imperative sentences. An *imperative* sentence is a sentence that makes a command or request. It ends in a period. The subject of an imperative sentence is always "you," which is usually understood without being expressed. Nevertheless, such a sentence is considered a complete sentence, as shown in the following examples:

Bring me the book.

Close your eyes and go to sleep.

Please, tell me a story.

Paul, take this money, go to the store, buy a loaf of bread, which we need for sandwiches, and give me the change.

Sentence fragments. A *sentence fragment* is a group of words that does not make a grammatical sentence. Often sentence fragments do not have a subject or a verb, or both; they are incomplete.

There are, however, many acceptable uses of sentence fragments:

Sentence fragments are acceptable as exclamations:

What fun!   How lovely!

Sentence fragments are acceptable as questions, provided that a previous statement or question establishes the nature of the question:

Mr. Smith is away on vacation.   *For how long?*
He will be back soon.   *When?*

Sentence fragments are acceptable as answers to questions:

> Where did he go? *Upstairs to his room.*
> Do you like him? *No.*
> When will he return? *Next week.*

Sometimes writers use sentence fragments to accomplish a purpose — perhaps to establish a certain pace, or to suggest a disjointed quality. The chief danger of using sentence fragments lies in giving the impression that they are sentences. In business writing, therefore, it is best to avoid the use of sentence fragments. If you must use them, use them sparingly. The following example illustrates the errors that can occur when sentence fragments are incorrectly used:

> Strolling the ancient city's streets, I seemed to hear the ghosts of history telling of its founding centuries ago. Of its trade with the Scythians and with tribes up and down the Danube. Telling of Alexander the Great.

Why is each of the last two word groupings a phrase rather than a sentence? Let us examine each of them:

> Of its trade with the Scythians, and with the tribes up and down the Danube.

This phrase has no verb and none of the nouns (*trade, Scythians, tribes, Danube*) is the subject. All the nouns are objects of prepositions.

> Telling of Alexander the Great.

In this phrase, the verb *telling* is the present participle of *tell*. But this verb is without a subject: the noun *Alexander the Great* is the object of a preposition verb.

There are several ways in which this paragraph could be changed to make all the fragments into sentences.

The entire paragraph can be rewritten as one sentence:

> Strolling the ancient city's streets, I seemed to hear the ghosts of history telling of its founding centuries ago, of its trade with

the Scythians and with tribes up and down the Danube, and also of Alexander the Great.

Or it can be rewritten by adding a subject to the two fragment sentences:

Strolling the ancient city's streets, I seemed to hear the ghosts of history telling of its founding centuries ago. The ghosts seemed to tell of trade with the Scythians and with tribes up and down the Danube. The ghosts also tell of Alexander the Great.

Sentence fragments may be long or short. If you recognize them for the incomplete sentences that they are, you will be able to use them or correct them as desired.

PARAGRAPHS

A paragraph consists of one or more sentences that introduce, develop, and conclude an idea about one subject. Each new paragraph explores a new idea, which is often stated in a paragraph's topic sentence. The remaining sentences in the paragraph expand on the topic sentence by giving specifics. The topic sentence is often, but not always, the first sentence of the paragraph.

Within a paragraph, the ideas contained in one sentence should logically develop from the ideas presented in the previous sentence. This progression should be clear and smooth and as apparent to the reader as it is to the writer.

What is true for each paragraph is also true for groups of paragraphs. There should be a clear, logical progression from paragraph to paragraph. Often the progression of ideas can be seen just by reading the topic sentences in each paragraph.

These are some general rules for developing paragraphs:

✔ Each paragraph should present a unit. It must be a grouping of sentences that are related to each other and to the main idea.

✔ Each paragraph should present a complete thought and expand on it fully before ending the paragraph and beginning the next.

✔ Within the paragraph, there should be a logical progression: from general to specific statements; from specific to general statements; from the beginning to the end of action; from a statement to a refutation to a re-examination of the original statement. The possibilities are numerous.

- ✔ There should be a good balance of types of sentences. At times it works well to repeat the same structure in sentence after sentence within a paragraph. But this stylistic device can be overused. It is generally more effective to vary the rhythm, length, and construction of sentences.
- ✔ Maintain the same person throughout a paragraph. Switching from "you" to "one" to "they" can be disconcerting to your reader.
- ✔ Maintain the same tense for the same subject within a paragraph. Events in the past should not be described in the present and also in the past. At times, some of the events in a paragraph may have taken place in the far past, others over a period of time. The sequence of tenses should make the time relationship clear.

Some paragraphs serve special functions within a written work and therefore require special attention.

The opening paragraph

The opening paragraph is the first paragraph of a written work. A major function of the opening paragraph is to engage the reader's attention. There are several customary ways of doing this:

- ✔ You can ask a question. The question should go to the heart of the material you deal with. The question may be asked as a direct question: "What weaving techniques were used by the indigenous peoples of the Yucatán?", or as an indirect question: "We wanted to know what weaving techniques were used by the indigenous peoples of the Yucatán."
- ✔ You can make a statement. The statement should be clearly worded. No qualifying phrases should offset the force of the statement. The statement may be the basic theme of the work or it may be the reason for writing the work: "There is

no good published material on the weaving techniques used by the indigenous peoples of the Yucatán."

✔ You can begin with a quotation with which you to agree or disagree. In either case, the quotation should be directly related to the theme of the work.

✔ You can present a short anecdote. The anecdote may be directly or obliquely related to the rest of the piece.

✔ You can cite an opinion by an authority or offer a common view with which you agree or disagree.

Transitional paragraphs

In a sense, every paragraph makes a transition from the paragraph that precedes it to the paragraph that follows. Some paragraphs, however, must make a major transition from one block of ideas to another block of ideas. You can use several devices to make transitions flow more smoothly:

✔ You can summarize what has gone before and lead in to the next theme by using a transitional word or phrase such as *moreover, on the other hand,* or *however.*

✔ You can use a short paragraph that picks up a word or phrase from the preceding paragraph then introduce a main idea for what will follow.

Concluding paragraphs

A concluding paragraph is the finishing touch to a piece of writing. It serves to tie together the sequence of ideas presented in the paragraphs and to give closure to the document by reemphasizing its main purpose. There are several ways this may be accomplished:

✔ You can summarize the ideas that have gone on before. This technique is effective only with long pieces of writing.

✔ You can draw conclusions about what has been said.

- ✔ You can state further questions to be explored at another time.
- ✔ You can end with a quotation from a respected authority on the subject.
- ✔ You can end with an anecdote that illustrates the main ideas of the document.

USAGE GUIDE

Correct word choice is an important ingredient in successful communication. Using the wrong word in conversation or written messages can cause someone to reach the wrong conclusion, and it can make you appear unprofessional; it can even be embarrassing. To avoid this, be alert to some common ways in which words are misused.

The usage notes that follow are pertinent to the English language usage that is most frequently used in our businesses, schools, government, and other institutions. Usage that is characteristic of the spoken language is usually not considered appropriate in written prose used in ceremonial or business communications and therefore is not considered here.

The material in this section attempts to provide guidance to usage problems that are basic and recurrent, especially within the context of the written word with its more exacting standards.

a, an   *A* is used before a word beginning with a consonant (*a building*) or a consonant sound (*a university*); *an* is used before a word beginning with a vowel (*an employee*) or a vowel sound (*an hour*). Both *a* and *an* have been used before some words in which an initial *h* is pronounced in an unaccented syllable (*a historian; an historic occasion*). It is never wrong to use *a* in such situations, but *an* is often considered unacceptable. The best rule is to use *a* before all words beginning with *h* except those in which the *h* is not pronounced (*an honor*).

about   The construction *not about to* is sometimes used informally to express determination: We are *not about to* negotiate with strikebreakers. But many people still consider it to be unacceptable in formal situations, and it may be misunderstood by people whose first language is not English.

above The use of *above* as an adjective or noun in referring to preceding text is common in some business and legal writing. In general writing, its use as an adjective (the *above* figures) is acceptable, but its use as a noun (read the *above*) has not become standard.

acquiesce When *acquiesce* takes a preposition, it is usually used with *in* (*acquiesced in* the ruling) but sometimes with *to* (*acquiesced to* his mother's wishes).

admission, admittance *Admission* and *admittance* have different meanings. *Admission* means "achieving entry to a group or institution," whereas *admittance* means "obtaining physical access to a place." One pays *admission* to a theater (a price paid to become a member of the audience) to be allowed *admittance* (physical entry to the theater itself).

adopted, adoptive One refers to an *adopted* child but to *adoptive* parents.

advance, advancement *Advance*, as a noun, is used for forward movement (We are satisfied with the *advance* of our salespeople into the new market) or for progress or improvement in a figurative sense (The corporation achieved a sales *advance* of 35 percent this year). *Advancement* is often used in the figurative sense: There are a number of achievements necessary to career *advancement* in this particular company. In these uses *advancement* often implies the existence of an agent or outside force, but *advance* does not. Thus the *advance* of research means simply the progress of the company's efforts in research, whereas the *advancement* of research implies progress resulting from the action of an agent or force: The addition of $1.5 million to the budget has resulted in the *advancement* of our research efforts.

adverse See *averse, adverse.*

advise *Advise* in the sense "to counsel or give advice" is always acceptable in business contexts: The president *advised* employees to observe the new regulations. Avoid the pretentious use of *advise* for *say, tell,* or *let you know* in business correspondence.

affect, effect *Affect* and *effect* have no sense in common. As a verb, *affect* is most commonly used in the sense "to influence": How will bad weather *affect* deliveries? *Effect* as a verb means "to bring about or execute": The layoffs are designed to *effect* savings. As a noun it means "a result": The demonstration was one *effect* of the new policy.

affinity *Affinity* may be followed by *of, between,* or *with: affinity of* persons, *between* two persons, or *with* another person. In technical writing *affinity,* meaning "a chemical or physical attraction," is followed by *for:* This dye exhibits an *affinity for* synthetic fabrics.

affirmative The expressions *in the affirmative* and *in the negative* are generally regarded as pompous: The professor answered *in the affirmative.* A better expression would be a simpler one: The professor answered *yes.*

agenda *Agenda,* meaning "list" or "program," is well established as a singular noun. Its plural form is *agendas.*

ago *Ago* may be followed by *that* or *when:* It was a week *ago that* (or *when*) I saw Janine. It should not be followed by *since:* It was a week *ago since* my order arrived. *Since* is properly used without *ago:* It has been a week *since* my order arrived.

alibi The noun *alibi* in its nonlegal sense, "an excuse," is generally acceptable in written usage, but as a verb (They never *alibi*), it is generally considered unacceptable.

all, all of, all that Constructions like *all us students* should be avoided in business and legal writing; use *all of us students*. The construction *all that* is used informally in questions and negative sentences to mean "to the degree expected": Orientation week was not *all that* exciting this year. This usage is generally considered unacceptable in business writing.

alleged   An *alleged burglar* is someone who is said to be a burglar but against whom no charges have yet been proved. An *alleged incident* is an event that is said to have taken place but which has not yet been verified. In their zeal to protect the rights of the accused, newspapers and law enforcement officials sometimes misuse *alleged*. A man arrested for murder may be only an *alleged murderer*, for example, but he is a real, not an *alleged, suspect* in that his status as a suspect is not in doubt.

all right, alright   The word *alright* is still considered an error in standard usage, despite the parallel to words like *already* and *altogether* and despite the fact that in casual speech the expression is often pronounced as if it were one word. Use *all right* instead in your formal written communications.

allude/allusion, refer/reference   *Allude* and *allusion* are often used where *refer* and *reference* would be more appropriate. *Allude* and *allusion* apply to indirect reference that does not identify specifically: He *alluded to* her car accident when he asked if she had run into any old friends today. *Refer* and *reference*, unless qualified, usually imply specific mention of something: She made *reference* to the book in her speech.

alternative   *Alternative* is widely used to mean "one of a set of possible courses of action," but because the word comes from a Latin word meaning "the other of two," some people would restrict its use to situations in which only two possible choices present themselves: The *alternatives* are to attend a traditional college or to enter a vocational school. In this stricter sense, *alternative* is incompatible with all numerals (There are *three* *alternatives*), and even the use of *two* is unacceptable for being redundant (The *two alternatives* are life and death). For similar reasons, the familiar phrase *no other alternative* is often considered a redundancy.

altogether, all together   *Altogether* should be distinguished from *all together*. *All together* is used with a group to indicate that its members performed or underwent an action collectively: The new computers were stored *all together* in an empty office. *All together* can be used only if it is possible to rephrase the sentence so that *all* and *together* may be separated by other words: The new computers were *all* stored *together*. *Altogether* is used to mean "entirely" or "completely": It is *altogether* possible that we will lose the game.

alumni   *Alumni* is used to refer to male graduates of an institution. Female graduates are *alumnae*. When the graduates are of both sexes, traditional use allows the masculine form *alumni,* but some people require both terms in the interest of fairness, and others use the combined form *alumnae/i.*

A.M.   See **ante meridiem.**

among   See **between, among.**

and   Although *and* has long been used to begin sentences, the practice tends to lend a conversational tone to what is written. It may be best to avoid this practice in business and legal writing. See also **but.**

and/or   Although *and/or* is widely used in business writing to mean "one or the other or both," this usage may be misunderstood, particularly in international correspondence.

ante meridiem   *Ante meridiem* is used chiefly in the abbreviated form of *a.m.* or *A.M.* to specify an hour of the day between midnight and noon: She had an 8:30 *A.M.* appointment with her optometrist on Thursday. The abbreviated form *p.m.* or

P.M., in contrast, refers to *post meridiem* and is used to specify an hour between noon and midnight: Following their 3:30 *P.M.* meeting, the union members had a small get-together to celebrate the ratification of the new contract.

Strictly speaking, *12 A.M.* denotes midnight and *12 P.M.* denotes noon, but because there is so much confusion over these uses, you should use *12 noon* and *12 midnight* in your writing.

anticipate, expect Some traditionalists hold that *anticipate* should not be used simply as a synonym for *expect*. They restrict its use to senses in which it suggests some advance action, either to fulfill (*anticipate* my desires) or to forestall (*anticipate* the competition's next move). Others accept the word's use in the senses "to feel or realize beforehand" and "to look forward to" (often with the implication of foretasting pleasure): They are *anticipating* (or *expecting*) a relaxing vacation.

any The phrase *of any* is sometimes used in informal contexts to mean "of all": That scientist is the best *of any* living authority on the subject. However, many find this construction unacceptable. *Any* is used to mean "at all" before a comparative adjective: Are the field office reports *any* better this month? The related use of *any* by itself to mean "at all" should be avoided in formal writing: It didn't matter *at all* (not *any*) when they arrived.

anyone, any one The one-word form *anyone* is used to mean "whatsoever person or persons." The two-word form *any one* is used to mean "whatever one (person or thing) of a group." *Anyone* may join means admission is open to everybody. *Any one* may join means admission is open to a single individual among the people who are applying for admissions. When followed by *of*, only *any one* (two words) can be used: *Any one of* them could do the job. *Anyone* is often used in place of *everyone*: Dale is the most thrifty person *of anyone* I know. But the words *of anyone* are unnecessary in this context: Dale is the most thrifty person I know.

apparent   Used before a noun, *apparent* means "seeming": Despite its *apparent* wealth, the college was deeply in debt. Used after a form of the verb *to be*, however, *apparent* can mean either "seeming" (The virtues of the writing program were only *apparent*) or "obvious" (The effects of the drought are *apparent* to anyone seeing the parched fields). You should make sure that your intended meaning is clear from the context.

as . . . as, so . . . as   Comparisons with *as . . . as* may be used in any context, positive or negative: Their team is *as* good *as* ours. The *so . . . as* construction, when used, is restricted to negative comparisons, especially when the word *not* is involved: Their team is not *so* good *as* ours.

as, since   Both *as* and *since* can mean "because" or "inasmuch as." But *as* can also mean "at the same time that" and is sometimes misunderstood: *As* they were leaving, she walked to the door. The easiest way to avoid confusion is to use *since* when the meaning is "because": *Since* they were leaving, she walked to the door.

assure, ensure, insure   *Assure, ensure,* and *insure* all mean "to make sure or certain." Only *assure* is used with references to a person in the sense "to set the mind at rest": They *assured* the president of their commitment. Although *ensure* and *insure* are generally interchangeable, only *insure* is used in the commercial sense "to guarantee persons or property against risk." In the sense "to make certain," the British preference is *ensure;* American usage includes both *ensure* and *insure:* To *insure* (or *ensure*) success, the company did a thorough market study.

as well as   *As well as* in the sense "in addition to" does not have the conjunctive force of *and.* Consequently, the singular subjects remain singular and govern singular verbs: My niece, *as well as* most of her friends, attended the concert. *As well as* is redundant in combination with *both: Both in theory as well as in practice, the idea is unsound.*

averse, adverse *Averse* and *adverse* are often confused. *Averse* indicates opposition or strong disinclination on the subject's part: *Andy was averse to joining the chess club. Adverse* refers to something that opposes or hinders progress: *Currently, banks must deal with an adverse economy; They proceeded, despite the adverse circumstances.*

aweigh See *way, under way, aweigh.*

awhile, a while *Awhile,* an adverb, is never preceded by a preposition such as *for,* but the two-word form *a while* may be preceded by a preposition. In writing, each of the following is acceptable: *stay awhile; stay for a while; stay a while* (but not *stay for awhile*).

back The expression *back of* is an informal variant of *in back of* and should be avoided in writing: *There was a small loading dock in back of* (not *back of*) *the factory.*

backward The adverb may be spelled *backward* or *backwards,* and the forms are interchangeable: *They each stepped backward* in response to the noise; *The mirror was facing backwards.* Only *backward* is an adjective: *The book presented a backward view of rural life.*

bad, badly Traditional usage requires the adjective *bad,* not *badly,* after linking verbs such as *feel* and *look: I felt bad* (not *badly*) *about missing the party.* Formal usage bans the use of *bad* and *good* as adverbs: *My tooth hurts badly* (not *bad*). *He drives well* (not *good*).

baleful, baneful *Baleful* and *baneful* overlap in meaning, but *baleful* usually applies to that which menaces or foreshadows evil. *Baneful* is used most often for that which is actually harmful or destructive: Although the *baneful* effects of littering in public parks are well-known, many people still fail to deposit trash in waste containers.

because of, due to, owing to *Because of* is used with nonlinking verbs: He was exhausted *because* of lack of sleep. *Due to* means "caused by" and may follow a linking verb: His exhaustion was *due to* lack of sleep. *Owing to* is used as a compound preposition: His policies were successful *owing to* his firm commitment to progress. See also **due, due to**.

behalf *In behalf of* and *on behalf of* have distinct senses and should not be used interchangeably. *In behalf of* means "in the interest of" or "for the benefit of": We raised money *in behalf of* the United Way. *On behalf of* means "as the agent of" or "on the part of": The lawyer signed the papers *on behalf of* the client.

beside, besides The senses "in addition to" and "except for" are conveyed more often by *besides* than *beside:* We had few options *besides* the course we ultimately took. *Beside,* as a preposition, usually means "next to": His computer is positioned *beside* the printer. Watch out for ambiguity with *beside:* There was no one *beside* me at the table. This sentence means that the seats next to you were not occupied but could be misinterpreted to mean that you were alone.

better, best In standard usage *better* is used in a comparison of two: Which of the two accounting firms does the *better* job? *Best* is used to compare three or more: Which of these four methods works *best? Best* is also used idiomatically with reference to two in certain expressions: May the *best* team win!

between, among *Between* is used when just two entities are involved: the rivalry *between* Ford and General Motors. When more than two entities are involved, the choice of *between* or *among* depends on the intended meaning. *Among* is used to indicate that an entity has been chosen from the members of a group: *Among* the three candidates, Sarah seems most likely to become the next president. *Among* is also used to indicate a relation of inclusion in a group: He is *among* the best songwriters of our time. *Between* is used to indicate the area bounded by several points: We have narrowed the search to the area *between* Philadelphia, New York, and Scranton. In other cases either *between* or *among* may be used. Thus if a hot-air balloon comes down *among* the houses, it lands in the area of the houses, and possibly on top of one. If it comes down *between* the houses, it lands in the space between the houses, hitting none.

bias Historically, *bias* means "a preference or inclination" and may be for or against someone or something. But *bias* now often implies an injustice: Congress included a provision in the Civil Rights Act of 1964 banning racial *bias* in employment.

bimonthly, semimonthly *Bimonthly* and *biweekly* mean "once every two months" and "once every two weeks." For "twice a month" and "twice a week," the words *semimonthly* and *semiweekly* should be used. But there is a great deal of confusion over the distinction, and a writer is well advised to substitute expressions like "every two months" or "twice a month" whenever possible. However, the word *bimonthly* is unavoidable when used as a noun to mean "a publication that appears every two months."

black When used to refer to African-Americans, the noun and the adjective *black* are often capitalized to reflect the parallel status of Blacks with other ethnic groups and nationalities.

blatant, flagrant *Blatant* and *flagrant* are often confused. In the sense that causes the confusion, *blatant* has the meaning "totally or offensively conspicuous or obtrusive." *Flagrant* emphasizes wrong or evil that is glaring or notorious. Therefore, one who blunders may be guilty of a *blatant* (but not a *flagrant*) error; one who intentionally and ostentatiously violates a pledge commits a *flagrant* act.

born, borne   In its literal sense the past participle *born* is used only in passive constructions (using a form of *be*) relating to birth: The baby was *born* today. *Born* may also be used figuratively: Out of that meeting a great project was *born*. *Borne* is used for all other senses of *bear,* including the act of giving birth: She has *borne* three children; The soil has *borne* abundant crops; Such a burden cannot be *borne* by anyone.

borrow   In spoken English, people sometimes use the expression *borrow off* in place of *borrow from*. In written contexts use only *borrow from*: Gale *borrowed* $500 *from* (not *off*) the bank.

both   *Both* indicates that the action or state denoted by a verb applies equally to two entities. Saying that *both* packages weigh more than five pounds means that each package weighs more than five pounds by itself. Used in conjunction with certain words, *both* is redundant. It is illogical to say they are *both alike,* since neither could be "alike" if the other were not. Similarly, *both* is unnecessary in a sentence saying that they *both* appeared together, since neither one can "appear together" individually.   In possessive constructions, *of both* is usually preferred: the works *of both* authors (rather than *both their* works).

bring, take   *Bring* usually denotes movement *toward* the place of speaking or the point from which the action is regarded: *Bring* the letter to me now. *Take* denotes movement *away* from such a place. Thus you normally *take* checks to the bank and *bring* home cash, though from the banker's point of view, you have *brought* checks to the bank in order to *take* away cash.

burgeon   The verb *burgeon* and its participle *burgeoning,* used as an adjective, are traditionally restricted to the actual or the figurative sense "to bud or sprout" or "to emerge": The *burgeoning* talent of the young cellist was apparent to all. Burgeon is not normally considered a synonym for the more general *expand, grow,* or *thrive:* The *burgeoning* population of Seattle presents some problems for city planners. This use of the present participle has become more acceptable in recent years, however.

but *But* is sometimes used as a preposition to mean "except" and so pronouns that follow it should be in the objective case: No one *but me* can read it. *But* is redundant when combined with *however:* But the division, *however,* went on with its own plans. Using *but* when it means "no more than" or "only" is unnecessary in negative sentences: It won't take *but* an hour. The expression *But what* is not normally used in standard writing: I don't know *but what* (*whether*) we'll arrive first. Similarly, standard practice bans the use of *but* instead of *than* in this type of sentence: It no sooner started *but* (*than*) it stopped. Beginning a sentence with *but* is now widely accepted, even in business English. See also **and.**

callous, callus The noun is spelled *callus* (a *callus* on my foot), but the adjective is spelled *callous:* The terrorists displayed a *callous* disregard for human rights.

can, may Traditionally, *can* has been used only to express the capacity to do something and *may* to indicate permission: The supervisor said that anyone who wants an extra day off *may* have one; *May* I have that pencil? In informal speech, however, *can* is often used to express permission. The negative contraction *can't* is frequently used in coaxing and wheedling questions: *Can't* I have the car tonight?

cannot In the phrase *cannot but,* which is criticized as a double negative, *but* is used in the sense of "except": You *cannot but* admire the view (you cannot do otherwise than admire the view). Alternative phrasings are *can but admire, can only admire, cannot help admiring.*

capital, capitol The term for a town or city that serves as a seat of government is spelled *capital.* The term for the building in which a legislative assembly meets is spelled *capitol.* It is capitalized (*Capitol*) in references to the seat of the U.S. Congress.

celebrant, celebrator *Celebrant* should be reserved for an official participant in a religious ceremony or rite (the *celebrant* of a wedding). It is also considered acceptable in the general sense of "participant in a celebration": The town filled with New Year's Eve *celebrants. Celebrator* is an undisputed alternative for this general sense.

center As a verb *center* is used with *on, upon, in,* or *at:* Our thoughts *centered on* the flood victims; The business is *centered in* New York. Traditionalists maintain that *center* should not be used with *around,* since the word *center* refers to a point of focus: The discussion *centered on* (not *around*) the meaning of the law. Alternatives to *center around* include *revolve around, focus on, concern,* or *involve:* The discussion *focused on* the meaning of the law.

ceremonial, ceremonious *Ceremonial* (adjective) is applicable chiefly to things; *ceremonious* (also an adjective), to persons and things. *Ceremonial* means simply "having to do with ceremony": There were many *ceremonial* occasions for the family this year; *Ceremonial* garb was required at the ritual. *Ceremonious,* when applied to a person, means "devoted to forms and ritual" or "standing on ceremony": She was regarded as a *ceremonious* chief of protocol.

certain Although *certain* appears to be an absolute term (Nothing is more *certain* than death and taxes), it is frequently qualified by adverbs: We are *fairly* certain.

cite   See **quote, cite.**

commentate   The verb *commentate* has long been in use in the sense "to give a commentary." But in the sense "to provide a running commentary on," it is usually unacceptable: The announcer *commentated* (*gave a commentary*) on the tennis tournament.

common   See **mutual, common.**

compare, contrast   *Compare* means "to examine something for similarity or difference" and is followed by *with* or *to.* Use *with* when you examine two things for similarities or differences: We *compared* our program *with* theirs. Use *to* when you compare dissimilar things: They *compared* the copy *to* the original. The verb *contrast* means "to show only differences." It is often followed by *with:* The senator's views *contrast* sharply *with* his predecessor's. As a noun *contrast* is often followed by *to:* My cousins, in *contrast to* me and my brothers, are fluent in both English and Spanish.

complement, compliment   *Complement* and *compliment,* though distinct in meaning, are sometimes confused because they are pronounced the same. *Complement* means "something that completes or brings to perfection": The thick carpet was a perfect *complement* to the expensive furniture. *Compliment* means "an expression of courtesy or praise": She received many *compliments* on her winning essay.

complete   *Complete* is generally held to be an absolute term like *perfect* or *chief,* which is not subject to comparison. Nevertheless, it is sometimes qualified by *more* or *less:* A *more complete* failure I could not imagine; That book is the *most complete* treatment of the subject available today.

comprise, compose   The traditional rule states that the whole *comprises* the parts; the parts *compose* the whole: The Union *comprises* 50 states; Fifty states *compose* (or *constitute* or *make up*) the Union. However, *comprise* is used informally, especially in the passive, in place of *compose: The Union is *comprised* of 50 states.*

continuance, continuation, continuity   *Continuance* is sometimes interchangeable with *continuation. Continuance,* however, is used to refer to the duration of a state or condition: The president's *continuance* in office was troubling to some people. *Continuation* applies especially to prolongation or resumption of action (This meeting is a *continuation* of the council meeting) or to physical extension (The *continuation* of the railroad spur beyond our town means more rail traffic throughout the day). *Continuity* is used to refer to consistency over time: The *continuity* of foreign policy was secured by her appointment. The *continuity* of a story is its internal coherence from one episode to the next; the *continuation* of a story is that part of the story that takes up after a break in its recitation.

contrast   See **compare, contrast.**

convince, persuade   Traditionally, one *persuades* someone to act but *convinces* someone of the truth of a statement or proposition: By *convincing* me that I was as qualified as the other applicants, the guidance counselor *persuaded* me to try for the scholarship. If the distinction is accepted, then *convince* should not be used with an infinitive: They *persuaded* (not *convinced*) me to go.

council, counsel, consul   *Council, counsel,* and *consul* are never interchangeable, although their meanings are related. *Council* and *councilor* refer principally to a deliberative assembly (a *city council* or *student council*) and one of its members. *Counsel* and *counselor* pertain chiefly to advice and guidance and to a person who provides it: We're proceeding according to the *counsel* of our attorney. *Consul* denotes an officer in the foreign service of a country: The *consul* in Bogota was welcomed by the country's new leaders.

couple *Couple,* when used to refer to two people who function socially as a unit, may take either a singular or a plural verb. Whatever the choice, usage should be consistent: The *couple are* now finishing *their* joint research (or The *couple is* now finishing *its* joint research).

criteria, criterion *Criteria* is a plural form only (The *criteria* for making a decision *are* clear) and should not be substituted for the singular *criterion:* His sole *criterion* for opposing the project is its cost.

critique *Critique* is widely used as a verb (*critiqued* the survey) but is regarded by many as pretentious jargon. The use of it as a noun in phrases like *give a critique* or *offer a critique* is acceptable.

data Although *data* is the plural of the Latin word *datum,* it is usually treated as a singular noun: The *data is* nonconclusive. Using a plural verb with data is also acceptable, however.

debut *Debut* is widely used as a verb, both intransitively in the sense "to make a first appearance" (The play *debuts* at our new downtown theater tonight) and transitively in the sense "to present for the first time" (We will *debut* a new product line next week). However, both of these uses are widely objected to by traditionalists, who do not like the shift of *debut* from a noun to a verb.

depend *Depend,* indicating condition or contingency, is always followed by *on* or *upon:* It depends *on* who is in charge. In casual speech the preposition is sometimes omitted: It *depends* (*on*) who is in charge.

deprecate, depreciate The fully accepted meaning of *deprecate* is "to express disapproval of." But the word has steadily encroached upon the meaning of *depreciate.* It is now used, almost to the exclusion of *depreciate,* in the sense "to belittle or mildly disparage": The cynical employee *deprecated* all of the good things the company had to offer. This newer sense is acceptable. *Depreciate* is primarily used to mean "to fall in price or value": A car *depreciates* immediately after you purchase it.

dilemma *Dilemma* applies to a choice between evenly balanced alternatives, often unattractive ones: He faced the *dilemma* of choosing between a higher salary in another state or a lower salary close to home. It is not properly used as a synonym for *problem* or *predicament:* Shoplifting has become a big *problem* (not *dilemma*) for this supermarket.

disinterested, uninterested Traditionally, a *disinterested* party is one who has no stake in a dispute and is therefore presumed to be impartial. One is *uninterested* in something when one is indifferent to it. These two terms should not be used interchangeably: I suggested finding a disinterested person to settle the argument, but they were uninterested in my opinion.

distinct, distinctive A thing is *distinct* if it is sharply distinguished from other things: a *distinct* honor. A property or attribute is *distinctive* if it enables us to distinguish one thing from another: This carpeting has a *distinctive* feel to it (meaning that the feel of the carpet enables us to distinguish it from other carpets). By contrast: Thick-pile carpeting is a *distinct* type of floor covering (meaning that thick-pile carpeting falls into a clearly defined category of floor coverings).

done *Done* means "completely accomplished" or "finished": The entire project will not be *done* until next year. In some contexts, however, this use of *done* can be unclear: The work will be *done* next week. Does that mean that it will be finished next week or that someone will do the work next week? Alternatives, dependent on the meaning, would be: The work will *get done* next week; The work will *be done by* next week.

doubt, doubtful   *Doubt* and *doubtful* are often followed by clauses introduced by *that, whether,* or *if.* Often *that* is used when the intention is to express more or less complete rejection of a statement: I *doubt that* they will even try. In the negative *doubt* is often used to express more or less complete acceptance: I don't *doubt that* you are right. When the intention is to express real uncertainty, the choice is usually *whether:* We *doubt whether* they can succeed. In fact, *whether* is the traditional choice in such examples, although some experts would accept *if* (which is more informal) or *that.* *Doubt* is frequently used in informal speech, both as a verb and as a noun, together with *but:* I don't *doubt but* (or *but what*) they will come. However, *doubt but* should be avoided in formal writing.

drunk, drunken   *Drunk* (adjective) is used predicatively: The guard was *drunk.* For attributive use before a noun, the choice is usually *drunken:* a *drunken* guest. The attributive use of *drunk* is generally unacceptable. But its use in the phrase *drunk driver* is supported by usage and statute. A *drunk driver* is a driver who has exceeded the legal limit of alcohol consumption; a *drunken driver* is a driver who is inebriated, whether in excess of the legal limit or not.

due, due to   The phrase *due to* is always acceptable when *due* functions as a predicate adjective following a linking verb: Our hesitancy was *due to* fear. But when *due to* is used as a prepositional phrase (We hesitated *due to* fear), the construction is considered by many to be unacceptable. Generally accepted alternatives are *because of* or *on account of.* See also **because of, due to, owing to.**

each   When the subject of a sentence begins with *each,* it is grammatically singular, and the verb and following pronouns must be singular as well: *Each* of the designers *has his* or *her* distinctive style. When *each* follows a plural subject, however, the verb and following pronouns generally remain plural: *The editors each have their* jobs to do. The redundant expression *each and every* should be avoided.

each other, one another   Traditionally, *each other* refers to two, and *one another* refers to more than two: Bob and Jane wrote to *each other*; The nurses help *one another*. When speaking of an ordered series of events or stages, only *one another* can be used: The Caesars exceeded *one another* in cruelty, meaning that each Caesar was crueler than the previous one. *Each other* should not be used as the subject of a clause: We know what *each other* are thinking. A better construction would be: *Each* of us knows what the *other* is thinking. The possessive forms of *each other* and *one another* are written *each other's* and *one another's:* The machinists wore *each other's* hardhats.

effect   See **affect, effect.**

either   Traditionally, *either* is used only to refer to one of two items. When referring to more than two items, *any* or *any one* is the preferred term. *Either* takes a singular verb: *Either plant grows* in the shade; I doubt whether *either of* them *is* available.

elder, eldest   *Elder* and *eldest* apply only to persons, unlike *older* and *oldest,* which also apply to things. *Elder* and *eldest* are used principally with reference to seniority: *elder* statesman; Pat the *Elder.* Unlike *older, elder* is also a noun: the town *elders;* Listen to your *elders.*

else   *Else* is often used redundantly in combination with prepositions such as *but, except,* and *besides: No one* (not *no one else*) *but* that witness saw the accident. When a pronoun is followed by *else,* the possessive form is generally written as *someone else's* (not *someone's else*). Both *who else's* and *whose else* are in use, but not *whose else's: Who else's* notebook could it have been? *Whose else* could it have been?

emigrate See migrate, emigrate, immigrate.

ensure See assure, ensure, insure.

errata The plural *errata* is sometimes employed in the collective sense of a list of errors. Nevertheless, *errata* always takes a plural verb: The *errata are* noted in an attached memo.

everyplace, every place *Everyplace* and *every place* used adverbially for *everywhere* are found principally in informal writing or speech: *Everyplace* (or *every place*) I go, I hear raves about that movie. A better construction would be: *Everywhere* I go, I hear raves about that movie. *Every place* as a combination of adjective and noun is standard English: I searched in *every place* possible.

everywhere The only acceptable word is *everywhere*, not *everywheres*. The use of *that* with *everywhere* (*everywhere that* I go) is superfluous.

except *Except* in the sense "with the exclusion of" or "other than" is generally construed as a preposition, not a conjunction. A personal pronoun that follows *except* is therefore in the objective case: No one *except them* knew it; Every guest arrived late *except me*.

excuse The expression *excuse away* has no meaning beyond that of *excuse* (unlike *explain away*, which has a different meaning from *explain*). *Excuse away* is unacceptable: The sales clerk's rude behavior cannot be *excused* (not *excused away*).

expect See anticipate, expect.

explicit, express *Explicit* and *express* both apply to something that is clearly stated rather than implied. *Explicit* applies more particularly to that which is carefully spelled out: The *explicit* requirements for graduating early are contained in the school handbook. *Express* applies particularly to a clear expression of intention or will: The corporation made an *express* prohibition against dealers' selling cars below list prices.

farther, further Traditionally, *farther* is used for physical distance: The freight train went *farther* down the line. *Further* is used for nonphysical distance, as when referring to degree or time: The accident pushed us *further* into debt; The company took *further* steps to advertise its product. In some cases, however, especially in contemporary writing, either word is acceptable. You may say *further* from the truth or *farther* from the truth.

fatal, fateful Although the senses of *fatal* and *fateful* have tended to merge, each has a different core meaning. The contrast between *fatal,* in the sense "leading to death or destruction," and *fateful,* in the sense "affecting one's destiny or future," is illustrated by the following sentence: The *fateful* decision to relax safety standards led directly to the *fatal* car crash.

fault *Fault* used as a transitive verb meaning "to criticize or find fault with" is now widely acceptable: One cannot *fault* the lead actor's performance; To *fault* them is grossly unfair.

fewer, less *Fewer,* referring to a smaller number, is correctly used in writing only before a plural noun: *fewer* reasons, *fewer* gains on the stock market. *Less,* referring to not as great an amount or quantity, is used before a mass noun: *less* music; *less* sugar; *less* trouble. *Less than* is also used before a plural noun that denotes a measure of time, amount, or distance: It has been *less than* three weeks since the announcement; Her parents are *less than* 60 years old; The ski equipment cost *less than* $400.

finalize *Finalize* is business jargon that is avoided by many careful writers: We will *finalize* plans to remodel 12 stores this year. A better construction would be: We will *complete* (*finish, make final*) plans to remodel 12 stores this year.

firstly *Firstly, secondly, thirdly,* and so on are less desirable substitutes for *first, second, third,* and so on.

flagrant See **blatant, flagrant.**

flammable, inflammable *Flammable* and *inflammable* are identical in meaning. *Flammable* has been adopted by safety authorities for the labeling of combustible materials because the *in–* of *inflammable* was incorrectly believed by some people to mean "not": The liquid is *flammable.*

flaunt, flout *Flaunt* and *flout* are often confused. *Flaunt* as a transitive verb means "to exhibit ostentatiously": The champion *flaunted* a gold-plated trophy. To *flout* means "to defy openly": They *flouted* all social proprieties.

flounder See **founder, flounder.**

forbid *Forbid* may be used with an infinitive (I *forbid* you *to smoke* in the elevators); or with a gerund (I *forbid* your *smoking*) Avoid using it with *from:* I *forbid* you *from* smoking.

forceful, forcible, forced *Forceful, forcible,* and *forced* have distinct, if related meanings. *Forceful* is used to describe something that suggests strength or force: a *forceful* argument; *Forceful* measures may or may not involve the use of actual physical force. *Forcible* is most often used concerning actions accomplished by the application of physical force: There had clearly been a *forcible* entry into the storeroom; The suspect had to be *forcibly* restrained. *Forced* is used to describe a condition brought about by control or by an outside influence: Products made by *forced* labor are generally shunned in the international marketplace; It became necessary for the pilot to make a *forced* landing; Her displeasure was evident in her *forced* smile.

former The word *former* is used when referring to the first of two persons or things mentioned: If I had to choose between an analog and a digital watch, I would choose *the former.* It is best not to use *former* when referring to the first of three or more. For that purpose one may use *the first* or *the first-named* or, preferably, repeat the name itself: Computers, scanners, and copiers are integrated in many offices, with *computers* representing the dominant technology.

fortuitous, fortunate *Fortuitous* is often confused with *fortunate*. *Fortuitous* means "happening by chance." *Fortunate* means "having unexpected good fortune." A *fortuitous* meeting may have either fortunate or unfortunate consequences. In common usage some of the meaning of *fortunate* has rubbed off on *fortuitous* so that even when it is properly used, *fortuitous* often carries an implication of lucky chance rather than unlucky chance. But the word is not synonymous with *fortunate* and is best used when it refers to something that came about by chance or accident: Thanks to a *fortuitous* meeting with Steve, I now know how to get to the new mall.

forward, forwards *Forwards* should not be used in place of *forward* except in the adverbial sense of "toward the front": The bus driver asked the passenger to move *forward* (or *forwards*). In specific phrases the choice of one or the other is often idiomatic: Look *forward;* Her life change from that day *forward;* The seaweed moved backward and *forward* as dictated by the movement of the water.

founder, flounder The verbs *founder* and *flounder* are often confused. *Founder* comes from a Latin word meaning "bottom" (*foundation*) and originally referred to knocking enemies down; it is now used to mean "to sink below the water" and "to fail utterly, collapse." *Flounder* means "to move clumsily; thrash about," and hence "to proceed in confusion." If the railroad's business between Chicago and Peoria *founders,* expect the line to be shut down; If the restaurant is *floundering,* longer hours and lower prices may still save it.

fulsome   *Fulsome* is often used, especially in the phrase *fulsome praise,* as the equivalent of *full and abundant.* This could lead to possible confusion because of the sense "offensively flattering or insincere"; hence *fulsome praise* could be taken to mean insincere, unctuous compliments.

further   See **farther, further.**

get   *Get* has a great number of uses, some of which are acceptable at all levels and others of which are generally felt to be casual. In business writing, it is best to avoid the use of *get* in place of *be* or *become:* They *get* discouraged easily. Avoid the use of *get* or *get to* in place of *start* or *begin:* Let's *get* (or *get to*) working now. Also, avoid the use of *have got* in place of *must:* I *have got to* go now.

gift   As a verb *gift* traditionally was used in the sense "to present as a gift; to endow": We *gifted* the charity with a $1,000 donation. In current use, however, *gift* in this sense is considered affected and should be avoided. *Gift* as a noun meaning "a present" is standard: We received your *gift.*

good, well   *Good* is used as an adjective with linking verbs such as *be, seem,* or *appear:* The future looks *good. Well* should be used as an adverb: The motor runs *well.*

government   In American usage *government* always takes a singular verb: The *government is* too bureaucratic. In British usage *government,* in the sense of a governing group of officials, is usually construed as a plural collective and therefore takes a plural verb: The *government are* determined to maintain strict reins on industry.

group   *Group* as a collective noun can be followed by a singular or plural verb. It takes a singular verb when the persons or things that make up the group are considered collectively: The *group is* ready to present its report. *Group* takes a plural verb when the persons or things that make it up are considered individually: The *group were* divided in their loyalties.

half The phrases *a half, half of,* and *half a* are all correct, though they may differ slightly in meaning. For example, *a half day* is used when *day* has the special sense "a working day," and the phrase then means "four hours." *Half of a day* and *half a day* are not restricted in this way and can mean either 4 or 12 hours. When the accompanying word is a pronoun, however, the phrase with *of* must be used: *half of them.* The phrase *a half a* is unacceptable in standard usage.

hanged *Hanged,* as the past tense and past participle of *hang,* is used in the sense "put to death by hanging": Frontier courts *hanged* (not *hung*) many a prisoner after a summary trial. In all other senses of the word, *hung* is the preferred form as past tense and past participle: He *hung* the calendar by his desk.

hardly *Hardly* has the force of a negative, therefore, it is not used with another negative: I *could hardly* see (not *couldn't hardly* see). A clause following *hardly* is introduced by *when* or, less often, by *before:* We had *hardly* finished one report *when* (or *before*) another was assigned. Such a clause is not introduced by *than* in formal style: *Hardly* had I walked inside *when* (not *than*) the downpour started.

he Traditionally, the pronouns *he, him,* and *his* are used as generic singular pronouns in formal writing: No one seems to take pride in *his* work anymore. This usage has been criticized as sexist, however, and writers have developed numerous strategies to avoid it. One is to use compound pronouns such as *he or she* and *she/he.* These are acceptable but often cumbersome. Another strategy is to alternate generic *he* with generic *she,* in chapters, paragraphs, or even sentences if the subject matter will allow it. A solution that is very common in speech is to use *they, their,* and *them* to refer to singular nouns and pronouns: Everyone must finish *their* work on time. This practice violates the grammatical rule of number agreement for pronouns, but many choose to employ it anyway. Perhaps the best solution is to write consistently in the plural: All employees must finish *their* work on time.

headquarter, headquarters The verb *headquarter* is used informally in both transitive and intransitive senses: Our European sales team will *headquarter* in Paris; The management consulting firm has *headquartered* its people in the New York Hyatt. Many people dislike this use of *headquarter* because it evokes business jargon. As a noun *headquarters* is properly used with either a singular or a plural verb. A plural verb is more common: The committee's *headquarters* are upstairs. But a singular verb is sometimes preferred when reference is to authority rather than to physical location: *Headquarters* has approved the purchase of desktop computers for our engineers.

help *Help* in the sense "avoid" or "refrain from" is frequently used in an expression such as *I cannot help but think*. Other ways of saying the same thing include *I cannot help thinking* and *I cannot but think*. Another idiomatic use of *help* is exemplified by this sentence: Don't change it any more than you can *help* (any more than you have to). Some grammarians condemn this usage on the ground that *help* in this sense means "avoid" and logically requires a negative, but the expression is well-established.

here In constructions introduced by *here is* and *here are*, the number of the verb is governed by the subject, which appears after the verb: *Here is* the *cake* I promised to bring; *Here are* the *cupcakes* I promised to bring.

historic, historical *Historic* and *historical* are differentiated in usage, although their senses overlap. *Historic* refers to what is important in history: The *historic* first voyage to outer space. It is also used in regard to what is famous or interesting because of its association with persons or events in history: Frederick Douglass' home is considered to be a *historic* site. *Historical* refers to whatever existed in the past, whether regarded as important or not: The novel contained several *historical* characters. Events are *historical* if they happened, *historic* only if they are regarded as important. *Historical* refers also to anything concerned with history or the study of the past: The city supports its *historical* society well; He was well known for his *historical* novels.

hopefully The use of *hopefully* to mean "it is to be hoped" (*Hopefully*, we'll exceed last year's sales volume) can be justified by analogy to the similar uses of *happily* and *mercifully*. However, it is best to avoid using *hopefully* this way because many people consider it an error.

how The use of *as how* for *that* (They said *as how* they would go) is not considered standard, and should be avoided. For similar reasons, the expressions *seeing as how* and *being as how* should also be avoided in formal writing.

however *However* is redundant in combination with *but*. One or the other should be used: We had an invitation *but* didn't go; We had an invitation; *however,* we didn't go. The use of *however* as the first word of a sentence is generally acceptable.

identical Some language critics insist that *with* is the preferred preposition after *identical*. But both *with* and *to* are acceptable: This year's model is identical *with* (or *to*) last year's.

idle *Idle* may be used in the transitive sense "to make idle." The following example is acceptable: The dock strike had *idled* many crews and their ships.

if *If* may be substituted for *whether* to introduce a clause indicating uncertainty after a verb such as *ask, doubt, know, learn,* or *see:* We shall soon learn *if* (or *whether*) it is true. *If* should be avoided when it may be ambiguous: Please inform the registrar *if* you intend to be present. (Does it mean *whether or not* you intend to be or *only if* you intend to be present?) Often *if not* is also ambiguous: The discovery offered persuasive, *if not* conclusive evidence. This could mean "persuasive and perhaps conclusive" or "persuasive but not conclusive." Traditionally, the subjunctive (*if I were*) is used for a situation contrary to fact: If I *were* the president, I *would* (or *should*) make June 1 a national holiday. The indicative is required when the situation described by the *if* clause is assumed to be true: If I *was* short with you a moment ago, it is only because I wasn't paying attention. When an *if* clause is preceded by *ask* or *wonder,* use the indicative: He *asked if* Napoleon *was* a great general. Using *would have* in place of the subjunctive in contrary-to-fact *if* clauses is incorrect: If I *had been* (not If I *would have been*) promoted.

immigrate   See **migrate, emigrate, immigrate.**

impact   As a verb *impact* is sometimes used transitively: These taxes *impact* small businesses. It is also used intransitively with *on:* Social pathologies, such as those common to the inner city, *impact* heavily *on* public education. Many language critics object to these usages as typical of bureaucratic jargon.

imply   See **infer, imply.**

important   The adjective *important* is sometimes used to modify a clause: The shareholders' opinion is evident; *more important,* it will prevail. Grammarians often object to this usage. The adverb *importantly* is also used in this way and can cause no objections: The shareholders' opinion is evident; *more importantly,* it will prevail.

impractical, impracticable   *Impractical* can refer to that which is not sensible or prudent: Your suggestion that we use balloons to convey messages across town is *impractical*. *Impracticable* applies to that which is not capable of being carried out or put into practice: Building a new stadium in the marsh has proved to be *impracticable*. A plan may be *impractical* if it involves undue cost or effort and still not be *impracticable*. The distinction between these words is subtle, and *impractical* is often used where *impracticable* would be more precise.

infer, imply   *Infer* is sometimes confused with *imply*, but the distinction between the two words is useful. To *imply* is "to state indirectly." To *infer* is "to draw a conclusion." One should write: The quarterly report *implies* that sales are down because of the recession. Because of that implication, investors have *inferred* that we have something to hide, and our stock has fallen three points.

inflammable   See **flammable, inflammable.**

input   *Input* is a technical term referring to information fed into a computer. When used in nontechnical contexts, it can seem a pretentious substitute for *information*. In some contexts *input* can be ambiguous: The advisor had no *input* on the dress code. This sentence can mean that the advisor received no information from others or that the advisor provided no information.

inside, inside of   *Inside* and *inside of* have the same meaning. *Inside* is generally preferred, especially in writing, when the reference is to position or location: The materials are *inside* the warehouse. *Inside of* is used more acceptably when the reference is to time: The 300-page manuscript was photocopied *inside of* 10 minutes. A better construction would be: The 300-page manuscript was photocopied *in less than* 10 minutes.

insure   See **assure, ensure, insure.**

intense, intensive   *Intensive* is often used interchangeably with *intense*. However, it refers especially to the strength or concentration of an activity when imposed from without. Thus one speaks of *intense* dislike but *intensive* training.

its, it's   *Its,* the possessive form of the pronoun *it,* is never written with an apostrophe. The contraction *it's* (for *it is* or *it has*) is always written with an apostrophe.

joint   See reciprocal, joint.

kind   The use of the plurals *these* and *those* with *kind* (*these kind* of films) has been defended by some as a sensible idiom, but one that should be avoided in writing. Substitute *this* (or *that*) *kind of* or *these* (or *those*) *kinds of* and take care that the following nouns and verbs agree in number with *kind: This kind of* film *has had* a lot of success in foreign markets. *Those are* the *kinds of* books that *capture* the public imagination. When *kind of* is used to mean "more or less," it is properly preceded by the indefinite article *a* in formal writing: The work showed *a kind of* genius (not *kind of a* genius). The use of *kind of* to mean "somewhat" (We were *kind of* sleepy) should be avoided in formal writing.

kudos   *Kudos* is one of those words, like *congeries,* that looks plural but is historically singular. So it is correctly used with a singular verb: *Kudos is* due the committee for organizing a successful picnic.

lack   As an intransitive verb meaning "to be deficient," *lack* is used chiefly in the present participle with *in:* You will not *lack in* support from the finance committee. In the sense "to be in need of something," it requires no preposition but is sometimes used with *for:* You will not *lack* (or *lack for*) support from the graduation committee. In some cases, however, the two phrasings can convey different meanings: The millionaire *lacks* nothing (has everything); The millionaire *lacks for* nothing (has everything he needs).

latter   *Latter,* as used in contrast to *former,* refers to the second of two: Jones and Smith have been mentioned for transfer to our London office, but the *latter* may decline the post. *Latter* is not appropriate when more than two are named: Jones, Smith, and Kowalski have been nominated. Kowalski should then be referred to as *the last, the last named,* or preferably, simply *Kowalski.*

lay, lie   *Lay* ("to put, place, or prepare") and *lie* ("to recline or be situated") are frequently confused. *Lay* is a transitive verb and takes an object. *Lay* and its principal parts (*laid, laid, laying*) are correctly used in the following examples: Please *lay* the books on the floor; The messenger *laid* (not *lay*) the computer printouts on the desk; The table *was laid* for four; He was *laying* the tray down when I came in. *Lie* is an intransitive verb and does not take an object. *Lie* and its principal parts (*lay, lain, lying*) are correctly used in the following examples: The founder of the company often *lies* (not *lays*) down after lunch. When I *lay* (not *laid*) down, I fell asleep; The rubbish had *lain* (not *laid*) in the bin for a week; I *was lying* (not *laying*) in bed when I received the call; The valley *lies* to the east. There are a few exceptions to these rules. The idioms *lay low* and *lay for* and the nautical sense of *lay* (*lay* at anchor), though intransitive, are well established.

leave alone, let alone   *Leave alone* may be substituted for *let alone* in the sense of "to refrain from disturbing or interfering": *Leave* the salespeople *alone* and they will produce; *Left alone,* they were quite productive. Those who do not accept this substitution generally believe *leave alone* should be restricted to the sense of "to depart and leave one in solitude": They were *left alone* in the wilderness. In formal writing *leave* is not an acceptable substitute for *let* in the sense "to allow or permit." Only *let* is acceptable in these examples: *Let* me be; *Let* us not quarrel; *Let* matters stand.

lend   See loan, lend.

less   See fewer, less.

lie   See lay, lie.

lighted, lit   *Lighted* and *lit* are equally acceptable as past tense and past participle of *light*. Both forms are also well established as adjectives: The only thing that could be seen in the shuttered room was a *lighted* (or *lit*) candle.

like   There is a traditional injunction against using *like* as a conjunction: The machine responds *as* (not *like*) it should. Constructions like *looks like, sounds like,* and *tastes like* are not objectionable, but *as if* should be substituted in formal writing: It looks *as if* there will be no action on the bill before Congress recesses. There is less objection to the use of *like* as a conjunction when the verb following it is not expressed: The new senator took to politics *like* a duck to water.

likewise   *Likewise* is not a conjunction and cannot take the place of a connective such as *and* or *together with*: The mayor risked his credibility, *likewise* his honor. A better construction would be: The mayor risked his credibility *and* (or *and likewise*) his honor.

literally   *Literally* means "in a manner that accords precisely with the words." It is often used as if it meant "figuratively" or "in a manner of speaking," which is almost the opposite of its true meaning: Mary was *literally* breathing fire.

loan, lend   Both *lend* and *loan* are acceptable verbs in standard English, although some people hold that *lend* is preferable and that *loan* should be used only as a noun. *Lend* is preferred over *loan* in the following examples: One who *lends* money to a friend may lose a friend; When I refused to *lend* my car, I was kicked out of the carpool. Only *lend* has figurative uses: All I ask is that you *lend* an ear to my plea; Some say distance *lends* enchantment, but others contend that out-of-sight means out-of-mind.

lost The phrase *lost to* can sometimes be ambiguous: As a result of poor preparation, the court battle was *lost to* the defense attorney. Was it lost by the defendant's attorney or lost by the plaintiff's attorney to the defendant's attorney? Unless the context makes the meaning clear, the sentence should be reworded: As a result of poor preparation, the court battle was *lost by* the defense attorney.

majority When *majority* refers to a particular number of votes, it takes a singular verb: Her *majority* was five votes. When it refers to a group of persons or things that are in the majority, it may take either a plural or singular verb, depending on whether the group is considered as a whole or as a set of people considered individually. For example, when we refer to an election accomplished by a group as a whole, we say "The *majority elects* the candidate *it wants*," but when we speak of something done individually, such as living within five miles of an office, we say "The *majority* of our employees *live* within five miles of the office." *Majority* is often preceded by *great* (but not by *greater*) in emphatically expressing the sense of "most of": The *great majority* has decided not to throw good money after bad. The phrase *greater majority* is appropriate only when considering two majorities: A *greater majority* of the workers has accepted this year's contract than accepted last year's.

man Many people consider the word *man* to be sexist when it is used as a synonym for *humankind* or for the generic pronoun *one*. To avoid the implication of sexism, use *man* only when referring to a male person. Gender-neutral substitutes for *man* include *one, man or woman, human,* and *humanity.*

–man compounds Compounds ending in *–man* are considered by many people to be sexist when these words are used to stand for the representative or typical member of groups containing both sexes. A variety of gender-neutral terms have been coined recently as substitutes for compounds ending in –*man*: *police officer, firefighter, flight attendant, letter carrier, member of Congress, spokesperson,* and so on: *Every* citizen (not *man*) should have the opportunity to work. See also **–person.**

masterful   *Masterful* means "strong-willed, imperious, domineering": *Her* masterful *approach tended to keep the negotiations brief and to-the-point.* It also is used, as is *masterly,* in the sense "having the skill of a master." But the distinction between the two words should be respected: *His* masterly *recital brought to mind those of his mentor.*

materialize   *Materialize* as an intransitive verb has the primary sense "to assume material form" or, more generally, "to take effective shape": *If our plans* materialize, *we will be traveling to Paris in the spring.* Although *materialize* is widely used informally in the sense "appear" or "happen" (*Three more witnesses testified, but no new evidence* materialized), such usage should be avoided in formal writing.

may   See **can, may.**

means   In the sense "financial resources," *means* takes a plural verb: *Our* means are *adequate for this purchase.* In the sense "a way to an end," it may take a singular or plural verb; the choice of a modifier such as *any* or *all* generally determines the number of the verb: *Every* means was *tried; There* are *several* means *at our disposal.*

meantime, meanwhile   *Meantime* is more common than *meanwhile* as a noun: *In the* meantime, *we made alternative plans for our vacation.* In expressing the same sense as "in the meantime" as a single adverb, *meanwhile* is more common than *meantime:* Meanwhile, *we made alternative plans for our vacation.*

migrate, emigrate, immigrate   *Migrate* is used with reference to both the place of departure and the destination and can be followed by *from* or *to*. It is said of persons, animals, and birds and sometimes implies a lack of permanent settlement, especially as a result of seasonal or periodic movement. *Emigrate* pertains to a single move by a person and implies permanence. It refers specifically to the place of *departure* and emphasizes movement *from* that place. If the place is mentioned, the preposition is *from:* Since many people have *emigrated from* Russia, we see a new demand for Russian-language books. *Immigrate* also pertains to a single move by persons and likewise implies permanence. But it refers to *destination,* emphasizes movement there, and is followed by *to:* Many people have *immigrated to* the United States in recent months.

minimize   According to traditional grammar, *minimize* can mean only "to make as small as possible" and is therefore an absolute term, which cannot be modified by *greatly* or *somewhat,* which are appropriately used only with verbs like *reduce* and *lessen.* The informal use of *minimize* to mean "to make smaller than before," which can be so modified, should be avoided in formal writing.

mobile   See **movable, mobile.**

most, mostly   The adverb *most* is sometimes used informally in the sense of "almost": *Most* all the tapes were on sale last week. However, this usage should be avoided in business writing. In the sense "very," as an intensive where no explicit comparison is involved, *most* is acceptable both in writing and in speech: It proved to be a *most* ingenious solution. The adverb *mostly* means "for the greatest part, mainly" or "generally, usually": The trees are *mostly* evergreens. In writing, one should say *for the most part* (not *mostly*) in sentences like "*For the most part,* Northern Telephone is the supplier of our communications equipment."

movable, mobile   Something is *movable* if it can be moved: All our furniture is *movable;* There is a *movable* partition between our desks. It is *mobile* if it is designed for easy transportation (The van contained a *mobile* electric generating unit) or if it moves frequently (The company owned several *mobile* drilling rigs).

mutual, common   *Mutual* is often used to describe a relation between two or more things, and in this use it can be paraphrased with expressions involving *between* or *each other:* They met to discuss their *mutual* relations, meaning "their relations with each other" or "the relations between them." *Common* describes a relationship shared by the members of a group to something else (Their *common* interest is swimming) or in the expression *common knowledge,* "the knowledge shared by all." The phrase *mutual friend,* however, refers to a friend of each of the several members of a group: The skating partners were originally introduced by a *mutual friend.*

nauseous, nauseated   Traditionally, *nauseous* means "causing nausea"; *nauseated* means "suffering from nausea." People who adhere to tradition avoid using *nauseous* in the sense of *nauseated:* She was *nauseated* after eating in the cafeteria; His behavior is *nauseous.*

need   The verb *need* is used both as a main verb and as an auxiliary verb. As a main verb *need* must be agree with its subject and is followed by *to:* He *needs to* find a new job. As an auxiliary *need* primarily occurs in questions, negations, and *if* clauses. It does not agree with its subject and is not followed by *to:* He *need* not find a new job; *Need it be* done in a hurry? The auxiliary *need* means something like "to be obliged to": You *needn't* come (you are under no obligation to come). In this case there is an externally imposed obligation on the subject *you.* If there were no externally imposed obligation, the main verb could be used: Since I was there when it happened, I *don't need* to hear (not *needn't hear*) the television news account.

neither   *Neither* is construed as singular when it occurs as the subject of a sentence: *Neither of the reports is* finished. Accordingly, a pronoun with *neither* as an antecedent also must be singular: *Neither of the doctors in the lawsuit is* likely to reveal *his or her* identity.

no   When *no* introduces a compound phrase, its elements should be connected with *or* rather than with *nor:* James has *no* experience *or* interest in coaching hockey; *No* modification *or* change in the rules will be acceptable to them.

nominal   *Nominal* in one of its senses means "in name only." Hence a *nominal payment* is a token payment, bearing no relation to the real value of what is being paid for. The word is often extended in use, especially by sellers, to describe a low or bargain price: We also acquired an adjacent 600,000-barrel oil reserve at a *nominal* extra cost.

no sooner   *No sooner,* as a comparative adverb, should be followed by *than,* not *when: No sooner* had I arrived *than* I had to leave for an emergency meeting; I had *no sooner* made an offer *than* they said the property had been sold to another person.

not   Care should be taken with the placement of *not* and other negatives in a sentence to avoid ambiguity. *All issues are not speculative* could be taken to mean either "all of the issues are not speculative" or "not all of the issues are speculative." *We didn't sleep until noon* could mean either "We went to sleep at noon" or "We got up before noon."

nothing   *Nothing* takes a singular verb, even when it is followed by a phrase containing a plural noun or pronoun: *Nothing* except your fears *stands* in your path.

number As a collective noun *number* may take either a singular or a plural verb. It takes a singular verb when it is preceded by the definite article *the: The number* of concert pianists *is* small. It takes a plural verb when preceded by the indefinite article *a: A number* of the workers *are* unskilled.

odd *Odd,* when used to indicate a few more than a given number, should be preceded by a hyphen to avoid ambiguity: There are *thirty-odd* people in line. *Odd* in this sense is used only with round numbers.

off *Off* should not be followed by *of* or *from:* The speaker stepped *off* (not *off of* or *off from*) the platform. Nor should *off* be used for *from* to indicate a source in a sentence: I got a loan *from* (not *off*) the credit union.

on, onto, upon To indicate motion toward a position, both *on* and *onto* can be used: The dog jumped *on* (*onto*) the counter. *Onto* is more specific, however, in indicating that the motion was initiated from an outside point, such as from the floor. In constructions where *on* is an adverb attached to a verb, it should not be joined with *to* to form the single word *onto:* The lecturer moved *on to* (not *onto*) the next subject. In their uses to indicate spatial relations, *on* and *upon* are often interchangeable: The container was resting *on* (or *upon*) the counter. To indicate a relation between two things, however, instead of between an action and an end point, *upon* cannot always be used: Hand me the book *on* (not *upon*) the table.

one another See **each other, one another.**

onetime, one-time When spelled as a single word, *onetime* means "former." When hyphenated, *one-time* means "only once." Thus a former employee is a *onetime employee*; a mayor who served as mayor only once is a *one-time mayor*.

only When used as an adverb, *only* should be placed with care to avoid ambiguity. Generally, this means placing *only* next to the word or words that it limits: Dictators respect *only force;* they are not moved by words. Dictators *only respect* force; they do not worship it. She picked up the receiver *only when* he entered, not before. She *only picked up* the receiver when he entered; she didn't dial the number. Occasionally, placement of *only* earlier in the sentence seems more natural: I can (*only*) make my decision by Friday of next week *only* if I receive a copy of the latest report by tomorrow. Placement of *only* after *can* would serve the rhetorical function of warning the reader that a condition on the statement follows. *Only* is often used as a conjunction equivalent to *but* in the sense "were it not that": They would have come, *only* they were snowed in. This usage is not considered standard in business writing.

oral   See **verbal, oral.**

ought   *Ought to* is sometimes used without a following verb if the meaning is clear: Should we begin soon? Yes, we *ought to.* The omission of *to* (no, we *ought* not), however, is not standard. Usages like *one hadn't ought to come* and *one shouldn't ought to say that,* which are common in certain varieties of American English, should be avoided in standard English.

owing to   See **because, due to, owing to.**

pair   *Pair* as a noun can be followed by a singular or plural verb. The singular is always used when *pair* denotes the set taken as a single entity: This *pair* of shoes *is* a year old. A plural verb is used when the members are considered as individuals: The *pair are* working more harmoniously now.

parent   The use of *parent* as a verb is generally considered unacceptable. Since there is no acceptable one-word substitute for it, paraphrases like *perform the duties of parenthood* are recommended.

party   A person may be called a *party* in the sense of "participant": She was a *party* to the industrial espionage ring. Except in legal usage, *party* should not be used as a general synonym for *person:* The *person* (not *party*) who stole $12,000 from the treasury was arrested.

pass   The past tense and past participle of *pass* is *passed:* They *passed* (or *have passed*) right by the front gate. *Past* is the corresponding adjective (in centuries *past*), adverb (drove *past*), and preposition (*past* midnight; *past* the crisis).

people, persons   Traditionally, *people* and *persons* have been distinguished in usage. *People* is the proper term when referring to a large group of individuals, collectively and indefinitely: *People* use a wide variety of our products at work and at home. *Persons* is applicable to a specific and relatively small number: Two *persons* were fired. In modern usage, however, *people* is also acceptable with any plural number: I counted two *people*. The possessive form is *people's* (the *people's* rights) except when *people* is used in the plural to refer to two or more groups considered to be political or cultural entities: The Slavic *peoples'* history is marked by much tragedy and sorrow.

per   *Per* is used with reference to statistics and units of measurement: There is a 10 cent charge *per* mile; The *per*-day rate is $125 *per* person. In nontechnical writing, it is preferable to substitute *a* or *each* for *per:* A dozen additional dinner guests *a* (or *each*) day was not uncommon. Its more general use to mean "according to" (We will work *per* the terms of this contract, not beyond) is limited to business and legal writing.

percent, percentage   *Percent* is usually written as one word in business material and should be spelled out (that is, instead of using the percent sign) in nontechnical work: 20 *percent*. The number of the noun that follows it in a prepositional phrase or that is understood to follow it governs the number of the verb: Twenty *percent* of the stock *is* owned by a conglomerate; Forty-seven *percent* of our sales *come* from consumer appliances. *Percentage,* when preceded by *the,* takes a singular verb: The *percentage* of unskilled workers *is* small. When preceded by *a,* it takes either a singular or plural verb, depending on the number of the noun in the prepositional phrase that follows: A small *percentage* of the workers *are* unskilled; A large *percentage* of the order for that CD *was* never shipped.

perfect, perfectly   *Perfect* has been traditionally considered an absolute term, like *unique, chief,* and *prime,* and should not be subject to comparison with *more, less, almost,* and other modifiers of degree. The comparative form nonetheless is used in the United States Constitution in the phrase *a more perfect union.* It is generally regarded as correct when *perfect* is used to mean "ideal for the purposes": A *more perfect spot* for our broadcasting station could not be found. *Perfectly* is used in casual speech as an intensive meaning "quite," "altogether," or "just": They threw away a *perfectly good* coat; The food was *perfectly dreadful.* This use should be avoided in business writing.

–person compounds   *Person* is increasingly used to create compounds that may refer to either a man or a woman: *chairperson, spokesperson, anchorperson, salesperson.* These forms can be used when the reference is to the position itself, regardless of who might hold it: The committee should elect a new *chairperson* at its meeting. They are also appropriate when speaking of the specific individual holding the position: She was the best *anchorperson* the local station had ever had. In cases referring to specific people, alternatives such as *anchorwoman* and *spokesman* are also acceptable and might be preferred by the holder of the position.

persons   See **people, persons.**

personality   *Personality,* meaning "a celebrity" or "a notable," is widely used in speech and journalism. But it should be avoided in this sense in business writing.

persuade See convince, persuade.

plead In strict legal usage one is said to *plead guilty* or *plead not guilty* but not to *plead innocent*. In nonlegal contexts, however, *plead innocent* is sometimes used.

plus *Plus* does not have the conjunctive force of *and*. Therefore, when *plus* is used after a singular or plural subject, the verb remains singular: Two *plus* two *equals* four; Inadequate research *plus* careless writing *results* in a weak article. *Plus* is sometimes used loosely as a conjunction to connect two independent clauses: We had terrible weather this year, *plus* our water heater broke. But this use is not standard and should be avoided.

P.M. See ante meridiem.

poor In formal usage *poor* should be used as an adjective, not an adverb: Many devote their lives to helping *poor* people survive. It should not be used to qualify a verb as in *did poor* or *never worked poorer*. *Poorly* and *more poorly* are required in such examples.

practical, practicable *Practical* describes that which is sensible and useful: They devised a *practical* approach. *Practicable* means "usable" and "workable": Your idea is *practicable*. The distinction, however, is often subtle, and many writers use *practical* in both cases. This example illustrates the traditional distinction: It might be *practicable* to build a bullet train between New York and Omaha, but it would not be *practical*.

practically, virtually The primary sense of *practically* is "in a way that is practical": She expected the consultant to handle the project *practically*. It has also become almost interchangeable with *virtually*, meaning "in fact or to all purposes": The city was *practically* (or *virtually*) paralyzed by the snowstorm. Thus a man whose liabilities exceed his assets may be said to be *practically bankrupt,* even though he has not been legally declared insolvent. By a slight extension of this meaning, however, *practically* is often used to mean "nearly" or "all but": They had *practically* closed the restaurant by the time I arrived. Because of the potential for confusion, such use should be avoided, especially in business writing.

precipitate, precipitant, precipitous   The adjective *precipitate* and the adverb *precipitately* often refer to rash, overhasty human actions: It was a *precipitate* decision that he soon regretted. *Precipitant* and *precipitantly* are also used in the foregoing ways, with stress on rushing forward or falling headlong, literally or figuratively: The firm was not one to engage in *precipitant* action. *Precipitous* and *precipitously* are used primarily of physical steepness (a *precipitous* slope) or in the figurative extensions of such literal uses (a *precipitous* drop in interest rates).

premiere   *Premiere* is primarily used as a noun meaning "the first public performance": Many stars turned out for the *premiere* of the movie. It is generally unacceptable as a verb despite its wide use in the world of entertainment.

presently   *Presently* is used primarily in the sense "soon": Karen will arrive *presently.* It is also used in the sense "at the present time": He is *presently* (*now*) living in Chicago. When you use this word you should make sure that your meaning is clear from the context.

principle, principal   *Principal* and *principle* are often confused but have no meanings in common. *Principle* is only a noun, and all its senses are abstract: *principles* of nuclear physics. *Principal* is both a noun and an adjective. As a noun (aside from its specialized meaning in law and finance), it generally denotes a person who holds a high position or plays an important role: A meeting between all the *principals* in the transaction had been arranged; She is the new high school principal.

As an adjective it has the related sense of "chief" or "leading": Only the *principal* candidates, participated in the debate.

protagonist   *Protagonist* denotes the leading figure in a theatrical drama or, by extension, in any work or undertaking. Sometimes in modern usage the sense of singularity is lost: There are three *protagonists* in the takeover fight. This watered-down meaning should be avoided. *Protagonist* is also used to indicate a champion or advocate, another use that should be avoided.

prove, proved, proven   The regular form *proved* is the preferred past participle: You have *proved* your point; The theory has been *proved* by our mathematicians. The alternative *proven* in such examples is unacceptable to many language critics. *Proven* is a Scots variant made familiar through its legal use: The charges were not *proven*. But *proven* is more widely used as an adjective directly before a noun as in a *proven* talent or a *proven* point.

quick, quickly   Both *quick* and *quickly* can be used as adverbs. *Quick* is more frequent in conversation: Come *quick*! In writing the slightly more formal *quickly* is preferred: When the alarm was heard by the security guards, they responded *quickly*. In the latter example, *quick* would be unacceptable to most experts.

quote, cite   The verb *quote* is appropriate when words are being given exactly as they were originally written or spoken: He *quoted* the first paragraph of the report. When the reference is less exact, *cite* is preferable: He *cited* an advertising study. The noun *quote* as a substitute for *quotation* should be avoided in formal writing: The *quotation* (not *quote*) from Milton was the perfect end to her presentation.

raise, rise   *Raise* is properly used as a transitive verb: *Raise* the garage door. For intransitive uses, *rise* is standard: The elevator *rises*. However, *raise* is sometimes used as an intransitive verb:

The window *raises* easily. As a noun *raise,* rather than *rise,* is now standard in the United States for an increase in salary, although one still speaks of *a rise in prices.*

rare, scarce *Rare* and *scarce* are sometimes interchangeable, but *scarce* carries an additional implication that the quantities involved are insufficient or inadequate. Thus we speak of *rare books* or of *the rare qualities* of someone we admire but of increasingly *scarce* oil reserves.

rarely, seldom The use of *ever* after *rarely* or *seldom* is considered redundant: He *rarely* (not *rarely ever*) makes a mistake. The following constructions, using either *rarely* or *seldom,* are standard, however: *rarely if ever; rarely or never* (not *rarely or ever*).

rather *Rather* is usually preceded by *should* or *would* in expressing preference: They *would rather* not eat dinner at home tonight. But *had* is equally acceptable: I *had rather* work nights than be unemployed. In a contraction such as *he'd,* either *would* or *had* can be understood: *He'd rather* (He would or had rather) be bored than be unemployed. As a modifier, *rather* is frequently unnecessary and overused: *rather nice; rather cold; rather important.*

reciprocal, joint *Reciprocal,* like *mutual,* can apply to relations between the members of a group, often with reference to an exchange of goods or favors: They agreed on terms for *reciprocal* trade. *Joint* is often used to describe an undertaking in which several partners are involved: The *joint* efforts of federal and local officials will be required to eradicate acid rain.

refer/reference See allude/allusion, refer/reference.

regard, respects *Regard* is usually singular in the phrase *in* (or *with*) *regard to* (not *in regards to*). *Regarding* and *as regards* are used in the same sense "with reference to" but are not as widely acceptable. In the same sense *with respect to* is acceptable, but *respecting* is not. *Respects* is sometimes preferable to *regards* in the sense "particulars": In some *respects* (not *regards*) you are similar to my friend Robert.

relatively   *Relatively* is appropriate when a comparison is stated or implied: The first question was *relatively* easy (that is, in comparison to the others). *Relatively* should not be used to mean simply "fairly": I am *fairly* (not *relatively*) sure of it.

repel, repulse   The verbs *repel* and *repulse* both have the physical sense of "to drive back or off." They also may apply to rebuffing or rejecting discourteously, but only *repel* is used in the sense of "to cause distaste or aversion": Your arrogance *repelled* us; He rudely *repulsed* all of our attempts to help him.

replete   *Replete* means "abundantly supplied": The takeover battle was *replete* with scandal, mudslinging, and threats. It should not be used to mean simply "complete" or "equipped": The subdivision has a club *complete* (not *replete*) with pool, tennis courts, and golf courses.

responsible   Some usage experts believe that *responsible* should be used only with reference to persons, since only persons can be held accountable. The word is widely used, however, with reference to things: Defective welding was *responsible* for the buckled axle.

restive, restless   *Restive* and *restless* are used as equivalent terms. *Restive*, however, implies more than simply "nervous" or "fidgety." It implies resistance to some sort of restraint. Thus a patient who is sleeping poorly may be *restless*, but the same patient is *restive* only if kept in bed against his or her will.

rise   See raise, rise.

sacrilegious   The adjective *sacrilegious* is often misspelled through confusion with *religious*. It refers to gross irreverence toward something sacred: His profanity in church was *sacrilegious*.

said   As an adjective *said* is seldom appropriate to any but legal writing, where it is equivalent to *aforesaid:* The *said* tenant (named in a lease) agreed to maintain the yard; The *said* property has a lien on it. In similar contexts in general usage, *said* should be omitted as in *the tenant; the property.*

same   Only in legal writing is *the same* or just *same* used as a substitute for *it* or *them.* In general writing one should be specific: The charge is $5. Please send *your payment* (not *the same*) today.

scarce   See **rare, scarce.**

scarcely   *Scarcely* has the force of a negative; therefore, it is not properly used with another negative: I *could scarcely* believe it (not I *couldn't scarcely* believe it). A clause following *scarcely* is introduced by *when* or, less often, by *before* but not by *than:* The match had *scarcely* begun *when* (or *before*) it was rained out.

seasonal, seasonable   *Seasonal* and *seasonable,* though closely related, are differentiated in usage. *Seasonal* applies to what depends on or is controlled by the season of the year: There is always a *seasonal* rise in unemployment during the late winter months. *Seasonable* applies to what is appropriate to the season (*seasonable* clothing) or timely (a *seasonable* intervention). Rains are *seasonal* if they occur at a certain time of the year. They are *seasonable* at any time if they save the crops.

see that   The phrase *see where* sometimes occurs in conversation as an informal equivalent of *see that:* I *see that* (*see where*) everything is running smoothly at the rehearsal. The same applies to *read where.* These conversational usages should be avoided in business writing.

seldom   See rarely, seldom.

semimonthly   See bimonthly, semimonthly.

set, sit   Originally, *set* meant "to cause (something) to sit," so it is now in most cases a transitive verb: The worker *sets* his shovel down; One *sets* the table. *Sit* is generally an intransitive verb: They *sit* at the microphone. There are some exceptions: The sun *sets* (not *sits*); A hen *sets* (or *sits*) on her eggs.

shall, will   In formal writing *shall* is used in the first person to indicate futurity: I *shall* leave tomorrow. In the second and third persons the same sense of futurity is expressed by *will:* He *will* come this afternoon. Use of the auxiliaries *shall* and *will* is reversed when the writer wants to indicate conditions, such as determination, promise, obligation, command, compulsion, permission, or inevitability: I *will* leave tomorrow. In contemporary writing *will* is used in all three persons to indicate futurity: We *will* be in New York next week. *Shall* is still used in some first-person interrogatives (*Shall* we go? When *shall* we visit your sister?) and in a few set phrases (We *shall* overcome). In writing, a condition other than mere futurity is often expressed more clearly by an alternative to *shall* or *will,* such as *must* or *have to* (indicating determination, compulsion, or obligation) or by use of an intensifying word, such as *certainly* or *surely,* with *shall* or *will.* Informally, contractions such as *I'll, we'll,* and *you'll* are generally used without distinction between the functions of *shall* and *will* as formally defined.

should, would   Traditionally, the rules governing the use of *should* and *would* were based on the rules governing the use of *shall* and *will.* The rules have been eroded even more in the case of *should* and *would.* Either *should* or *would* is now used in the first person to express conditional futurity: If I had known that, I *should* (or *would*) have made a different reply. In the second and third persons, only *would* is acceptable: If he had known that, he *would* have made a different reply. *Would* cannot always be substituted for *should,* however. *Should* is used in all three persons in a conditional clause: If I (or *you* or *he* or *she*) *should* decide to go, we will give you a call. Should is also used in all three persons to express duty or obligation (the equivalent of *ought to*): I (or *you* or *he* or *she*) *should* go. Would is used to express volition or promise: I agreed that I *would* do it. Either *would* or *should* is possible as an auxiliary with *like, be inclined, be glad, prefer,* and related verbs: I *would* (or should) like to call your attention to an oversight in the accountant's report. But *would* is more common than *should. Should have* is sometimes incorrectly written *should of* by writers who have mistaken the source of the spoken contraction *should've.*

since See **as, since.**

sit See **set, sit.**

slow, slowly *Slow* is sometimes used as an informal variant of the adverb *slowly* when it comes after the verb: We drove the car *slow.* But *slowly* should be used in formal contexts. *Slow* is often used informally when brevity and forcefulness are sought: Drive *slow! Slow* is also the established idiomatic form with certain senses of common verbs: The watch runs *slow;* Take it *slow.*

so The conjunction *so* is followed by *that* when it introduces a clause stating the purpose of or reason for an action: The supervisor stayed late *so that* (in order that) he could catch up on his paperwork. *So* can stand alone, however, when it is used to introduce a clause that states the result or consequence of something: The canning process kills much of the flavor of food, *so* salt is added.

so . . . as See **as . . . as, so . . . as.**

sometime   *Sometime* as an adjective is properly used to mean "former." It is also used colloquially with the meaning "occasional": The team's *sometime* pitcher is a favorite of the fans.

stratum   The standard singular form is *stratum;* the standard plural is *strata* (or sometimes *stratums*) but not *stratas*.

take   See **bring, take.**

tend   *Tend* is an informal alternative to *attend* in the phrase *tend to,* meaning "to apply one's attention to": I stayed home today to *tend to* (*attend to*) my garden.

than, as   In comparisons, a pronoun following *than* or *as* may be taken as either the subject or the object of an implied verb whose sense is understood: John is older *than* I (*am*). The nominative *I* is required since the verb *am* is implied. Yet, in the sentence It does not surprise me *as much as him,* the use of the objective *him* can be justified by analogy to the sentence It does not surprise me *as much as* (it surprises) *him.*

this, that   *This* and *that* are both used as demonstrative pronouns to refer to a thought expressed earlier: The door was unopened; *that* (or *this*) in itself casts doubt on the guard's theory. *That* is sometimes prescribed as the better choice in referring to what has gone before (as in the preceding example). When the referent is yet to be mentioned, only *this* is used: *This* is what bothers me — we have no time to consider late applications. When used as an adjective, *this* often occurs speech as an emphatic variant of the indefinite article *a: This* friend of mine is moving to Portland; I have *this* terrible headache. But this usage is casual and should be avoided in business writing.

tight   *Tight* as an adverb appears after the verb when it follows verbs such as *squeeze, shut, close, tie,* and *hold:* The father told the child to hold on *tight* to the railing; Close it *tight*. In most cases the adverb *tightly* also may be used in this position: Close it *tightly*. In a few cases *tight* is the only form that may be used: They told us to sit *tight* and not to worry; Sleep *tight*, little one. Before a verb only *tightly* is used: The money supply will be *tightly* controlled.

together with   *Together with*, like *in addition to*, is often employed following the subject of a sentence or clause to introduce an addition. The addition, however, does not alter the number of the verb, which is governed by the subject: The chairperson (singular), *together with* two aides, *is* expected in an hour. The same is true of *along with, as well as, besides, in addition to*, and *like*: Common sense *as well as* training *is* a requisite for the job.

too   *Too* preceded by *not* or another negative is frequently used informally as a form of understatement to convey humor or sarcasm: The workers were *not too* pleased with the amount of their raises; This comedian is *not too* funny. *Not too*, when used to mean approximately "not very," is also considered casual: Passage of the bill is *not* now considered *too* likely. Such casual use should be avoided in business writing. *Too* can often be eliminated from such sentences without loss; but if deletion gives undue stress to the negative sense, the writer may find *not very* or *none too* preferable choices: The comedian is *not very* funny. *Too* is often used in writing in place of *moreover* or *in addition* to introduce a sentence: There has been a cutback in oil production; *too*, rates have been increasing. This usage also should be avoided in business writing.

torn   *Torn*, never *tore*, is the standard past participle of the verb *tear*. I have *torn* a page of the book.

tortuous, torturous   Although *tortuous* and *torturous* have a common Latin source, their primary meanings are distinct. *Tortuous* means "twisting" (a *tortuous* road) or by extension "extremely strained or devious" (*tortuous* reasoning). *Tortuous* refers primarily to the pain of torture. However, *torturous* also can be used in the sense of "twisted" or "strained," and *tortured* is an even stronger synonym as in *tortured reasoning*.

transpire   *Transpire* has long been used in the sense "to become known": It soon *transpired* that they intended to vote for my opponent. The meaning "to happen" or "to take place" has come into use more recently: Marcia wondered what would *transpire* next. This latter use should be avoided in business writing.

try and, try to   *Try and* is common in informal conversation for *try to,* especially in established combinations such as *try and stop me* and *try and get some rest.* In most contexts, however, it is not interchangeable with *try to* unless the situation is clearly informal. The following is unacceptable in formal writing: It is a mistake to *try and* force compliance with a rule that is so unpopular.

type   *Type* is followed by *of* in constructions like *that type of leather.* The variant form that omits *of,* as in *that type leather,* is generally unacceptable. *Type* is most appropriate when reference is being made to a well-defined or sharply distinct category: That *type* of chassis gives passengers a smooth ride; I do not get an upset stomach when I take this *type* of aspirin. When the categorization is vaguer or less well accepted, *kind* or *sort* is preferable. See also **kind.**

under way   See **way, under way, aweigh.**

unexceptional, unexceptionable   *Unexceptional* is often confused with *unexceptionable.* When the desired meaning is "not open to objection" or "above reproach," the term is *unexceptionable:* She presented *unexceptionable* arguments for her curious behavior on the train. *Unexceptional* should be used to mean "not exceptional": Although the course sounded like it would be complex and interesting, it proved to be *unexceptional.*

uninterested   See **disinterested, uninterested.**

upon   See **on, upon.**

various   *Various,* sometimes appearing as a collective noun followed by *of,* is not standard usage: He spoke to *various of* the members. It is correct as an adjective in the sense "of diverse kinds": She left early for *various* reasons.

verbal, oral   In the sense "by word of mouth," *verbal* is synonymous with *oral.* In other senses *verbal* has to do with words, whether written or spoken such as *verbal* communication (as opposed to communication through gestures or body language). *Verbal,* when applied to terms such as *agreement, promise, commitment,* and *understanding,* is well established as a synonym of *oral.* But anyone who fears misunderstanding may use *oral* instead: They struck an *oral* (or *verbal*) agreement.

virtually   See **practically, virtually.**

wait on, wait for   *Wait on* is correctly used in the sense "to serve." *Wait for* is used to mean "awaiting": We will *wait for* (not *on*) your decision.

want   When *want* is followed immediately by an infinitive construction, it does not take *for:* I *want you* to go (not *want for you*). When *want* and the infinitive are separated in the sentence, however, *for* is used: What I *want* is *for you* to finish that one first; I *want* very much *for you* to give me the recipe.

–ward, –wards   Since the suffix *–ward* indicates direction, there is no need to use *to the* with it: The cargo ship is sailing *westward* (or *to the west*).

way, under way, aweigh   *Way,* not *ways,* is the generally accepted form in writing when the term refers to distance:

We have a long *way* to go. The phrase *under way* (meaning "in motion" or "in progress") is written as two words or as one (*underway*), including reference to the nautical (*underway* not *under weigh*). Confusion sometimes arises because an anchor is *weighed* and, when off the bottom, is *aweigh*.

well   See **good, well.**

what   When *what* is the subject of a *clause,* it is singular if it is taken as equivalent to *that which* or *the thing which*: *What seems to be a personality conflict is creating problems in the cast.* It is plural if it is equivalent to *those which* or *the things which*: *What were at first minor incidents have now become major problems in the chemical disposal system.* When a *what* clause is the subject of a *sentence,* it is usually plural if the clause indicates plurality. But the conditions governing this choice are complicated, and an authority, such as *The American Heritage® Dictionary of the English Language, Third Edition,* should be consulted for further study.

whatever   *Whatever* (pronoun) and *what ever* are used in questions and statements: *Whatever* (or *what ever*) *made them say that?* Both forms are used, although the one-word form is more common. (The same is true of *whoever, whenever, wherever,* and *however* when used in corresponding senses.) For the adjective only the one-word form is used: *Take whatever office supplies you need.* When the phrase preceding a restrictive clause is introduced by *whatever, that* should not be used: *Whatever video that you want to view will be ordered.* A better construction would be: *Whatever video you want to view will be ordered.*

when   In casual speech *when* is used to mean "a situation or event in which": *A dilemma is when you don't know which way to turn.* This usage, however, should be avoided in business writing.

where   When *where* refers to "the place *from* which," it requires the preposition *from*: *Where* did you come *from*? When it refers to "the place *to* which," it requires no preposition: *Where* did they go (*to*)? When *where* refers to "the place *at* which," it also requires no preposition: *Where* are they (*at*)?

which   *Which* sometimes refers to an entire preceding statement rather than to a single word: The drilling failed to turn up any new reserves, *which* disturbed the geologist. In this acceptable example the reference is clear. But when *which* follows a noun, the antecedent may be in doubt and ambiguity may result: The inspector filed the complaint, *which* was a surprise. If *which* is intended to refer to the entire first clause rather than to *complaint,* the desired sense would be expressed more clearly by this construction: We learned that the inspector had filed the complaint, and that discovery came as a surprise to us.

whose   *Whose,* as the possessive form of a relative pronoun, can refer to both persons and things. Thus it functions as the possessive of both *who* and *which*. The following example, in which *whose* refers to an inanimate object, is acceptable: The car, *whose* design is ultramodern, is typical of the new styles. (The alternative possessive form *of which* is also used in referring to things but is sometimes cumbersome in application.)

why   *Why* is redundant in *the reason why*: The reason (*why*) they joined the new health club is not clear. The sentence could also be recast: Their reasons for joining the new health club are not clear.

will   See **shall, will.**

–wise   The suffix *–wise* has long been used to mean "in the manner or direction of": *clockwise, likewise, otherwise,* and *slantwise*. It is particularly overused as business jargon meaning "with relation to" and attachable to any noun such as *saleswise* and *inflationwise*. Generally considered vague and pretentious, the *–wise* suffix should be avoided in all forms of domestic and international communication: The report is not encouraging *saleswise; Taxwise,* however, it is an attractive arrangement. Rephrase such sentences: The report is not encouraging *in terms of potential sales;* For *tax savings,* it is an attractive arrangement.

with *With* does not have the conjunctive force of *and.* Consequently, in the following example the verb is governed by the singular subject and remains singular: The superintendant, *with* his assistant, is expected at the science fair on Monday.

would See **should, would.**

wreak *Wreak* is sometimes confused with *wreck,* perhaps because the *wreaking* of damage may leave a *wreck:* The storm *wreaked* havoc along the coast. The past tense and past participle of *wreak* is *wreaked,* not *wrought,* which is an alternative past tense and past participle of *work.* Thus the Bible says God *wreaked* punishment on sinners, but Samuel F. B. Morse properly asked "What hath God *wrought?*"

PICKING A PREPOSITION

The following list contains forms of verbs, adjectives, and nouns that regularly appear in combination with certain prepositions. Following in each entry word are the prepositions that are idiomatically linked with that word.

Picking the right preposition is often a matter of idiom. Related verbs such as *acquiesce, agree,* and *concur* might be thought to agree in every detail in the choice of prepositions, but they do not; therefore consulting a list of idiomatic expressions is the only sure method of avoiding error. Even people who work with the language every day — such as professional writers and speakers — often consult such a list. The list is not intended to imply that the entry word must be followed or preceded by a preposition but rather that in certain contexts it is often used with that preposition. Only usages that commonly give difficulty are contained in the list.

The prepositions listed are the ones most often used with the words in question; where the choice is determined by a particular sense of the entry word, the sense is indicated and illustrated when an example of the particular combination is not likely to readily come to mind. No adverbial usage is included, nor are the countless combinations of entry words followed by infinitives. Phrasal verbs, such as *bottom out* and *carry forward*, are also omitted.

abashed at
abhorrence of
abhorrent to
ability at *or* with (*at mechanics; with tools*)

abound in *or* with
absolve of *or* from
accede to
access to
accessible to

accession of or to (of property; to the throne)

acclimate or acclimatize to

accommodate to or with (to changing circumstances; with everything she requested)

accompanied by or with (by her husband; with every difficulty imaginable)

accord (n.) between, of, or with; (v.) to or with (accord every consideration to her; a statement that accords with the law)

account (v.) for or to (for things; to persons)

accrue to

acquiesce in

acquit of

adapt for, from, or to

addicted to (plus noun, but not plus infinitive: addicted to heroin; to taking heroin; not to take heroin)

adept at or in

adequate for or to (for a goal or purpose; to a need)

adjacent to

admit to, into, or of (admit one to or into a club; a passage admitting to the lobby; a matter that admits of several views)

adverse to

advocate (n.) of; (v.) for

affiliate (v.) with or to

affinity of, between, or with

akin to

alien (adj.) to or from

ally (v.) to or with

aloof from

amenable to

amused by or at

analogous in, to, or with (in qualities; to or with each other)

analogy of, between, to, or with

angry at, with, or about

antidote to, toward, or against

antipathy to, toward, or against

anxious for or about

apprehensive of or for (of danger; for one's welfare)

apprise of

apropos of

arrogate to or for

aspiration toward or after

aspire to, toward, or after

assent to

attempt (n.) at or on (at realizing an achievement; on a person's life)

attended by or with (by persons; by or with conditions or circumstances)

attest to

attune to

augment by or with

averse to

aversion for, to, or toward

basis for, in, or of (*for a rumor; in fact* or *in law; of a medicinal compound; of* or *for an official's authority*)

bid (*v.*) for or on (*for nomination; on property*)

blame (*v.*) for or on (*blame her for the delay; blame the delay on him*)

boast (*n., v.*) of or about

boggle at

capacity of or for (*of four quarts; for growth*)

capitalize at or on (*at $4 million; on an opponent's mistakes*)

careless about, in, or of (*about her attendance; in her speech; of* or *about the children's welfare*)

caution (*v.*) about or against

center (*v.*) on, upon, in, or at (but not *around*)

charge (*v.*) for or with (*for services; with manslaughter; with a duty; with strong emotion*)

clear (*adj.*) of; (*v.*) of or from

climb up (though usually redundant), or down

coincide with

common (*adj.*) to

comparable to or with

compare with or to (like things that are strictly comparable *with* each other; unlike things *to* each other; unlike things *to* each other in sense of *liken*; things *with* each other in sense of *be worthy of comparison*)

compatible with

complementary to

compliment (*n., v.*) on

concern (*n., v.*) about, in, or with

concur in or with (*in a plan* or *policy; with a person* or *view*)

conducive to

confide in or to

conform or conformity to or with

connive at or with (*at a fraud; with an accomplice*)

consequent (*adj.*) or consequential to, on, or upon

consist of or in (*an alloy consisting chiefly of nickel; treason, which consists in aiding the enemies of one's country*)

consistent with

contemporaneous with

contemporary with

contemptuous of

contend with, against, about, or over (*with* or *against rivals, enemies,* or *unfavorable circumstances; about* or *over disputed matters*)

contiguous to

contingent on or upon

contrast (*n.*) between, to, or

with (*between things; in contrast to* or *with*); (*v.*) with

conversant with

convict (*v.*) of

correspond to *or* with (*a statement not corresponding to* or *with his earlier account; a part that corresponds to the bore of a musket; when I corresponded with her*)

culminate in

cure (*v.*) of

decide on, upon, for, *or* against (*on* or *upon a matter* or *issue; for* or *against a principal in a legal action*)

deficient in

deprive of

derive from

desire (*n.*) for

desirous of

desist from

despair (*v.*) of

destined for (*for an end, use,* or *purpose; for a locality*)

destitute of

destructive to *or* of

deviate (*v.*) from

devoid of

devolve from, on, to *or* upon

differ from, on, over, *or* with (*from another person in outlook; on* or *over issues; with a second party to an argument*)

different from *or* than (*a job different from his; an outcome different from what we expected; how different things seem now than yesterday*). *Different from* is the preferred form when it works readily — when *from* is followed by a single word or short clause. *Different than* is most acceptable when it aids conciseness — when *from* could not be used except ponderously and when *than* is followed by a condensed clause.

differentiate between, among, *or* from

diminution of

disappointed by, in, *or* with (*by* or *in a person; in* or *with a thing*)

discourage from

disdain (*n.*) for

disengage from

disgusted with, at, *or* by (*with a person* or *an action; by a personal quality, action,* or *behavior*)

dislike of

dispossess of *or* from

disqualify for *or* from

dissent (*n., v.*) from

dissimilar to

dissociate from

dissuade from

distaste for

distinguish from, between, *or*

among (*distinguish one species from another; distinguish between* or *among shades of meaning*)

distrustful of

divest of

dote on

emanate from

embellish with

emigrate from

empty (*adj.*) of

enamored of *or* with

encroach on *or* upon

end (*v.*) with *or* in (*with a light dessert* or *with a toast; in divorce*)

endow with

entrust to *or* with (*entrust a mission to a confidant; entrust a friend with a mission*)

envelop in

envious of

essential (*adj.*) to *or* for; (*n.*) of

estrange from

exclusive of

excuse (*v.*) for *or* from (*for a fault; from an obligation* or *duty*)

exonerate of *or* from

expect from *or* of (*expect an apology from a mistaken person; expect integrity of a partner*)

experience (*n.*) in *or* of

expert (*adj., n.*) in, at, *or* with

(*in* or *at weaving; with a loom*)

expressive of

exude from

favorable to, toward, *or* for

fear (*n.*) of *or* for (*of death; for my safety*)

fond of

fondness for

foreign to

free (*adj., v.*) of *or* from

freedom of *or* from

friend of *or* to

frightened at *or* by

fugitive (*n., adj.*) from

grateful to *or* for (*to a person; for a benefit*)

grieve for, after, *or* at

habitual with

hanker after

heal by *or* of

hinder from

hindrance to

hint (*v.*) at

honor (*v.*) by, for, *or* with (*by* or *with a citation for bravery; for his bravery; with one's presence*)

hope (*n.*) for *or* of; (*v.*) for

identical with *or* to

identity (oneself) with (*with the hero of a play*)

immigrate to

impatient at *or* with (*at a condition of affairs; with a person*)

impervious to

implicit in

impressed by *or* with

improve on *or* upon

inaccessible to

incentive (*n.*) to *or* for

incidental to

incongruous to

inconsistent with

incorporate in, into, *or* with

independent (*adj.*) of

infer from

inferior to

infested with

influence (*n.*) on, upon, over, *or* of

infuse with

inimical to *or* toward

initiate into

innocent of

inquire about, after, *or* into

inroad into

insight into

inspire by *or* with

instruct in

intention of

intercede with, for, *or* on behalf of

intrude on, upon, *or* into

inundated with

invest in *or* with (*in bonds; with the rank and duties of an office*)

involve in

isolate from

jealous of *or* for (*of his power; for her rights and welfare*)

justified in

lack (*v.*) in (*lacking in support*); transitive usage (*lack support*)

laden with

lament (*n., v.*) for *or* over

laugh (*n.*) at *or* over; (*v.*) at

level (*v.*) at *or* with (*level a gun or a charge at a person; level wood with a plane; with a person — that is, be honest in dealing*)

liable for *or* to (*for an act; for or to a duty or service; to a superior*)

liken to

martyr (*n.*) to; (*v.*) for

mastery of *or* over (*of a subject; of or over an adversary or obstacle*)

means of, for, *or* to

meddle in *or* with

mediate between *or* among

mediate on *or* upon

militate against *or* (rarely) for

mindful of

mistrustful of

mock at

monopoly of

muse on, upon, *or* over

necessary (*adj., n.*) for *or* to

necessity for, to, *or* of

need (*n.*) for *or* of

neglectful of

negligent in *or* of

oblivious of *or* to

observant of

obtrude on *or* upon

occasion for or of (for rejoicing; of my visit)
occupied by or with
offend against
opportunity of or for
opposite (adj.) to or from; (n.) of
opt for or against
original (adj.) with
originate in or with
overwhelm by or with
parallel (adj.) to; (n.) between or with
partake in or of
patient (adj.) with or of
peculiar to
permeate into or through
permeated by
permit (v.) of (a rule that permits of two interpretations)
persevere in or against
persist in
persuaded by, of, or into
pertinent to
pervert (v.) from
possessed of, by, or with (of great wealth; of a keen wit; by or with an urge to kill)
possibility of or for
precedence of or over
precedent (adj.) to; (n.) for or of (for a ruling; of seating members according to rank)
preclude from
prefer to (prefer live jazz to recordings)

pregnant by or with (by a person; with significance)
prejudicial to
preoccupied by or with
preparatory to
prerequisite (adj.) to; (n.) of
preside at or over
presume on or upon
prevail over, against, on, upon, or with (over or against an adversary; on, upon, or with a person to provide a service)
prodigal (adj.) of
productive of
proficient in or at
profit (v.) by or from
prohibit from
prone to
provide for, against, or with (for or against an emergency; for a dependent child; for annual elections, by law; with food and medicine)
pursuant to
qualify for or as
receptive to
reconcile to or with (to hard times; one's belief with another's)
redolent of
regard (n.) for or to (for a person; in or with regard to a matter)
repent of
replete with

respect (*n.*) for, to, *or* of (*for a person; with* or *in respect to; in respect of*)
responsibility for
restrain from
revel in
rich in
rob of
satiate with
saturate with
scared at *or* by
secure (*adj.*) in
similar to
slave (*n.*) to *or* of
solicitous of, about, *or* for
subject (*adj.*) to
suffer from
suitable for *or* to
superior (*adj.*) to
sympathetic to *or* toward
sympathy for, toward, *or* with (*for* or *toward a person or cause; in sympathy with a cause*)
tendency to *or* toward
thrill (*v.*) to, at, *or* with (*to or at a source of delight; with delight*)
tolerance for, toward, *or* of (*for, toward, of persons or causes; of pain; of a scientific instrument*)
treat (*v.*) as, to, of, *or* with (*as a friend; to a meal; of a subject* or *topic; with another person in negotiations*)
vary from
vest (*v.*) in *or* with (*authority vested in an official; an official vested with authority*)
vie for
void (*adj.*) of
vulnerable to
wait (*v.*) for *or* on (*for one who was delayed; on a customer or patient*)
want (*n.*) of; (*v.*) for (*did not want for money*)
wanting (*adj.*) in
wary of
yearn for, after, *or* over
zeal for *or* in

A GUIDE TO
WRITING

FORMS OF ADDRESS

Forms of address do not always follow set guidelines; the type of salutation is often determined by the relationship between correspondents or by the purpose and content of the letter. However, the following general styles apply to most occasions. For informal salutations, use "Mr." for a man; use "Ms." or "Mrs." or "Miss" for a woman, according to her stated preference. For formal salutations, avoid gender-specific forms in favor of simpler forms that can be used to address either a man or a woman.

	FORM OF ADDRESS	SALUTATION
College and university officials		
dean, assistant dean	Dean Joseph (Jane) Stone *or* Dr. (Mr., Ms.) Joseph (Jane) Stone Dean, School of _____ *or* Assistant Dean, School of _____	Dear Sir (Madam): Dear Dr. (Mr., Ms.) Stone: Dear Dean Stone:
instructor	Mr. (Ms.) Joseph (Jane) Stone Department of _____	Dear Sir (Madam): Dear Mr. (Ms.):
president, chancellor	President *or* Chancellor Joseph (Jane) Stone *or* Dr. (Mr., Ms.) Joseph (Jane) Stone President, _____ *or* Chancellor, _____	Dear President Stone: *or* Dear Chancellor Stone: Dear Dr. (Mr., Ms.) Stone:

FORM OF ADDRESS	SALUTATION
professor, assistant professor, or *associate professor*	Professor, Assistant Professor, *or* Associate Professor Joseph (Jane) Stone *or* Dr. (Mr., Ms.) Joseph (Jane) Stone Department of _____	Dear Professor Stone: Dear Dr. (Mr., Ms.) Stone:

Clerical and religious orders

abbot, Roman Catholic	The Right Reverend Joseph Stone Abbot of _____	Right Reverend Abbot:
archbishop, Eastern Orthodox	His Eminence Archbishop Joseph Stone	Your Eminence:
archbishop, Roman Catholic	The Most Reverend Joseph Stone Archbishop of _____	Your Excellency:
archdeacon, Protestant Episcopal	The Venerable Joseph (Jane) Stone Archdeacon of _____	Dear Archdeacon Stone:
bishop, Protestant Episcopal	The Right Reverend Joseph (Jane) Stone Bishop of _____	Dear Bishop Stone:
bishop, Eastern Orthodox	The Right Reverend Joseph Stone	Your Grace:
bishop, Methodist	The Reverend Joseph Stone Methodist Bishop	Dear Bishop Stone: Reverend Sir:
bishop, Roman Catholic	The Most Reverend Joseph Stone Bishop of _____	Most Reverend Stone: Sir:

	FORM OF ADDRESS	SALUTATION

brother,
    Roman Catholic
	Brother Joseph Stone	Dear Brother:
		Dear Brother
		    Joseph:

canon,
    Protestant
    Episcopal
	The Reverend Joseph
	    (Jane) Stone
	Canon of _____
		Dear Canon Stone:
		Reverend Sir
		    (Madam):

cantor	Cantor Joseph (Jane) Stone	Dear Cantor Stone:

cardinal	His Eminence Joseph
	    Cardinal Stone
		Your Eminence:
		Dear Cardinal
		    Stone:

clergyman,
    Protestant
	The Reverend Joseph
	    (Jane) Stone
		Dear Dr. (Mr., Ms.)
		    Stone:

elder, Presbyterian	Elder Joseph (Jane) Stone	Dear Elder Stone:

dean,
    Protestant
    Episcopal
	The Very Reverend
	    Joseph (Jane) Stone
	Dean of _____
		Dear Dean Stone:

general secretary,
    Baptist
	The Reverend Joseph
	    Stone:
		Dear Reverend
		    Stone:

minister, Protestant	The Reverend Joseph
	    (Jane) Stone
		Dear Reverend
		    Stone:

monsignor,
    Roman Catholic
	The Right Reverend
	    Monsignor Joseph
	    Stone
		Right Reverend
		    Monsignor:
		Dear Monsignor
		    Stone:

mufti, Islam	The Mufti of _____	Your Eminence:

patriarch,
    Eastern Orthodox
	His All Holiness Patriarch
	    Demetrios
		Your All Holiness:

pope	His Holiness, The Pope *or* His Holiness, John Paul II	Your Holiness: Most Holy Father:

	FORM OF ADDRESS	SALUTATION
president, *Mormon Church*	President Joseph Stone Church of Jesus Christ of Latter-day Saints	Dear President Stone:
priest, *Eastern Orthodox*	The Reverend Joseph Stone	Dear Reverend Stone: Dear Reverend Father:
priest, *Roman Catholic*	The Reverend Joseph Stone	Dear Reverend Father: Dear Father: Dear Father Stone:
rabbi, Jewish	Rabbi Joseph (Jane) Stone	Dear Rabbi Stone:
sisterhood, *member of,* *Roman Catholic*	Sister Mary Stone	Dear Sister: Dear Sister Stone:

Diplomats

	FORM OF ADDRESS	SALUTATION
ambassador, U.S.	The Honorable Joseph (Jane) Stone Ambassador of the United States	Dear Ambassador Stone:
ambassador *to the U.S.*	His (Her) Excellency Joseph (Jane) Stone Ambassador of _____	Excellency: Dear Ambassador Stone:
chargé d'affaires, *U.S.*	Joseph (Jane) Stone, Esq. American Chargé d'Affaires	Dear Mr. (Ms.) Stone:
chargé d'affaires *to the U.S.*	Joseph (Jane) Stone, Esq. Chargé d'Affaires of _____	Dear Mr. (Ms.) Stone:
consul, U.S.	Mr. Joseph (Jane) Stone American Consul	Dear Mr. (Ms.) Stone:

	FORM OF ADDRESS	SALUTATION
minister, U.S.	The Honorable Joseph (Jane) Stone Minister of the United States	Dear Mr. (Ms.) Minister:
minister to the U.S.	The Honorable Joseph (Jane) Stone Minister of _____	Dear Mr. (Ms.) Minister:
president, premier, or *prime minister,* *of a nation*	His (Her) Excellency Joseph (Jane) Stone President, Premier, *or* Prime Minister of _____	Excellency: Dear Mr. (Madam) President, Premier, *or* Prime Minister:
secretary general, *United Nations*	His (Her) Excellency Joseph (Jane) Stone Secretary-General of the United Nations	Excellency: Dear Secretary General Stone:
U.S. representative to *the United* *Nations*	The Honorable Joseph (Jane) Stone United States Representative to the United Nations	Dear Mr. (Ms.) Stone: Dear Ambassador Stone:
Federal, state, and **local officials** **(government)**		
alderman, *alderwoman*	Alderman (Alderwoman) Joseph (Jane) Stone	Dear Mr. (Ms.) Stone:
cabinet member	The Honorable Joseph (Jane) Stone Secretary of _____	Dear Secretary Stone:

	FORM OF ADDRESS	SALUTATION
chairperson, *U.S. House* or *Senate Committee*	The Honorable Joseph (Jane) Stone Chairman (Chairwoman), Committee on _____ United States House of Representatives *or* Chairman (Chairwoman), Committee on _____ United States Senate	Dear Mr. Chairman: *or* Dear Madam Chairwoman:
commissioner, *federal, state,* *or local*	The Honorable Joseph (Jane) Stone	Dear Mr. (Ms.) Stone:
governor	The Honorable Joseph (Jane) Stone Governor of _____	Dear Governor Stone:
judge, federal	The Honorable Joseph (Jane) Stone Judge of the United States _____ Court	Dear Judge Stone:
judge, state or local	The Honorable Joseph (Jane) Stone Judge of the _____ Court of _____	Dear Judge Stone:
lieutenant governor	The Honorable Joseph (Jane) Stone Lieutenant Governor of _____	Dear Mr. (Ms.) Stone:
mayor	The Honorable Joseph (Jane) Stone Mayor of _____	Dear Mayor Stone:

	FORM OF ADDRESS	SALUTATION
speaker, U.S. or state House of Representatives	The Honorable Joseph (Jane) Stone Speaker of the House of Representatives *or* Speaker of the House of Representatives of the State of _____	Dear Mr. (Ms.) Stone:
state attorney general	The Honorable Joseph (Jane) Stone Attorney General State of _____	Dear Attorney General Stone:
state representative, delegate, or assembly member	The Honorable Joseph (Jane) Stone House of Representatives, House of Delegates of _____, *or* _____ Assembly State Capitol	Dear Mr. (Ms.) Stone:
state senator	The Honorable Joseph (Jane) Stone The State Senate State Capitol	Dear Senator Stone:
U.S. associate justice, Supreme Court	Justice Stone The Supreme Court of the United States	Dear Justice Stone:
U.S. attorney general	The Honorable Joseph (Jane) Stone Attorney General of the United States	Dear Mr. (Madam) Attorney General:
U.S. chief justice, Supreme Court	The Chief Justice of the United States The Supreme Court of the United States	Dear Chief Justice Stone:

	FORM OF ADDRESS	SALUTATION
U.S. postmaster general	The Honorable Joseph (Jane) Stone Postmaster General of the United States	Dear Mr. (Ms.) Stone:
U.S. president	The President The White House	Dear Mr. (Madam) President:
U.S. president, former	The Honorable Joseph Stone	Dear Mr. Stone:
U.S. representative	The Honorable Joseph (Jane) Stone United States House of Representatives	Dear Mr. (Ms.) Stone:
U.S. senator	The Honorable Joseph (Jane) Stone United States Senate	Dear Senator Stone:
U.S. vice president	The Vice President Executive Office Building	Dear Vice President Stone:
undersecretary of a department	The Honorable Joseph (Jane) Stone Undersecretary of _____	Dear Mr. (Ms.) Stone:

FORM OF ADDRESS	SALUTATION

Military
(designations:
USAF, U.S. Air Force;
USA, U.S. Army;
USCG, U.S. Coast
Guard; USMC,
U.S. Marine Corps;
USN, U.S. Navy)

admiral, vice admiral, or *rear admiral (navy)*	Admiral, Vice Admiral, or Rear Admiral Joseph (Jane) Stone, USN	Dear Admiral Stone: or Dear Vice Admiral Stone: or Dear Rear Admiral Stone:
captain or *commander (army, coast guard, marine corps, navy)*	Captain or Commander Joseph (Jane) Stone, appropriate service designation	Dear Captain Stone: or Dear Commander Stone:
chief petty officer (coast guard, navy)	Chief Petty Officer Joseph (Jane) Stone, appropriate service designation	Dear Mr. (Ms.) Stone: or Dear Chief Stone:
chief warrant officer (air force, army, coast guard, marine corps, navy)	Chief Warrant Officer Joseph (Jane) Stone, appropriate service designation	Dear Mr. (Ms.) Stone:
colonel, lieutenant colonel, or *major (air force, army, marine corps)*	Colonel, Lieutenant Colonel, or Major Joseph (Jane) Stone, appropriate service designation	Dear Colonel Stone: or Dear Lieutenant Colonel Stone: or Dear Major Stone:

	FORM OF ADDRESS	SALUTATION
commodore (navy)	Commodore Joseph (Jane) Stone, USN	Dear Commodore Stone:
first lieutenant or *second lieutenant (air force, army, marine corps)*	First Lieutenant or Second Lieutenant Joseph (Jane) Stone, appropriate service designation	Dear Lieutenant Stone: *or* Dear Second Lieutenant Stone:
general, lieutenant general, major general, or *brigadier general (air force, army, marine corps)*	General, Lieutenant General, Major General, *or* Brigadier General Joseph (Jane) Stone, appropriate service designation	Dear General Stone: *or* Dear Lieutenant General Stone: *or* Dear Major General Stone: *or* Dear Brigadier General Stone:
lieutenant commander, lieutenant, lieutenant (jg), or *ensign (coast guard, navy)*	Lieutenant Commander, Lieutenant, Lieutenant (JG), *or* Ensign Joseph (Jane) Stone, appropriate service designation	Dear Commander Stone: *or* Dear Lieutenant Stone: *or* Dear Lieutenant (JG) Stone: *or* Dear Ensign Stone:

THE RÉSUMÉ

A résumé is a short description of your history in work and at school. Many jobs require a résumé from any prospective employee. What the résumé reveals about you may determine whether or not you are actually interviewed for a job.

The résumé should be well designed so that both the overall organization and the individual sections are clear to the reader. Spelling and grammar should be correct. If it is typed, it should be neat and error-free. If a word processor is used, be sure to electronically search for misspelled words and to read the document carefully for misplaced words or other such errors. It is also advisable to have someone else read over what you have written before you send it out.

The printed document should be produced on white or off-white letter-sized paper using a good quality printer, such as a laser printer, or a quality copying process, such as offset printing. If photocopies are made of the original, they also should be produced on good quality paper.

Format

Résumés have a fairly standard format. At the very top is the heading. It should state your name, address, and telephone number including area code. It is not necessary to include information such as your age, marital status, height, weight, or sex. If you choose to volunteer the information, you must judge whether it will assist you in your job search or will work against you.

The next item in the résumé is a brief paragraph that may be labeled "Objectives." In this paragraph, you indicate what job you are looking for and your major qualifications for such a job. Or you may simply use this paragraph to state your basic strengths and the nature of your past work.

Following this is the record of your work experience. This record is the main part of the résumé (except if you are looking for your first full-time job). Your work experience is listed with your most recent job first. The job before that is listed next, and so on with your first job listed last.

Usually, you give your title for each job and the name of the company (and division when relevant). If you do not want to reveal the name of your current employer in your résumé, then you may write a descriptive phrase, such as "independent engineering consultant firm."

The descriptions of your previous jobs should be short summaries of your responsibilities, accomplishments, and contributions to the positions. Verbs should be active and sentences should be short.

Résumés are generally kept to one page. If you have worked for a long time at a variety of different jobs, it may be necessary to prepare a two-page résumé.

After the record of your work experience, list your schooling, any degrees, relevant noncredit courses, hobbies, honors, and affiliations that you consider worth including. If you belong to professional societies, you should definitely list them. If you belong to social, civic, or volunteer organizations, list them only if you believe your membership in them is an asset. List any awards or honors you have received whether or not they are job-related.

Looking for your first job

If you are looking for your first full-time job, you must review your work history somewhat differently. If you have held some sort of part-time or summer job or worked at volunteer jobs, these should be included. If you have participated in school extracurricular activities, these are worth mentioning. Your school record is also an indication of your ability and seriousness of purpose.

In seeking a first job, you must state your field of knowledge, your reliability, and your ability to work well with others.

In any résumé that you prepare, you should be sure to account for all time between the end of schooling and the present. If you have taken off a year and traveled, say so. If you have attempted unsuccessfully to start your own business, say so. It is far better to state what you have been involved in than to allow a prospective employer to wonder what you have been doing with your time.

Sample résumés

On the following pages are two sample résumés. The first is for a person looking for a first job. The second résumé is for a person who has held several jobs. This second résumé is written to indicate that each job has involved more responsibility and skills than its predecessor.

Leslie Gray
987 East Road
Elmwood, New Jersey 03103
987-6543

Objective
To find an entry-level job in sales with a large international company.
Would like to utilize my knowledge of French.

Work experience
Summers 1992, 1993
Group leader in a European teen-travel summer trip. We traveled in
bicycles and by boat. Many of the arrangements had been made in
advance, but I often had to make substitute arrangements because
of unforeseen events.

Summer 1991
Spent three months in France working as a volunteer on a farm.
Did so to improve my spoken French.

Part-time employment 1991, 1992, 1993
Salesperson, college bookstore during school year.

School record
1994 B.A. in French Literature and Language. Minor in History.
       Princeton University.
1990 Elmwood High School. Honors in language and science.

Extracurricular activities
Member of soccer team in high school and college.
Contributor to school magazine in college.
President of French Club in high school.

Speak and write French fluently.
Have working knowledge of Spanish.

Courtney Green
123 Lincoln Street
Deerfield, Illinois 60015
789-3456

<u>Objectives</u>
To find a job that would utilize a broad range of my managerial and
business skills and offer the potential for advancement in a large company.

<u>Record of work experience</u>
1987 to present   Public Relations Director for a small manufacturing
                   company

Responsible for creating and maintaining a favorable public image
by preparing and disseminating news releases, arranging press
conferences, contests, conferences, and other activities that keep the
company in the public eye. Supervise a staff of six and work with various
other departments including art, advertising, and production.

1983 to 1987   Publicity Writer for the Widget Company

Wrote copy for publicity releases and other public-relations material.
Know paper, printing, art styles. Two-person office meant I had more
responsibility than a publicity writer normally encounters.

1980 to 1983   Copy editor for Deerfield Gazette

Corrected copy and did proofreading for the local paper. Did some
rewrite and occasional reporting.

<u>Educational background</u>
M.B.A. University of Illinois, 1987.

B.A. University of Illinois, 1980.
Major in Journalism. Received award for Most Promising Student.

Extracurricular: Worked on college newspaper; member of swim team.

<u>Affiliations and hobbies</u>
Member of Illinois Society of Publicity Writers
Vice President of Alumni Association, University of Illinois

Hobbies include swimming, tennis, and directing amateur theater.

The cover letter

A résumé that will be mailed to a prospective employer should be accompanied by a cover letter. The cover letter should be straightforward and brief; it should not be a repetition of all the information contained in the résumé. You should state the specific position you are interested in, briefly discuss your experience, and refer the reader to the enclosed résumé. At the end of the letter you may wish to indicate that you will telephone the prospective employer for an interview.

You will, of course, have to write a separate cover letter for each specific position you want to apply for. The cover letter, like the résumé, should be neat and should be printed on quality paper. Remember that the cover letter serves as your introduction to a prospective employer and that first impressions are very important. Be sure that the spelling and grammar are correct and that you have spelled all names and addresses properly.

Dear Sir or Madam:

    I am applying for the position of sales manager, advertised in Sunday's *Chicago Tribune*. I have held a number of selling jobs and am currently working in the sales department of a large manufacturing company.

    The enclosed resume will furnish additional information on my background. I will telephone you next week for an interview. Thank you for your consideration.

Sincerely,

Ellen Kovalcik

Ms. Ellen Kovalcik

BUSINESS LETTERS

The formats of the following three letters are typical of those used in business correspondence, although other variations certainly exist.

Most letters are single-spaced, with double spacing between paragraphs. In the full-block and the simplified formats, the first line of each paragraph aligns with the left-hand margin. The first line of each paragraph of the modified-block format begins five spaces from the left-hand margin.

Full-block format

1 Date
2 Inside address
3 Salutation
4 Subject line
5 Body of letter
6 Complimentary close
7 Signature block
8 Identifying initials
9 Enclosure notation
10 Copy notation
11 2 to 4 lines
12 2 to 12 lines
13 Double spaces
14 4 lines

Houghton Mifflin Company

222 Berkeley Street, Boston, Massachusetts 02116-3764
(617) 351-5000 Fax: (617) 351-1112

Trade & Reference Division

11

1 April 3, 19 —

12

Ms. Marion Stone
Vice President, Corporate Plans
2 CBA Corporation
43 Hunting Towers, Suite 100
City, ST 98765

3 Dear Ms. Stone:

4 Subject: Full-Block Letter Format

In this letter format, all elements are aligned with the left margin.
Spacing between letter parts is indicated by the key lines. Individual
5 paragraphs in the body of the letter are single-spaced internally.

If the letter exceeds one page, a continuation sheet may be used. The
heading begins six lines from the top of the page and includes the name
of the addressee, the date, and the page number.

Ms. Stone
Page 2
April 3, 19 —

The message continues four lines below the heading. At least three
message lines must be carried over to the continuation sheet.

13

The writer's corporate title is shown under the typewritten signature.
Identifying initials, enclosure notation, and copy recipients are
typewritten flush with the left margin and are spaced as shown.

6 Sincerely,

14

7 Candice B. Stillor
Director of Marketing

8 CBS: amm

9 Encs.: 2

10 cc: J.P. Patwell

Modified-block format

1 Fax notation
2 Date
3 Inside address
4 Salutation
5 Subject line
6 Body of letter
7 Complimentary close
8 Signature block
9 Identifying initials
10 Enclosure notation
11 Copy notation
12 2 to 4 lines
13 2 to 12 lines
14 Double spaces
15 4 lines

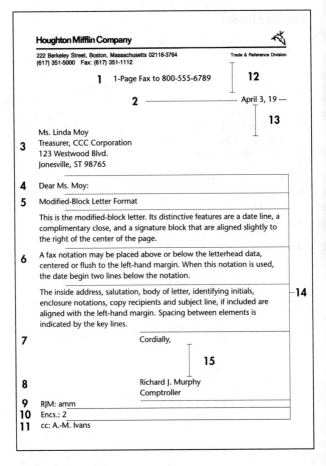

Houghton Mifflin Company

222 Berkeley Street, Boston, Massachusetts 02116-3764
(617) 351-5000 Fax: (617) 351-1112

Trade & Reference Division

1 1-Page Fax to 800-555-6789

12

2 ———————————————— April 3, 19 —

13

3 Ms. Linda Moy
Treasurer, CCC Corporation
123 Westwood Blvd.
Jonesville, ST 98765

4 Dear Ms. Moy:

5 Modified-Block Letter Format

This is the modified-block letter. Its distinctive features are a date line, a complimentary close, and a signature block that are aligned slightly to the right of the center of the page.

6 A fax notation may be placed above or below the letterhead data, centered or flush to the left-hand margin. When this notation is used, the date begin two lines below the notation.

The inside address, salutation, body of letter, identifying initials, enclosure notations, copy recipients and subject line, if included are aligned with the left-hand margin. Spacing between elements is indicated by the key lines.

—14

7   Cordially,

15

8   Richard J. Murphy
                                 Comptroller

9 RJM: amm
10 Encs.: 2
11 cc: A.-M. Ivans

Simplified format

1 Date
2 Inside address
3 Subject line
4 Body of letter
5 Signature line
6 Identifying initials
7 Copy notation
8 Enclosure notation
9 2 to 4 lines
10 2 to 12 lines
11 3 lines
12 Double spaces
13 5 lines

Houghton Mifflin Company

222 Berkeley Street, Boston, Massachusetts 02116-3764
(617) 351-5000   Fax: (617) 351-1112   Trade & Reference Division

9

1   April 3, 19 —

     ⌐ **10**

Ms. Rosemary Andrews
2   HCI Corporation
One State Street
City, ST 98765

3   Simplified Letter Format   — **11**

4   Ms. Andrews, this is a model of the simplified letter format. It is a clean,
modern format preferred by many corporations.

All elements are aligned with the left-hand margin. Spacing between
paragraphs of the body of the letter is indicated by the key lines.

There is no salutation, but the addressee's name is mentioned in the first
and final paragraphs. In addition, there is no complimentary close.
Therefore, Ms. Andrews, the signature line includes the writer's name,
usually in all capital letters, followed by a short title.

                    13   — **12**

5   DANIEL PACKARD — SENIOR EDITOR

6   amm

7   cc: K. Marx
     S. Schwartz

8   Encs.: 3

MINUTES OF MEETINGS

Agenda

An agenda lists all the specific procedures to be covered at a meeting. The agenda may be formal and may include such items as "Reading the minutes of the previous meeting" and "Adjournment." Or it may simply be an informal list of general topics to be discussed.

When preparing an agenda, you must ask every person invited to the meeting if he or she has something to be included. All items should be numbered, and subsections, when used, should carry lowercase letters. The document should be triple-spaced to leave room for notes.

Format

Minutes are a brief and official record of the meeting of a group. They are prepared either by a recording secretary or by a designated member of the group.

Depending upon the group or the nature of the meeting, minutes may be formal or informal. Many organizations have preferred formats for minutes, and certain kinds of meetings, such as directors' or stockholders' meetings, have specific required formats. Regardless of format, the following information is always included.

✔ Name of the group
✔ Type of meeting: regular, special, or a similar designation
✔ Date, time, and place
✔ Names of those present and absent
✔ Names of presiding officer and recording secretary

✔ Proceedings:
   Presentation, amendments (if necessary),
      and approval of previous minutes
   Unfinished business
   New business
✔ Date of next meeting
✔ Hour of adjournment
✔ Signature of secretary

Style

In preparing minutes you should keep the exact wording of resolutions and motions passed and the names of the proposers. Reports that are appended to the minutes or kept separate may be summarized. Frequently you will find it helpful to summarize the discussion.

It is important to remember that in addition to informing absent members of what took place at a meeting, minutes are an official record that may subsequently be referred to for a variety of purposes. Therefore they must be written cogently and accurately. Even though minutes present only the crucial points of a meeting, you should take full notes to ensure that nothing has been missed. It is very helpful if copies of reports of other material to be presented at the meeting can be obtained beforehand.

Whether minutes are written up in formal or informal format, care should be taken to ensure clarity and accessibility. The following style points may be used as general guidelines:

✔ Minutes may be either single- or double-spaced. Generous margins should be provided when single-spacing minutes.
✔ Pages should be numbered consecutively.
✔ The substance of the minutes should be presented in a direct manner. The object is to relate as clearly as possible what was discussed, what was decided, and what was left undecided.

If the minutes are long and complex, organizational devices such as headings, subheadings, paragraph headings, and underscoring may be used. Paragraphs or sections may be numbered according to the numbered items on the agenda. Short meetings involving small groups or limited subjects lend themselves to a concise treatment similar to an outline. It is more common, however, for minutes to be written in narrative form. In the latter case, the person preparing the minutes must be especially careful that summarized information is complete enough to convey what transpired. Above all, it is important that the significant points of a meeting stand out and can be easily located.

Minutes should always be written in objective language. All personal opinions and biases should be excluded.

Index

Various kinds of meetings will require an index of important subjects discussed and actions taken. The index is kept in the form of a card index, with one subject to a card. References are listed chronologically and give the page number of the appropriate minutes.

PAPERS AND REPORTS

Planning and research

There are as many reasons for writing as there are subjects to investigate — a paper or report may be undertaken as a school assignment, a job assignment, or a professional opportunity (presenting a paper at a meeting or publishing an article).

At times, a very specific topic is assigned to you. At other times, you may choose any subject that interests you. Often, you are asked to look into a general subject area and choose a specific topic within it. Whatever your reasons for writing, you want the final product to represent your best work.

It is the purpose of this section to provide general guidelines for research and writing that will help you from the preliminary stages to the final draft. Certain techniques will be useful to you in preparing papers on any subject and will be suitable for a wide variety of source materials.

Whatever the purpose of your writing, the final version will reflect how well you prepared yourself from the start. Trying to take shortcuts along the way will result in an inferior piece of work. Care and time invested during the preliminary stages will provide the foundation for a well-written essay or report.

Basic research procedures. There is a great deal of work to be done before you begin to write. A good way to begin is to formulate a tentative title (which may or may not be the final title of your paper). The tentative theme may be too broad or too narrow, or it may be a topic that you do not have the facilities to research. At this point, the title is merely a first statement of the general area of your paper and can help you focus your research.

By definition, all research papers are based on some kind of data; they also require that the writer collect, organize, present, and evaluate data. Some papers rely very heavily on other people's evaluations, while other papers rely more heavily on the writer's opinions. In either case, it is not enough simply to reproduce sources.

The source materials. Before you commit yourself to a topic, consider the materials you will need: books, magazine articles, newspaper clippings, maps, recordings, sheet music, statistics, informants, and the like. Begin to check libraries to find out which resources are available to you and make preliminary inquiries about where to look for other sources. Can you find what you need in one library? If not, you will have to look farther afield, or you may have to restate your topic.

Certain practical considerations should determine how you plan your research. For example, research that requires travel must be planned carefully. If you plan to interview experts for your paper, you'll need to schedule time with them well in advance. Sometimes it is necessary to wait for a reserved book or an interlibrary loan. Time must be allotted realistically. Some extra time should always be allowed for the unexpected.

Breaking down the topic. It is usually necessary to make some preliminary notes for an outline. These outline notes may be revised, expanded, or totally reorganized once your research is under way. The data you encounter may not be what you expect to find, or it may cause you to change your thinking and approach the subject from a different angle. Before you start to research your topic, you need to organize your ideas and make some preliminary notes.

Take one topic as an example:

What will the world's population be in the year 2025?
  Reasons for asking the question
  Predictions:
    On what basis are they made?
    Do experts agree?
    Are there areas of general agreement?
    Are there areas of major disagreement?
  The unpredictable:
    What events could alter predictions?
    How likely are those events?
    Have events ever altered past predictions?

Remember to keep notes of your own evaluations of the source materials you encounter.

As you begin to read, you may want to narrow the focus of your outline to stress a particular aspect of the topic:

Shifts in the ratio of older people
Relation of population growth to Earth's resources
Differences in population trends in developed and developing nations

Planning the work. Begin your research by reading a general book or article about your topic. You may be fortunate enough to find an article that provides a good overall picture of the subject. Encyclopedias contain general articles written by experts in the field that will suggest different aspects you may want to investigate. Such general essays may provide a short list of sources you can use to get started on your own research. Each source you consult will lead you to others. As you proceed with your research, you will be sifting and weighing a lot of material. When you begin to do research, it's difficult to predict the direction in which the work will go. Often, it's not until you're well into the research process that you can decide how to organize the information you're finding. What seems significant at one point may not be worth including when you start to write.

One of the most difficult aspects of preparing and organizing information is deciding what to include and what to omit.

Taking notes. As you work, you will need to keep notes of what you learn. It is advisable to equip yourself with two kinds of index cards (either two sizes or two colors). One set of cards will be used to record your sources. Each card will represent a different source. The second set of cards will be used to take notes of specific information gained from a source. These cards will contain much of the substance of your paper. They will record quotes, opinions, analyses, and other data. They may also contain your own opinions of what you encounter.

In addition to the cards, some of your "notes" may be photocopies of library materials that you will need for reference. Copying machines allow you to duplicate charts, tables, and statistics as well as long quotations that you may want to use or consult. As you duplicate material for your reference, though, keep in mind the copyright laws that govern the extent to which you can legally photocopy copyrighted material. Photocopy machines usually have these laws displayed near them.

If you have a personal computer and access to a full-page or hand-held scanner, you may be able to scan information from your sources directly into a file rather than relying on handwritten index cards.

However you take your notes, exercise care and keep track of your sources so that you'll have the information you'll need for notes and a bibliography.

Source cards. Even if you are scanning text into a computer file, you should make out an index card for every source you consult. When the time comes to begin writing, you may not quote every book and article, or even refer to each specifically, but you will probably want to include all your sources in your bibliography so your readers will know the works you consulted.

During the writing process, source cards provide the data for notes; once the paper or report is finished, the same cards, alphabetically arranged, enable you to type up your bibliography. You can record your own general comments about each source on the appropriate card. And, because you have the full data on the source card, you will not need to repeat all the information on each information card.

In general, bibliographical information includes whatever your readers will need to know if they want to consult the same source. Most of the bibliographical information for a book will be found on the title page and the reverse of the title page (the copyright page). Use the publisher's name as it appears on that book. Indicate only the first city listed.

The *MLA Handbook for Writers of Research Papers*, Fourth ed., by Joseph Gibaldi (New York: The Modern Language Association of America, 1995) suggests the following format for recording the bibliographical information of a book:

Gibaldi, Joseph. *MLA Handbook for Writers of Research Papers.*
    4th ed. New York: Modern Language Association of
    America, 1995.

There are also other kinds of information you may need to include for book-length sources, such as the name of a translator, editor, or reviser. The *MLA Handbook* or another equally authoritative source (including those from other professional organizations, such as the American Psychological Association and The Linguistic Society of America, which publish their own style sheets for their respective disciplines) will illustrate the many different formats for recording bibliographical information.

In addition to books, you will probably consult other sources, such as magazines and scholarly journals, which are called periodicals. These sources require a slightly different bibliographical format.

Ross, Gary Noel. "Butterfly Wrangling in Louisiana." *Natural History* 104 (1995): 36-42.

You will need to keep the bibliographical information for maps, sketches, works of art, recordings, filmstrips, and any other material you use. Again, consult the *MLA Handbook* or another standard text for the proper bibliographical format for these different media. Make notes of the relevant numbers, the location (such as "city hall"), title (if any), and anything else that would enable you or someone else to find that same item again. If you decide you want to include figures, graphs, or photos from one of your sources, you will have to write to the author or authors or the publisher and obtain permission to reproduce the work.

Be sure to record the source of any material you photocopy.

Information cards. Most of your notes will record facts or opinions you encounter in your sources. Because some quotations may be quite long, consider using 5″ × 8″ index cards. You may find yourself making a considerable number of information cards from one source and very few cards from another. Some notes will record specific statements, others will summarize ideas. Still others will contain brief quotations (in quotation marks). Because information cards contain different kinds of data, be sure to indicate whether the card contains a direct quotation, your paraphrase of the source, or your opinion of it. When you begin writing, these notations will tell you what information you need to put in a note as well as what material you need to put within quotation marks (all whole or partial direct quotations).

All cards should show the author's name and the page number(s) from which the data was taken. If you are using more than one book or article by the same author, the title may substitute for the author's name. Here you need only sufficient information to ensure that you give proper credit to your sources; you have full bibliographic information on your source cards.

Much of what you learned in your research will not be taken in notes. You will be forming ideas about the topic and the manner in which you intend to pursue it. Before you reach the end of your research, you should be able to prepare an outline that will show the final plan of the paper you will write.

Outlines

A substantial paper or report needs a well-balanced outline. In the finished product, the framework may be obvious or hidden, but it must be there. There are always several different methods for organizing information, so you may want to experiment before you settle on one way of outlining. For instance, if you're writing about someone's life or a nation's development, a chronological outline might seem to be the best way to organize your material, but you may try organizing the information to emphasize the person's achievements or the major industries of the nation.

A good outline has a structure of major divisions and subdivisions:

I. Roman numerals (I., II., III., etc.) mark off the major divisions of ideas in the paper.
   A. Capital letters (A., B., C., etc.) are used to subdivide ideas within each Roman numeral group.
      1. Arabic numerals (1., 2., 3., etc.) subdivide the ideas within each capital letter group.
         a. Lower-case letters (a., b., c., etc.) form the subgroups within the Arabic numeral divisions.

It is not necessary to subdivide each topic. No topic, however, should have an *A.* subhead without also having a *B.* subhead. Similarly, if there is a *1.*, there must be a *2.*; if there is an *a.*, there must be a *b.* In other words, if a category is to be sub-divided, it should have at least two subdivisions.

The subdivisions within an outline should be balanced. The *I.* topic should be as important as the *II.* and *III.* topics. Within each further division, there should also be balance.

Let us examine some possible outlines for the subject "What will the world's population be in the year 2025?" Note that in each example below, the title and the basic point (major thesis) of the outline in the paragraph following the title have been restated to suit the particular subject eventually chosen. Your major thesis, or some version of it, should appear in your first paragraph.

Outline 1. This is an example of a phrasal outline. Here, the thesis is the only portion described in a full sentence format.

PLANNING FOR AN OLDER POPULATION

All evidence indicates that the proportion of old people to young people in U.S. society is increasing. The shift will require new planning for the future.

I. Evidence of the shift
   A. The declining birthrate
   B. The changing death rate
   C. Population profiles for the future
      1. Profiles based on current rates
      2. Profiles based on various predictions for the future
         a. Same birthrate, lower death rate
         b. Lower birthrate, same death rate
         c. Lower birth and death rates

II. Implications of the population shift
   A. For work and retirement patterns
      1. Current patterns
      2. Prospective patterns
   B. For government planning
      1. Government income
      2. Government services
      3. Need for public institutions
   C. For people planning careers
   D. For industries

III. Planning for the future
   A. Fitting current data into planning schemes
   B. Monitoring future changes

IV. Steps to begin to take now

Outline 2. This outline maintains the organization of Outline 1 but presents a fuller version of its contents. It is usually advisable to produce a more fully developed outline since it will make the writing process less difficult.

PLANNING FOR AN OLDER POPULATION

All evidence indicates that the proportion of old people to young people in U.S. society is increasing. The shift will require new planning for the future.

I. Evidence of the shift in the ratio of older people in the population is available in our present statistics.
   A. The birthrate is declining because many women are choosing to have fewer children.
   B. The death rate is decreasing because more people are living longer.
   C. From present statistics we can provide a profile of future population ratios. All profiles will suggest an older population.
      1. We can project future population ratios by using the same birthrate and a lower death rate.
      2. We can assume a lower birthrate and the same death rate.
      3. We can assume both lower birth and death rates based on current trends.

II. The shift in the population, an increase in the number of older people, has important implications for future planning.
   A. We need to consider this shift in the population when we make projections about work and retirement patterns.
      1. Our projections must begin with an understanding of current work and retirement patterns.
      2. Based on current patterns, we can project how the increase in our older population will affect future work and retirement patterns.
   B. The government will need to consider the population shift in every sphere of its planning for the future.
      1. An older population will affect the amount of government income derived from taxation.

2. An older population will mean a restructuring of the government services provided, such as Medicare and Medicaid, and how money is allocated to such services.
3. An older population will also mean an increased need for publicly supported hospitals, rehabilitation centers, and home care providers.
C. People planning careers will want to consider the requirements of an older population, such as increased leisure time and increased need for occupational therapy.
D. People involved in industrial planning will also need to consider the different needs of an older population.
III. An increasingly older population will affect planning for the future.
A. The trends indicated in current data will have to be incorporated into planning for the future.
B. Planners will have to continue to monitor changes as they affect projections for the future.
IV. There are steps we can take now to incorporate this information into our plans for the future.

The outline in sentence form is much clearer than the phrasal outline. A sentence outline can help to clarify thinking about a subject. It will reveal the strengths and weaknesses of the structure better than a phrasal outline will. If a sentence outline is well thought out, each topic may be incorporated into the essay or report as a heading, sub-heading, or topic sentence of a paragraph.

An outline will take various shapes depending on the nature of the data and the way you assemble it. By the time the outline is prepared, you should know what data is available. Sometimes the outline will reveal the need for additional information in particular areas.

Relation of information cards to outline. Each writer has a distinct style of relating information cards to the outline. Some people prepare the outline itself by arranging the cards to create a pattern. Other people develop a mental image of an outline as research progresses, then arrange the cards to suit the outline. Whatever system is used, at some point the cards must be organized to fit the outline. It is advisable to make notations of pertinent subtopics on an upper corner of each card.

A finished paper should never read like an assortment of cards. The data on the cards will be used indirectly in some instances and directly in others. Sometimes a card will merely serve as a way of reminding you to include an idea. Other cards may have been made before a final outline was drafted, and their data may be irrelevant to the final topic. Do not hesitate to eliminate irrelevant information. One of the most important aspects of planning a well-written, coherent report or essay is a sense of what is relevant and what is not. Irrelevant information detracts from the coherence of your writing and confuses your readers.

Formats

Style points. How you present your work affects the way your readers respond to it. A clean and inviting appearance is one of the most important considerations when putting a piece of writing into final form, whether you are composing an original paper based on your own research or organizing and styling a report based on another person's work. All job applicants know the importance of first impressions and hence the need to present a neat appearance when first meeting a prospective employer. Similarly, a cleanly typed and styled paper will encourage readers to take it seriously. A sloppy or careless presentation will, in contrast, indicate to your audience that you don't feel your own work is important. If you haven't bothered to make your work presentable, you cannot expect anyone else to want to read it.

What will the final piece look like? Much depends on the purpose and audience for the writing. Papers and reports can be written in either a formal or informal format. A formal paper, as you shall see, has a complex structure and often presents the results of original research or a compilation and synthesis of other people's work (secondary sources). Academic essays, business reports, and technical papers are all formal and require care and precision in their final presentation. An informal paper, on the other hand, may comprise only a short text with a title or a few pages of notes from which you improvise, depending on how well you know your topic. At its simplest a written presentation may take the form of a business letter.

Regardless of the format used, the following stylistic points should be observed:

- ✔ All papers and reports need a cover or title page giving the title, the name of the writer, the date, and the name of the class or organization to which the project is being submitted.
- ✔ All pages should be numbered in the same position, either centered at the top or in the upper-right hand corner.
- ✔ All margins should be uniform, and they should not be skimpy.
- ✔ Any charts, graphs, or similar material should be numbered. A standard style for the title and legend of figures should be maintained.
- ✔ The paper or report should be double-spaced. Any quotation of five lines or more should be single-spaced and indented. Quotation marks should not be used for long quotations. Legends may also be single-spaced.
- ✔ Most papers and reports are typed or printed out on stan-

dard 8½" by 11" white paper. Certain organizations or kinds of projects require the use of pre-ruled or otherwise nonstandard paper. In any case use only high-quality paper for your original copy. If you have access to a personal computer, a laser printer will produce a much better copy than a dot-matrix printer can, even one that prints in near-letter quality.

A personal computer will make it much easier to produce an attractive final draft of your report or essay. Word-processing programs include instructions for setting margins, numbering pages, and setting up numerous other elements that make a print presentation of information both easy and pleasurable to read. Most word-processing software also has the following tools: a thesaurus, to help you find the right words; a grammar, against which you can check your prose for faulty sentences; and a tool for checking your spelling. But remember that the computer will accept any correctly spelled word in the language, and so it will not warn you about the most common spelling errors, such as *their/there*, *its/it's*, or about typographical errors, such as writing *then* for *than* or *ant* for *and*. These are problems you will have to watch for yourself.

Word-processing programs also provide templates for some of the most common documents: résumés, personal letters, business letters, memos, and proposals. You can modify and customize these templates to suit your needs.

There are numerous graphics programs now available that enable you to incorporate charts and graphs in your text. A full-page or hand-held scanner will allow you to copy artwork, photographs, and other visual elements into your text. But remember that using the work of other people without their permission is against the law.

Organization is the second important consideration when planning the final format of a paper or report. Your work's inviting appearance will encourage someone to begin reading, but only clarity of presentation and substance will get that person to read your paper or report through to the end and to consider it seriously.

Headings. The first decision you must make is whether a paper or report will benefit from the use of headings. A relatively brief or uncomplicated paper will usually require no headings. If well-planned, the framework should be apparent because the finished work is a logical and natural sequence of thought. A long or complicated paper, a technical report, or a promotional brochure, however, usually requires headings to distinguish among many topics and subtopics and to guide readers through your presentation. If you are writing a paper or report from an outline, the outline itself will provide the headings and subheadings. If you are working from raw data or a rough outline, you will need to formulate headings. Headings should be brief and informative. Use a single word or a phrase instead of a complete sentence.

If, for example, you decided to write a paper titled "Planning for an Older Population," and to work from Outline 1, the paper might have the following headings:

EVIDENCE OF THE SHIFT TO AN OLDER POPULATION
The Declining Birthrate
The Changing Death Rate

IMPLICATIONS OF THE POPULATION SHIFT
For Work and Retirement Patterns
    Current patterns
    Prospective patterns
For Government Planning
    Government income
    Government services

Note that the gradation in importance of the headings is conveyed by the different styles in which they are printed. Each category of heading should be treated identically.

The formal report. A formal paper or report is made up of different parts, each having a distinct purpose. Many organizations have a preferred format; word-processing programs also provide templates for such documents. What follows is the general format of a formal report; it is intended only as a guide and its various sections are adaptable to the needs of a specific project. However, a formal report always includes sections 1, 4, and 5.

1. Title page and/or cover
2. Introduction/preface or letter of transmittal
3. Abstract or summary
4. Table of contents and/or
   List of tables and illustrations
5. Text
   a. Introduction
   b. Discussion
   c. Conclusions and/or recommendations
6. Appendix
7. Bibliography
8. Index

Title page. This page contains the title of the paper, the name of the writer (and his or her position, if applicable), the name and address of the department or company (if the paper is written as a job assignment), the department and university or college (if the paper reports academic research), or the name of the class (if the paper is written as a school project), and the date.

Cover. An informal paper usually dispenses with a full title page and instead has a cover giving the title, the writer's name, and sometimes the name of the company or class to which it is submitted. A formal paper may have both a title page and a cover.

Introduction/preface or letter of transmittal. An introduction or preface is a short statement of the subject, purpose, and scope of the paper along with any necessary information about its writer or background about its preparation. A letter of transmittal (or a cover letter) is more formal than, and is used in place of, an introduction. It is typed on regular business letterhead. In addition to giving some or all of the information contained in an introduction, it is directed specifically to the authorization or request for the paper.

Any acknowledgments, as of contributors, assistants, or sources that are not mentioned elsewhere, should appear in a separate paragraph at the end of the introduction or letter of transmittal.

Abstract or summary. This is a brief synopsis, normally in one or two paragraphs, of the problem dealt with in the paper, the methodology used in examining it, and the conclusions reached. Once found almost exclusively in technical studies, the abstract is now widely used in academic and business papers. Its condensed form makes it useful in research and as accessible reference material; hence it has become one of the most important parts of a formal paper or report.

Table of contents. This lists the titles of the chapters or principal sections of the paper (and their numbers, if any are used); the subheadings or subtopics within each chapter or section; the appendix, bibliography, and index; and the page number on which each begins. Since the actual text of any paper always begins on page 1, all pages preceding the text (including the table of contents) are numbered in Roman numerals and should be so listed in the contents table if you choose to include them. Everything listed in the table of contents should be entered in the exact order in which it appears in the finished work.

The heading of the page, always centered, is *Contents* (*Table of* is now considered extraneous). The table itself begins an inch or two below the heading and is set up in outline form. Chapters, sections, and similar divisions are placed on the left side of the page and page numbers on the right. You may use a string of periods as a leader to connect the left-hand entry to the page number if you wish. In addition, many people use the subheadings *Chapter* and *Page* on top of the left- and right-hand columns respectively.

List of tables and illustrations. Many papers make extensive use of tables and illustrations (all illustrations are individually referred to in text as *figures*). These lists follow the table of contents and have the headings *Tables* or *Illustrations*. If the contents page is set with column subheadings, these lists should conform to style, using *Table* or *Figure* on the left and *Page* on the right. If the tables and figures are to be inserted later, you should indicate where they are to be placed in the text. (Style sheets provided by some professional groups and businesses give their preferred method for the placement and appearance of tables and illustrations.)

Text. The text of a paper or report should be logically organized and clearly written. An introduction states the purpose and scope of the project, the methodology used, pertinent background information, and a brief statement of the conclusions drawn. The discussion is a detailed study of the subject, presented as briefly and succinctly as possible. The final section of the text presents a full explanation of the conclusions and/or recommendations produced by the study.

Appendix. All supplementary materials, such as maps, charts, or graphs, that provide background to or amplification of the topic are listed in the appendix. If there are two or more appendixes, they should be distinguished by letters (capitals) or numbers (Arabic or Roman, although the latter should be used only if they are not used to refer to chapters or sections). A glossary of pertinent terms or a list of abbreviations may be placed in the appendix or in a separate section immediately following.

Bibliography. A paper or report that makes use of material from outside sources (including such things as unpublished articles or reports and speeches) requires a bibliography citing those sources (see p. 193).

Index. An index is used primarily in a long and involved work. It lists in alphabetical order all the main topics covered in the paper or report and can usually be put together by rearranging the table of contents. Certain works, however, require a detailed index that goes beyond the contents page listings and can only be drawn from the text itself. This can be a difficult task and there is a specific method to follow (see p. 197).

Writing the paper

It is not necessary to be a great writer to produce a good paper or report. It is necessary, though, to have a good grasp of the major ideas, good information, and a good outline. By the time you are ready to write, you should be familiar with any words or terms currently used in the field and you should be capable of explaining them.

The most difficult part of a document to write is the first paragraph. A first paragraph may raise an interesting question that you will answer or attempt to answer later in the paper. It may propose an idea to be examined, argue a cause, state a conclusion, or do any of a number of other things. At times, a first paragraph may begin with a quotation that will serve as a theme for agreement or disagreement. Above all, the first paragraph should be interesting and should be related to the rest of the paper. Because your written work is likely to be revised several times before you consider it ready to be seen by others, you may find it easiest to write your introduction or opening paragraph after you've finished the report or paper.

Keep your writing as simple as possible. Use unfamiliar or technical words when they are appropriate, but do not try to introduce learned words just to sound learned. If the subject you are dealing with has its own vocabulary, use that vocabulary. Your goal is readability and understanding. Try to avoid sentences that must be read and reread to arrive at their meaning. During the process of revision, break such sentences into their components and rewrite them with greater clarity.

There should be a logical flow from sentence to sentence and paragraph to paragraph. One idea will flow into the next and your writing will be persuasive. Often when a flow of ideas is lacking, it is because the writer has not absorbed the material well and is simply recording one note after another. A logic should also exist from section to section of a work. Transition sentences or paragraphs prepare the way for the introduction of new subject matter.

Many people believe that clear writing is related to clear thinking. If you are having a great deal of trouble putting your thoughts into writing, reexamine your thinking. Are you confident of your ideas and your data? Can other conclusions be drawn from your work? If so, how will you deal with them? If you are not confident of your material, do you have enough time to do some more research? If not, can you redefine and limit your topic to material with which you are comfortable?

Good writers aren't born. Good writing is the result of discipline, attention to details, and lots of practice, and it is something that can can learned. An often overlooked requirement for excellent written work is revision, revision, and revision. The more you reread what you're writing, the more confident you will become; the more adept you become at spotting your own particular writing weaknesses and correcting them, the easier writing will become. One draft of a document, or even two drafts, is simply not enough. It is also helpful to have someone whose opinion you respect read over a later draft and point out places where your logic isn't clear or where there are weaknesses in your presentation.

The process of revision is considerably simpler now than it was in the past when changes were made by cutting up the typewritten pages and pasting or taping the revisions into their new location. Computer software for editing provides instructions for highlighting only the portion of a text you wish to move and then transferring it to its new position. This simple method of revising a text is one of the ways computers can help you to improve the final versions of your work. Revising is now so easy that all writers should feel compelled to revise their material until it is as good as it can be.

One other requirement for good writing should be mentioned: always write with your intended audience in mind. Try not to write over the heads of your audience, and never write down to them. You do not want to offend your readers, so pay particular attention to your word choice. What is considered offensive language differs from one person or group to another, but, in general, you should monitor your usage in the following areas:

✔ *Gender:* Avoid using gender-specific terms, such as *man, mankind,* and *he,* to refer to all people. There are lots of words that do include women and men, such as *people, humanity,* and *humankind,* and using a plural noun, such as *readers* and *advertisers,* will remove any need to resort to awkward phrases like *he or she* or infrequent substitutes such as *s/he,* which the use of singular nouns will entail. What is known as "singular *they*" (*they* used to substitute for a singular noun) has been used in English for centuries and is very common in speech; its use is discussed in the "Usage Guide" under the word **he.**

✔ *Race and ethnicity:* There is almost no circumstance when explicit racism is tolerated, in speech or in writing, and words used to refer degradingly to a group of people are never appropriate in a formal writing context.

✔ *Handicaps and disabilities:* There are no positive words in English to refer to people with disabilities, and many times the available euphemisms (e.g., *hearing-impaired, physically-challenged*) are considered more offensive than the negative words and phrases. Avoid using the word *blind* to mean "ignorant" or *crippled* or *paralyzed* to mean "unable to function."

There are many other areas of the English vocabulary, like age, class, sexual orientation, and geographic origin, that contain offensive words (such as *hick, rube,* and *bumpkin*). As you write, remember that you want your readers to listen to you. What is important is writing in a way that people will continue to read your work for the value of its ideas. Avoiding offensive language has nothing to do with censorship. It is a matter of courtesy and respect for the feelings and experiences of other people. Attending to how people might react to your writing will only improve it.

Whatever the purpose of your writing, its preparation offers an opportunity for you to examine new topics, learn new research procedures, and sharpen writing skills. Some papers may be more successful than others, but over the years you will gain confidence and facility in preparing them.

Preparing notes

Most style manuals discuss two kinds of notes, distinguished by where they are placed: footnotes and endnotes. The *MLA Handbook* recommends endnotes, as do many writing guides for other disciplines, because essential bibliographic information can now be provided parenthetically within the text (author[s], year of publication, and page number[s]), thus reserving the notes for comments, additional references that might be of interest to your readers, and the like. Endnotes are all placed together at the end of the document; footnotes are placed at the bottom of the same text page on which a reference occurs. Both have the same uses.

Regardless of which format you choose, the notes are an important element in any paper or report because they can convey many kinds of information. They must, however, be used judiciously; the absence of one important citation or an abundance of notes referencing the same source can ruin the finished work. Again, you must decide which information is absolutely crucial and discard that which is irrelevant.

Using notes

The bibliographic information you include in your notes will come from what you wrote at the top of your information cards, so long as you carefully wrote down everything you need. Notes are used for specific purposes:

✔ To give the source of quotations, charts, tables, graphs, or statistics that you copy as found or to provide readers with additional sources for the same idea.
✔ To give the source of ideas, arguments, facts, or other data that you present in your own words or in diagrams.
✔ To give the source of something that is not gleaned from general research.
✔ To substantiate your own arguments.
✔ To offer comments that are not part of the main idea.

Notes that do not provide some sort of substantial information are now generally discouraged.

Notes differ in form from the style used for bibliographies. The following list the preferred format for notes:

✔ The author's name is given first name first and last name last, followed by a comma.

- ✔ The title of the work appears in italics; if a book, within quotation marks; if a poem, essay, or short story, followed by a comma.
- ✔ The city of publication is followed by a colon. The publisher, followed by a comma, and the year of publication are enclosed within parentheses and are followed by a period if the source is a book. For poems, essays, and short stories, the parenthetical information is followed by a comma and then by the page number(s) on which the cited work occurs.

A note is indicated in the text by a superscript numeral typed in the appropriate place, such as at the end of a sentence. The note itself, identified by a matching number followed by a space, appears at the end of the text (endnote) or at the bottom of the page (footnote).

Endnotes are now the preferred method of citation. Notes placed at the end of a section have the centered heading *Notes*. If you use this format, double-space them in a list at the end of each section or at the end of the text itself. If all the notes are placed at the end of the text, you will need to provide the appropriate chapter or section headings. If you choose to use footnotes, they should appear single-spaced at the bottom of the appropriate page, separated from the text by a short line, with a double space between them if there are two or more. You must be careful when typing your paper to leave enough room at the bottom to fit in all the footnotes that belong on the page. If you are using a word processor to format and place your footnotes, the spacing should follow the guidelines you would use if you were typing them in place.

Notes have a particular style and differ in some ways from the form used to present bibliographic entries. They begin with a number typed half space above the line. This number is followed by a full space and then by the remaining data. In such notes, authors' given names precede their last names (Monique Wittig, not Wittig, Monique), followed by a comma, the title, and, in parentheses, the place of publication, the publisher and the date, followed by a comma; page numbers are given only as figures. The entire note ends with a period. The first reference to a book or article is usually given in full. Further references are given in short form. Below are some examples of notes:

First mention of a book:
[1] John Walsh, *Samuel Johnson* (New York: The Viking Press, 1974), 183.

Further references to the same book:
[2] Walsh, 187.

Two books by same author or authors:
[3] Carl Bernstein and Bob Woodward, *All the President's Men* (New York: Simon and Schuster, 1974), 71.

Further references:
[4] Bernstein and Woodward, *President's Men*, 92.
[5] Bob Woodward and Carl Bernstein, *The Final Days* (New York: Simon and Schuster, 1976), 77.

Further references:
[6] Woodward and Bernstein, *Final Days*, 283.
(Note that even though the authors have listed their names in reverse order on the second book, it is advisable to repeat the title in further references to avoid confusion.)

Footnote for a book with an editor, but no author:
[7] Fred L. Israel, ed., *1897 Sears Roebuck Catalog* (New York: Chelsea House, 1968), 149.

For an article in an anthology:
[8] John T. Hitchcock, "Fieldwork in Ghurka Country," in *Being an Anthropologist*, ed. George D. Spindler (New York: Holt, Rinehart and Winston, 1970), 164-165.

Further references:
[9] Hitchcock, 173.

For a signed magazine article:
  [10] Edwin S. Dethlefsen and Kenneth Jensen, "Social Commentary from the Cemetery," *Natural History*, June–July 1977, 34.
  Further references:
  [11] Dethlefsen and Jensen, 37.

For an unsigned magazine article:
  [12] "Estrogen Therapy: The Dangerous Road to Shangri-La," *Consumer Reports,* Nov. 1976, 642.
  Further references:
  [13] "Estrogen Therapy," 644.

For a signed encyclopedia article:
  [14] Philip James, "Orchestration," *Encyclopedia International*, 1972, Vol. 13, 464-466.

For a famous play:
  [15] *Much Ado about Nothing*, III, iii, 53-55.

For a sound recording:
  [16] Melissa Etheridge, "I'm the Only One," *Yes I Am,* Island, 1993.

For material accessed through a computer service:
  [17] Natalie Angier, "Chemists Learn Why Vegetables Are Good for You," *New York Times* 13 Apr. 1993, late ed.: C1, *New York Times Online*, online, Nexis, 10 Feb. 1994.

There are now numerous databases and other electronic sources used in doing research, and you should not overlook this wealth of materials. Each of these sources — CD-ROMs, diskettes, magnetic tape, television and radio — has its own form for bibliographic citation, but the principle of providing full and accurate information to your readers remains the same. Additional information, including detailed examples of the proper form for many different kinds of notes, can be found in the *MLA Handbook*.

For material accessed from a periodically published database on CD-ROM:
  [18] Natalie Angier, "Chemists Learn Why Vegetables Are Good For

You," *New York Times* 13 Apr. 1993, late ed.: C1, *New York Times Ondisc,* CD–ROM, UMI-Proquest, Oct. 1993.

For a nonperiodical publication on CD–ROM:
[19] "Albatross," *The Oxford English Dictionary*, 2nd ed., CD–ROM (Oxford: Oxford UP, 1992).

For a publication on diskette:
[20] Michael Joyce, *Afternoon: A Story*, diskette (Watertown: Eastgate, 1987).

For a publication on magnetic tape:
[21] "Agnes Scott College," Peterson's College Database, magnetic tape (Princeton: Peterson's, 1992).

For a television or radio program:
[22] "Roseanne," Fox, 2 Aug. 1995.

The styles of notes used to add commentary or asides may vary. The following is one possibility:

[23] The *Oxford English Dictionary* gives an obsolete meaning for population as "devastating, laying waste." Many who fear the effects of overpopulation might tend to support this definition. (Note that the *Oxford English Dictionary* is a standard general reference. Unlike other references cited, it would not normally appear in a bibliography.)

All works listed in your notes, as well as other works that might be quoted directly, are listed in the bibliography.

Preparing a bibliography

Strictly speaking, a bibliography is a list of books or printed articles, but it may also include material other than printed matter, such as interviews, graphic works, and filmstrips.

Items in a bibliography follow a particular format that is slightly different from the form used for notes:

✔ Author's name is given last name first. If there is more than one author, all the authors after the first are listed first name

first. All books by one author are listed before the books in which that author collaborated with another. A period follows the author's name.
✔ Full titles are given and underlined if they are titles of books. Titles of stories, poems, and articles are given in quotation marks. A period follows the title; if the title is in quotation marks, the period goes inside the quotation marks.
✔ City of publication is provided, followed by a colon, the publisher (as shown on the title page and the copyright date.
✔ For articles, stories, and poems, the pages on which they appear are given.

What do you list in a bibliography? Certainly, you list all the books or articles you've cited in notes. It is likely you will also list other books or articles that proved useful as general background but not as a source of specific notes. Do not list books that were consulted but did not prove helpful.

Preparing a "Works Cited" section

An alternative to providing notes and a bibliography to document the sources you used in your research is to provide a "Works Cited" section at the end of your paper. In this documentation method, all sources of the words, ideas, and evidence you used in your research are arranged alphabetically at the end of your document. The reader is guided to this information by brief parenthetical citations placed within the text.

The following are general guidelines recommended by the *MLA Handbook* for the preparation of a "Works Cited" section:
✔ Paginate the section as a continuation of your text.
✔ Double-space within and between entries.
✔ Begin the first line of an entry at the left margin and indent successive lines five spaces from the left-hand margin.

- ✔ List entries in alphabetical order according to the last name of the author.
- ✔ If you are listing more than one work by the same author, alphabetize that author's works according to title. In place of the author's name in the second and following entries, type three hyphens and a period.
- ✔ Underline the titles of independent works, such as books, plays, and films. Use quotation marks around the titles of shorter works, such as poems, sections of a larger work, or unpublished works.
- ✔ Whenever possible, use shortened forms for the publisher's name (Houghton instead of Houghton Mifflin Co.)
- ✔ Separate author, title, and publication information with a period followed by two spaces.
- ✔ Use a colon to separate the column number and the year of a periodical from the page numbers.

Sample entries:

Two or more books by the same author:

Hirsch, E. D., Jr. <u>Cultural Literacy: What Every American Needs to Know</u>. Boston: Houghton, 1987.

—. <u>The Philosophy of Composition</u>. Chicago: U of Chicago P, 1977.

An article in a magazine:

Clottes, Jean. "Rhinos and Lions and Bears (Oh, MY!)." <u>Natural History</u> May 1995: 30-35.

A review:

Aveni, Anthony F. "A Bumpy Ride." Rev. of <u>Voyage to the Great Attractor: Exploring Intergalactic Space</u>, by Alan Dressler. <u>Natural History</u> May 1995: 76-9.

An article in a microform collection:

Chapman, Dan. "Panel Could Help Protect Children." <u>Winston-Salem Journal</u> 14 Jan. 1990: 14. <u>Newsbank: Welfare and Social Problems</u> 12 (1990): fiche 1, grids A8-11.

Material from a periodically published database on
CD–ROM:

> Angier, Natalie. "Chemists Learn Why Vegetables Are Good for You." <u>New York</u> <u>Times</u> 13 Apr. 1993, late ed.: C1. <u>New York</u> <u>Times Ondisc</u>. CD–ROM. UMI- Proquest. Oct. 1993.

A publication on diskette:

> Joyce, Michael. <u>Afternoon: A Story</u>. Diskette. Watertown: East-gate, 1987.

A publication on magnetic tape:

> "Children's Television Workshop." <u>Encyclopedia of Associations</u>. Magnetic tape. Detroit: Gale Research, 1994.

Documenting sources. To direct your reader to the materials listed in the "Works Cited" section, you would document sources within the text as follows:

✔ Cite the author's last name and the page number(s) of the source in parentheses at the end of the sentence but before the final period; *or*

✔ Use the author's last name in your sentence, and place only the page number(s) of the source in parentheses at the end of the sentence but before the final period; *or*

✔ Give the author's last name in your sentence when you are citing the entire work rather than a specific section or passage, and omit any parenthetical reference.

✔ Place a parenthetical reference within your sentence as close as possible to the part of the sentence it documents. Place it at the end of the clause after closing quotation marks but before the punctuation.

✔ When a reference documents a long quotation set off from the text, place the reference at the end of the passage quoted but after the final period.

Sample entry:

> One historian argues that since the invention of television "our

politics, religion, news, athletics, education and commerce have been transformed into congenial adjuncts of show business, largely without protest or even much popular notice" Postman 3-4).

The citation looks like this:

WORKS CITED

Postman, Neil. <u>Amusing Ourselves to Death: Public Discourse in the Age of Show Business</u>. New York: Penguin-Viking, 1985.

Preparing an index

An index is an alphabetical list of all the significant topics and individuals discussed in a paper, report, book, article, or other document, with the numbers of all the pages on which a specific subject or person is mentioned. It is made from the page proofs of a printed work or the final copy of a typed work to ensure that all page numbers are final, and it enables readers to consult specific topics in your work. In general, indexes are prepared only for long works of nonfiction, not for papers, articles, or reports under 100 pages. If you have access to a computer with a word-processing program, indexing your own manuscript is a fairly simple procedure.

Word-processing software for computers provides easy instructions for creating and updating an index. Generally, the procedure involves creating an index for your document and marking entries in your text that you wish to include in the index. Consult the user's manual for your software on the steps involved in creating an index.

If you do not have access to computer software with indexing capability, the following procedure is what has been used in the past to compile an index.

Working with the text, underline all items to be indexed; these include chapter or section headings and subheadings, important ideas and theories, and the names of events, places, people, and things.

The second step is to transfer the information to index cards. Write the subject in the top left, followed by a comma and the appropriate page number or numbers. Use a separate card for each item, including cross-references.

Next arrange the cards alphabetically by subject. During this step you should remove all insignificant items. An over-long index containing trivial entries will be of little use to the reader.

Finally, type the entries double-spaced in a list in either a single- or double-column format. The latter style is preferable and the entries in most indexes should be brief enough to accommodate it.

A number of points should be kept in mind. Entries should be as brief and specific as possible, usually a single word or a phrase. Always index according to the most important word in a phrase:

> address to, forms of, 348-360

Avoid if possible a string of page references following a single entry. In such a situation you will usually be able to develop subentries from the text to indicate what aspect of the entry is dealt with at each reference.

For cross-references use the words "See" or "See also." The former is a straight cross-reference and does not have page numbers, which are always entered at the primary index entry. Page numbers are entered when "See also" is used since the cross-reference is to additional information at another entry.

PROOFREADING

At one time or another everyone has done some simple proofreading, such as reading over a letter to see that everything is correct or checking over a list to see that nothing has been omitted.

The act of proofreading involves checking a typed or printed piece of copy against the original manuscript. Strict proofreading involves marking corrections in copy with textual symbols and marginal notations. Knowing how to use proofreaders' marks is helpful if you are proofing academic or office materials before or after they are typed or printed by someone else. While there is no single preferred method used in proofreading, there are basic guidelines.

Take as much time as you need to ensure accuracy. Most copy to be proofread, especially material that comes from a compositor, has very few mistakes. It is as easy to miss errors in clean copy as it is in dirty copy.

Read the copy through to the end once to understand its meaning, then forget about meaning. While some people appreciate suggestions, for example, of how wording could be improved, the proofreader's primary responsibility is to see that everything that is supposed to be in the text is in it and that the material is correct in all respects, such as spelling and spacing.

It is a good idea to read through the copy a number of times, checking for different things on each pass (such as spelling and punctuation or spacing and alignment). Read the copy three or four characters at a time, saying each letter, punctuation mark, and word space aloud. Remember that a misplaced comma is as crucial an error as a misspelled word. Complicated material, such as intricate tables and charts, is best proofread by two people, one reading from the original while the other checks the copy.

Take nothing for granted. Spelling and punctuation errors are missed by the proofreader who does not check every single word or mark about which he or she is unsure. Remember that even the original copy can contain spelling errors. Important pieces of copy should receive a second proofreading by another proofreader.

A sample of marked copy follows. A chart of proofreaders' marks is given on pages 202 and 203.

Sample copy

It is the proofreaders job to ensure that all typed or printed ma terial is properly spaced and aligned and contains grammatical typographical, or spellng errors. Mark all corrections in a color that is clearly distinguished that from of the copy Each correction requires a symbol in the text and a corresponding explanation in the marginnext to the line in which it is ffound. if there are 2 or more corrections in one line, write them in the margin the proper order and separate then with a slanting line Material to be inserted is written in the margin and its place is indicated by a caret. If you make you make an improper correction — and these things do happen do not erase it put a series of periods below what you have mistakenly crossed out in the text and write stet (which means "Let it stand" in the margin.

¶ Always remember to take your time. The proofreader has one goal total accuracy. Never assume or guess that something is Right. Check every word whose spelling you are unsure of in your copy of The American Heritage® Dictionary of the English Language, Third Edition.

Margin marks:

ⱽ

⌒

no | ∧ | i

tr / ⊙

| ⅀ | cap

sp

rom | in

⊙ | lf

in the text /

⌒ ‖

ṃ | ∧

stet

ꜱ/ꜱ | ⱶ

¶ | lf

⊙

lc

ital

Proofreaders' marks

Instruction	Mark in Margin	Mark in Type
Delete	*ℯ*	the ~~written~~ word
Insert indicated material	good	the word
Let it stand	*stet*	the written word
Make capital	*cap*	the word
Make lower case	*lc*	The Word
Set in small capitals	*sc*	See word.
Set in italic type	*ital*	The word is word.
Set in roman type	*rom*	the word
Set in boldface type	*bf*	the entry word
Set in lightface type	*lf*	the entry word
Transpose	*tr*	the word right
Close up space	⌒	the wo rd
Delete and close up space	⌿	the woord
Spell out	*sp*	2 words
Insert space	#	theword
Insert period	⊙	This is the word
Insert comma	⋀	words words, words
Insert hyphen	⸗	word for word test
Insert colon	⊙	The following words
Insert semicolon	⦵	Scan the words skim the words.
Insert apostrophe	⋁	Johns words

Instruction	Mark in Margin	Mark in Type
Insert quotation marks	ᵛ/ᵛ/	the word ˇword ˇ
Insert question mark	⸮	the word ‸
Insert parentheses	(/)/	The word word is in parentheses. ‸ ‸
Insert brackets	[/]/	He read from the Word the Bible. ‸ ‸
Insert en dash	⅟N	1964 1972 ‸
Insert em dash	⅟M/ ⅟M/	A dictionary ‸ how often it is needed belongs in every home. ‸
Start paragraph	¶	"Where is it?" ‸ "It's on the shelf."
Move left	[	[the word
Move right	]	⌐ the word
Center	][	⌐the word [
Align vertically	‖	the word ‖the word
Align horizontally, straighten type	═	the ₜword ═
Wrong font	ⓦⓕ	th⒠word
Broken type	x	th⒠word

THE LIBRARY

The card catalog

The card catalog is the best tool for finding books in the library published prior to 1980. Material on the cards will help you decide if that book will be helpful. The card catalog may also help you locate other materials such as records, filmstrips, microfilms, and microfiches though in some libraries, these materials may have their own reference systems. Periodicals and the issues available are generally listed in a vertical file or a computer printout.

What exactly is a card catalog? A card catalog is an index of books, arranged alphabetically on 3″ × 5″ cards in a set of file drawers. Each file drawer is usually labeled to show what portion of the alphabet it contains. The cards list the following information about the books: author, title, subject or subjects covered in the book. Some cards give cross-references to other cards. A few cards are information cards: these do not direct you to a particular book but instead tell you where to find cards or items that may be hard to locate.

No matter where a book is situated in the library, the catalog card will direct you to it. Although the cards are listed alphabetically, the books are not arranged alphabetically on the shelves. Librarians in the United States usually organize books by one of two systems: the Dewey Decimal System or the Library of Congress System. Both systems classify books into major fields of knowledge and will be explained in the section "Organization of the Library." Thus, mathematics books will be in one section, history books in another, and so on. Within each broad area of knowledge, there are subdivisions. While these systems create an orderly arrangement for the library, without the card catalog it would be very difficult for the average individual to find specific books.

Organization of the cards. Although new acquisitions are now generally added to libraries' computer catalogs, familiarity with the older card system will help you use computer catalogs. The card catalog is alphabetized word by word. That means that all the cards beginning, for example, with the word "New" will be placed before the cards beginning with "News" or "Newton." Thus the order will be

New astronomy theories	Newark
New Jersey	Newport
New mathematics	News
New ports	News gathering
New theories of science	Newton, Isaac
New York	Newtonian physics

The word-by-word method of alphabetizing differs from the method used by dictionaries. In dictionaries, each word or phrase is alphabetized as if it were written as one word. In a dictionary system, "Newark" would come before "New Jersey" and "New York."

In a card catalog, all abbreviations are listed as if they were spelled out. Thus, "Mt." would be listed as if spelled "mount" and "St." would be listed as if spelled "saint." "Mc" and "M" would be listed as if spelled "Mac." Articles (*a, an, the*) are not considered if they appear at the beginning of a title. (*The House of the Seven Gables* would be alphabetized at *House,* not at *The.*)

If a person is an author as well as a subject, all books written *by* him or her would be listed before all books written *about* him or her.

In very complicated situations, an information card will often clarify matters. For example, there are many kings named Henry from many countries. There are also people whose last names are Henry. How do you figure out which comes first? An information card will usually explain the order used in the catalog.

What the cards tell you. The cards in the catalog are designed to direct you to the books themselves. To find the books, you need to understand what can be learned from the cards.

In the first place, a card in the catalog tells you that the book you want is in the library's collection. The card will not tell you if someone else has the book out on loan, and, in many libraries, the card will not indicate whether the book is at the bindery for repairs. The card will let you know whether the book may be borrowed or must be used in the library. In some cases, one edition of a book is noncirculating, but another edition of the same book may be taken out on loan. There is usually a card in the catalog for each edition.

Other items that may be learned from a catalog card are the author's full name, date of birth, and date of death; and the title and subtitle, copyright date, number of pages, and publisher of the book. You can learn whether the book has illustrations, a bibliography, or an introduction by someone other than the author. Some cards will give the date when a book was first published if the book is a new edition or revision. At the bottom of the card, there are notations that indicate where other cards may be found in the catalog for that same book. These notations can be helpful by referring you to related subjects.

The most important thing that you can learn from the card is the book's call number, which will direct you to the shelf on which the book can be found. The call number may be classified by the Dewey Decimal System or the Library of Congress system (discussed in the section "Organization of the library"). Some books may have no call number. For instance, works of fiction — especially contemporary fiction — are often arranged by the author's last name in a separate fiction section, and the fiction cards may have Fic. or F. in the corner where one would normally find the call number. Some libraries may place nothing at all on the fiction cards. Biographies may also be treated as a separate category in some libraries. The call number on a biography book may be simply be a B (for biography) followed by the first initial of the last name of the person about whom the book is written. Thus, a biography about Sigmund Freud would have B-F where the call number would normally appear; a biography by Sigmund Freud about Woodrow Wilson would have B-W for the call number.

Author cards. Librarians consider the author card to be the basic catalog card. Most books have authors. Sometimes the author is one individual. Sometimes several people, a committee, a foundation, a magazine, or even the government may be the author of a book.

The author card lists the author's name, last name first. On the line below, it lists the title of the book. If there are ten books in the library by one author, there will be ten author cards, one for each book. Those cards will be listed alphabetically by their titles.

For example, if you wanted to find books written by Herman Kahn, you would look up "Kahn, Herman" and find:

```
U162
.K25      Kahn, Herman, 1922 —
              Thinking about the unthinkable. New York, Horizon
          Press, 1962.

          254p. 22cm.
          Includes bibliographical references.


          1. Strategy — Mathematical models. 2. Deterrence
          (Strategy). 3. Atomic warfare.   I. Title.

U162.K25                    355.43                    62-11235
Library of Congress
```

Another card you might find is:

```
HC        Kahn, Herman, 1922 —
59            The next 200 years: a scenerio for America
.K32      and the world/by Herman Kahn, William Brown, and
          Leon Martel. New York: Morrow, c1976.

          xv, 241p.; 22cm.
          Includes index.
          Bibliography:  p.

          1. Economic history — 1945– — Addresses, essays,
          lectures.2. Economic forecasting — Addresses, essays,
          lectures. 3. Technology and civilization — Addresses,
          essays, lectures. 4. United States — Economic conditions
          — 1971– .  I. Brown, William, joint author.  II. Martel,
          Leon, joint author.   III. T.

RG76 — 27008                              76 — 5425
HC59.K32                                  330.9/04
```

The first book, *Thinking about the Unthinkable,* was written in 1962 by Herman Kahn. It has 254 pages and bibliographical references. Other catalog cards may be found at strategy — mathematical models, deterrence, atomic warfare, and *Thinking about the Unthinkable.*

Most important, the card tells you that the book will be found on the shelf with other books having the number U162. (The U is for Military Science using the Library of Congress system).

The second book by Herman Kahn has a different number — HC59.K32 — and falls into a different subject area. It was written by Herman Kahn and other people. Its copyright date is 1976. The book has 241 pages and includes both an index and a bibliography. Other catalog cards for the same book may be found at economic history — 1945 — addresses, essays, lectures; economic forecasting — addresses, essays, lectures; technology and civilization — addresses, essays, lectures; United States — economic conditions — 1971; Brown, William; Martel, Leon; and *(The) Year 2000.*

Some authors do not write under their own names. The library may list the book at the pseudonym or at the real name. The card catalog will clarify the name and the spelling that the library uses.

All the catalog cards for Mark Twain will be found under

Twain, Mark, pseud.

    see

Clemens, Samuel Langhorne, 1835–1910.

"Clemens." Not all writers who use pseudonyms are listed at their real names. When you look up an author, look under the name that you are familiar with. The card catalog will inform you whether the author is listed by his or her pseudonym or real name.

The United States government and its branches may be the author of a book. If you try to look up "Library of Congress" in the card catalog, a cross-reference card will tell you to look under "U.S. Library of Congress." There you will find books with "U.S. Library of Congress" as the official author. You will find books about the Library of Congress filed after these author cards.

Title cards. On the title card, the title is usually typed in above the author's name. Below, the author's name is given and the title is repeated. A title card is really the basic author card with the title shown at the top.

If you know the title of a book but don't know who wrote it, the card catalog can help you find it. Titles, like authors, are listed in the card catalog in alphabetical order. If you wanted to find a book named *My Ántonia*, you would look under *My*.

```
PS3505      My Ántonia
.A87M8
1954        Cather, Willa Sibert, 1873–1947.
                My Ántonia. With illus. by W.T. Benda.
            Boston, Houghton Mifflin [c1954]

            371p.          illus.          22cm.

LC          I. Title.
```

There may not be a call number on this card because it is a work of fiction and would be found in the fiction section under "Cather." If a library uses the Library of Congress system, call number similar to the one in the above example would be on the card.

In addition to containing information on full works of fiction, the card catalog may help you find short novels. Usually, though, it will not help you find short stories, poems, plays, essays, and other short works published in collections or anthologies. To find these you need to use reference books.

The main thing to remember when looking for a title card is to ignore the article at the beginning of the title. Look for *A Tale of Two Cities* at *Tale*, not *A*. Look for *The Uses of Enchantment* at *Uses*, not at *The*.

Sometimes you may be unsure if the name by which you know a book is an author's name or the title. For example, if you want to find *The Guinness Book of World Records*, look it up under *Guinness*.

```
Ref.
AG243
.G85    The Guinness book of world records. 1956–
             New York,  Sterling Pub. Co. [etc.]

             v. illus., ports.          20-26cm.

             Vol. for 1962 issued as Worthwhile Sterling
        paperbacks, 901.
        Title varies:  1956, The Guinness book of superlatives.


          1. Curiosities.   I. Title: The Guinness book of
        superlatives.
```

The authors' names are omitted from this card, but a card for an older edition shows the authors were Norris McWhirter and Ross McWhirter, not a person named "Guinness."

Some books — such as reference books — have no official author since they are compiled by several individuals. When published, these books can be located by title.

Subject cards. Most researchers find that the subject cards are the most useful cards in the catalog. Some cards will refer you to books that cover a broad subject, and other cards will refer to books on subdivisions of a subject. There may also be an information card that leads you to related topics. Suppose that you are doing research on costumes to help you design and make costumes for a play set in 18th-century England. You look up the subject COSTUME in the card catalog. Note that the subject card is the basic author card with the subject in capital letters at the top of the card.

COSTUME.

GT510
.E8

Evans, Mary

    Costume throughout the ages, by Mary Evans . . .
frontispiece in color and 210 illustrations. Philadelphia,
London [etc.] J.B. Lippincott company [c1930].

xv, 358. incl. col. front., illus., plates. 22cm.

"References" at end of each chapter: "Bibliography
of history costume": p.318–329.

1. Costume. 2. Costume—Hist. I. Title.

Library of Congress   GT510.E8   30-26371
——————— Copy 2.

One book you see is *Costume throughout the Ages* by Mary Evans. It has illustrations and plates, and it has references and a bibliography. You should note that since the copyright date is 1930, any books listed in the bibliography will have been printed before 1930.

There is also a cross-reference card:

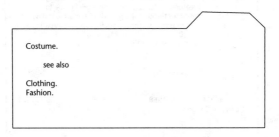

Costume.

    see also

Clothing.
Fashion.

These other subjects may or may not be useful in your research. You make a note of the subject that may help.

After the general subject COSTUME are books on particular aspects of the general subjects. For example:

    COSTUME — HISTORY   COSTUME, THEATRICAL

Each of these subcategories will likely be helpful in the research you are doing, and you note books listed under each one.

For example, this card may appear:

```
GT 1741       Theatrical costume and the amateur stage. Green,
.G4           Michael.

1968          Theatrical costume and the amateur stage: a book
              of simple methods in the making and altering of
              theatrical costumes, including a brief guide to
              costumes through the periods to the present day;
              drawings by William Langstaffe. London, Arco 1968.
                 150 p.     illus.     23cm. 36/ —
                 SBN 209-62630-5


              1. Costume.    I. Title

GT 1741.G4         1968              646.4          68-122121
Library of Congress
```

The book seems to be one that may help you actually make the costumes once you have decided what the costumes are to look like, so you make a note of it.

Using computer catalogs. The information that you will find in a computer catalog isn't much different from the card catalog. If you are unfamiliar with using computers in the library to look for research sources, ask a librarian to show you how to start an electronic search. One aid might be a book just produced by the American Library Association, *The American Library Association Guide to Information Access: A Complete Research Handbook and Directory,* edited by Sandra Whiteley

(New York: Random House, 1994). This book, which should be available in the reference section of most large libraries, provides a good introduction to basic research procedures, several chapters on what is available using electronic research methods, plus 35 chapters on specific research topics such as Automobiles, Consumer Information, Education, The Environment, Film, Jobs and Careers, Sexuality, Sports, Travel, and Women's Studies. In each chapter, the *ALA Guide* provides research sources in the following order:

General Sources of Information	Government Publications
Periodical Indexes	Government Agencies
Other Indexes	Associations
Electronic Sources	Libraries
Periodicals	Current LC Subject Headings
	Sources of Expert Advice

Since about 1980 (in some cases earlier), libraries have been gradually converting their cataloging systems from cards to computers; there are many types of cataloging software in use. You will need to ask the conversion date for the system used in the library you are working in. The information available in a computer catalog will be identical to or exceed what you can find in the card catalog. The following screens give you examples of the type of information that is often accessible when you use the cataloging software available at your local library.

Once you turn on the computer, you will get a screen that looks something like the following:

```
┌─────────────────────────────────────────────────────┐
│              Searching: Library Catalog               │
│                                                       │
│   Find        Options      Startover      Quit        │
│   Help                                                │
│   Author                                              │
│   Title                                               │
│   Subject                                             │
│   ─────                                               │
│                                                       │
│                                                       │
│   Author/Keyword                                      │
│   Title/Keyword      Choose letter option and         │
│   Subject/Keyword    press RETURN to begin searching  │
│   Keywords                       or                   │
│   Expert Keywords    hit the NEXT key                 │
│   ─────                                               │
│                                                       │
│                                                       │
│   Numeric                                             │
│                                                       │
│   ──────── Press the NEXT key for more                │
└─────────────────────────────────────────────────────┘
```

This menu offers you a choice of how to begin your information search: by using an Author, Title, or Subject or a Keyword in any of these areas, or the call number (numeric) of a book. The underlined letters (S for Subject, K for Keywords, and so on) are what you will type in on the keyboard if the computer isn't equipped with a mouse. If you are unsure of how to proceed, there is usually an option allowing you to call up a general information screen that provides additional directions.

Suppose you want to look up the books available in the library on the subject of pesticides. Type S for subject and hit the <Enter> key, or click on Subject with the mouse. The computer will show you a screen with the cursor blinking next to an arrow. Where the cursor is, type in "pesticides."

General

Use the arrow keys (left/right/up/down) to highlight an option and press the key labeled RETURN to execute that option. If an option is followed by an ellipsis (. . .), there are more options beneath it to choose from. Optionally,

Enter the SUBJECT and press RETURN
Press F10 to cancel.
->

Press the NEXT key for more, or the PREV key for previous page

The computer will begin to fill the screen with the subject listings for pesticides. You may, for example, notice that first listing provides you with alternative subject words containing pesticide-related titles. Other topic designations serve to further define the subject area, such as "Pesticides and the Environment" and "Pesticides and wildlife":

You searched SUBJECT for: pesticides

	Titles	Search Results	Headings 1-8
1	[18]	Pesticides	
2		Related Term: Herbicides	
3		Related Term: Insecticides	
4		Related Term: Natural pesticides	
5		Related Term: Pesticide resistance	
6		Related Term: Pests: Control	
		Pesticides and the Environment	
7			
		Use: Pesticides— Environmental aspects	
8	[4]	Pesticides and wildlife	

Type a number for more information, or press NEXT for other selections.

The numbers that precede two of the subject listings tell you the number of books the library has available on each particular subtopic. For example, there are four books in the library concerning pesticides and wildlife. At the bottom of the screen are instructions on how to display a record. Often the procedure is to type the number that is keyed to the line containing the information you want. Other software may ask you to use the directional keys (left/right/up/down) to move the highlight on the screen and then hit <Enter> to display the record you want.

Suppose you want to see what books the library has concerning pesticides and wildlife. Typing the number 8 will bring up a small box on the screen in which "8" will appear next to an arrow, and the computer will prompt you to hit <Enter> if indeed 8 is your choice. When <Enter> is hit, you will see the following screen, which looks like a streamlined version of the card in the card catalog:

```
Find        Options        Startover        Quit        Help

You searched SUBJECT for: pesticides

        SEARCH RESULTS          Titles 1-4 of 4

1    Carson, Rachel, 1907–1964. Silent spring. 25th anniversary
     ed. Boston: Houghton Mifflin Co. 1987.

2    Carson, Rachel Louise. Silent spring. Boston, Houghton
     Mifflin. 1962.

3    Hudson, R.H. (Rick H.). Handbook of toxicity of pesticides to
     wildlife. 2nd ed. 1984.

4    Rudd, Robert L. Pesticides and the living landscape. Madison,
     University of Wisconsin Press. 1964.


Type a number for more information, or press NEXT for other
selections.
```

Following the same procedure as you did when choosing to see the entries at "Pesticides and wildlife," you can select any of the numbers 1-4 and receive a full version of the book's catalog card. Selecting the first entry calls up the following screen:

Find	Options	Startover	Quit	Help

CALL NUMBER: SB959 .C3 1987x.
AUTHOR: Carson, Rachel, 1907–1964.
TITLE: Silent spring/ by Rachel Carson;
      drawings by Lois and Louis Darling;
      foreword by Paul Brooks.
EDITION: 25th anniversary ed.
PUBLISHED: Boston: Houghton Mifflin Co., [1987], c1962.

_____

Library Holdings at   <Press F13 to see other locations>

Your Local Library Adult

1. Call number: SB959 .C3 1987x — Nonfiction— Available

Along the top is the call number for Rachel Carson's book, *Silent Spring*. The bottom section tells you that there is one copy at the library you are working in and that it is currently available for you to check out.

You may wish to search for books by using keywords, titles, authors, series, or call numbers — whatever kind of information you have for beginning your search. If you decide at some point that you want to start your search over, simply hit <Esc> (escape), <Start Over>, or a similar key and the computer will return you to the opening screen.

Many libraries have a printer attached to each computer terminal with which you can print out a copy of the sources you decide to look at. Both the card and computer catalogs can lead you to books, but neither can help you determine if the books are what you need. To know if a book is useful, you must examine it.

There are now additional electronic services and data sources available at some libraries. Check at your library to find out what it has to offer.

Organization of the library

Today there are two organizational systems in the United States: the Dewey Decimal System and the Library of Congress System. When you enter a library, see if the books have Dewey Decimal call numbers (e.g., 792.42) or Library of Congress call numbers (e.g., PN 1993.5).

Call numbers stand for certain categories. The categories in the Dewey Decimal System differ from the categories in the Library of Congress System.

Dewey Decimal System. Call numbers in this system begin with Arabic numerals.

000 Generalities — bibliographies, encyclopedias, libraries, and the like
100 Philosophy and related disciplines
200 Religion
300 Social sciences — statistics, sociology, economics, law, education, and similar disciplines
400 Language — linguistics, other languages

500 Pure sciences — mathematics, astronomy, physics, chemistry, earth science, biological science, botany, zoology, and similar disciplines

600 Technology — medicine, engineering, agriculture, domestic science, business, and similar disciplines

700 The arts — architecture, sculpture, drawing, painting, photography, music, and recreational arts

800 Literature and rhetoric — American and English literature, literature from other languages

900 General geography, history, and similar disciplines

Each category is subdivided further (e.g., 401, 426, 492) and decimal numbers may be added to make further distinctions (e.g., 426.12, 792.42). On the shelf, all the books are arranged in numerical order. Books without the decimal are arranged before books with the decimal, as in the series 792, 792.12, 792.42.

Library of Congress System. Call numbers in this system begin with letters.

A   General works
B   Philosophy and religion
C   History and auxiliary sciences
D   History and topography (except America)
E&F America
G   Geography and anthropology
H   Social sciences
J   Political sciences
K   Law
L   Education
M   Music
N   Fine arts
P   Language and literature
Q   Science

R	Medicine
S	Agriculture
T	Technology
U	Military science
V	Naval science
Z	Bibliography and library science

Note that the letters I, O, W, X, and Y are not included. They may some day be used if further categories become necessary. Categories in the Library of Congress System are further subdivided with a second letter, then a numeral of one to four digits, then a decimal followed by a numeral or a letter and a numeral. Sometimes there is a further subdivision of categories introduced by a second decimal.

On the shelf, books are arranged alphabetically by letter category, as in P, PN, PS. Within each of the letter categories, books are arranged in numerical order from 1 to 9999, as in PN1, PN86, PN1993, PN1993.5, PN1994, PN6110.

Electronic research sources

If your library has the necessary computer system or if you have a personal computer and a modem, then the new world of information being made available through electronic sources is open to you. Such resources include on-line databases, CD-ROMs, document delivery services, electronic bulletin boards, and the Internet. Each source will provide you with information you often cannot obtain any other way.

On-line services. Databases have become important sources to check when you are conducting research. They are large files created by government agencies, scholarly groups, or private corporations. These files are often made available on-line to consumers by companies called vendors, such as Dialog®, BRS, and ORBIT®. There are more than 5000 databases, some that provide primarily bibliographic data, others that offer the full texts of articles and reports.

The *ALA Guide* categorizes vendors into three levels based on how much they charge, the training required to use them, the size of their audience, and the kind of data they offer.

Level 1 includes scholarly and professional services that are often found in offices and libraries: BRS, Human Resources Information Network (HRIN)®, Dialog®, NEXIS®, and NewsNet®. Easynet® is called a "gateway" because it provides access to 850 databases.

Level 2 systems are comprised of services for nonprofessional users: Knowledge Index® and BRS/AfterDark®. They are available at lower rates than the Level 1 services because they operate in the evening and on weekends when traffic is less heavy. People often use Level 2 systems on their PCs to do research at home.

Level 3 contains vendors who specialize in consumer services such as E-mail, access to bulletin boards, and a wide variety of research and entertainment options. CompuServe®, Prodigy®, and America Online® are three of the better-known vendors.

If you want to do an on-line search but don't have the equipment to access one of these vendors, your library may be willing to do it for you, but there will be a fee. There are also books listed in the *ALA Guide* that describe the vendors and their services and how to get the most out of them.

CD–ROM (Compact Disc–Read Only Memory). A CD–ROM, like an audio CD, uses laser technology to encode and read electronic data, the equivalent of about 300,000 print pages. A CD–ROM can be used only if you have a PC with a large-capacity hard drive and a special drive connected to your computer that enables you to "read" the disc or copy it into your computer. It is also now possible to access CD–ROM drives from homes and offices by telephone. In addition to encyclopedias and other major reference works, many of the databases available on-line from vendors are also available on CD–ROM. For up-to-date information about what is available on CD–ROM, there are two annual sources you can consult: CD–ROMS in Print (Meckler Publishing) or the Gale Directory of Databases (Gale Research).

Document delivery services. Just as electronic technology has changed the way research is done, it has also changed how we identify the information we need. Document delivery services greatly expand the potential range of your research activity. If, for example, you've found an article you need that's not available in your library, a document delivery service, such as CARL UnCover, Information Express®, UMI Article Clearinghouse, or The Information Store®, will fax or mail it to you for a fee (which includes what they must pay to the copyright holder). According to the *ALA Guide,* some libraries offer access to CARL's services.

Electronic bulletin boards (BBSs). There are more than 45,000 BBSs accessible to people in the United States, and many of them, accessible 24 hours a day, can be valuable research sources. Although there are some nonprofit bulletin boards, most charge a nominal annual fee for membership. The *ALA Guide* lists 110 BBSs of the federal government alone, ranging from ABLE INFORM, connected with the National Rehabilitation Center, to WSCA-BBS, a BBS connected to the Board of Wage & Service Contract Appeal.

Because most electronic bulletin boards have been set up by someone with a serious interest in a subject, many BBSs offer a lot of information on specific topics that cannot be obtained in any other way. If you want to find a bulletin board in one of your areas of interest or consult someone knowledgeable in a certain area, the *ALA Guide* suggests checking CompuServe®, which lists BBSs, or looking in the *National Directory of Bulletin Board Systems* by Patrick Dewey (Meckler Publishing).

The Internet. The global network known as the Internet connects millions of users in numerous countries. It is often likened to an "information superhighway." It began as a means for scholars to exchange information, but it now enables you to communicate with users who may not subscribe to your system and it provides virtually any kind of information you may want, including texts, archives of graphic materials, astronomical maps, and chemical formulas.

The Internet requires a standard address form and transfer protocol. For example, "Telnet" is the command you use to look at information on another computer. It is used to connect bulletin boards, library catalogs, and other resources. In order to log onto another computer, you have to know the machine name or the numeric address, which you'll find in a directory. There are also numerous tools that will make it easier for you to find what you're looking for on the Internet.

Most universities and colleges are now linked to the Internet, and some cities, such as Cleveland, offer "freenets," which provide local information and help people to connect with the Internet.

The *ALA Guide* offers a selective bibliography of books and articles for the novice.

Library reference sources

After you have searched through the card catalog and checked available electronic resources, you have not yet exhausted the resources of the library. Most libraries have reference sections — separate rooms or areas — containing books that are often consulted as sources. Some items may very clearly be reference books, such as encyclopedias, dictionaries, almanacs, and atlases. Other items may not fit as obviously into the category of reference books, such as anthologies and books of documents. In addition, some valuable reference material may be found not in the reference section but in the general collection.

There are two kinds of library reference sources. One kind supplies the required information — you look in the book and find what you want to know. The other kind directs you to the required information in another book, magazine, newspaper, or other source. Both types are needed for most reference projects. Read the introductions to the reference books carefully. Each book organizes material in its own way. Each has its own abbreviations and cross-references.

Reference works not available locally may be accessed through electronic sources such as CD–ROM or through another library on the Internet.

Indexes to newspapers and periodicals. An index is a guide to direct you to material on a subject or by an author. Using an index involves two processes. The first is finding out whether and where an article has been published. The second process is sometimes more difficult — finding a copy of the required newspaper or magazine. Large libraries may have bound volumes of periodicals and microfilm or microfiche copies of newspapers. Most magazines prepare an annual alphabetical list of the articles they've published during the year.

The *Readers' Guide to Periodical Literature* directs you to articles in the most widely read magazines in the United States. Regular supplements are available to bring you up to date. *Access* directs you to some periodicals not indexed in *Readers' Guide*.

Indexes to direct you to more specialized journals in particular fields are also available. A short list of examples includes:

Agricultural Index
Applied Science and Technology Index
Art Index

> *Business Periodicals Index*
> *Cumulative Book Index*
> *Education Index*
> *Humanities Index*
> *Index to Legal Periodicals*
> *Music Index*
> *Reader's Guide to Periodical Literature*
> *Social Science Index*
> *Ulrich's International Periodical Index* (Lists the names of periodicals in many languages. It does not index specific articles.)

Very few newspapers are indexed. It may be possible to find information on world or national events in one of the following newspaper indexes:

> *Index to the Christian Science Monitor*
> *The New York Times Index*
> *The Times Index, London*
> *The Newspaper Index* (indexes a few large American newspapers)

If your library has the material to which the indexes refer, it is probably on microfilm or microfiche. In general, finding and obtaining articles published in newspapers, especially if they are older than five or ten years, is difficult. The electronic newspaper listings that do exist don't contain more than a few years' worth of articles.

Local newspapers vary greatly in their manner of filing material about old stories and in their willingness to let people not on staff use the files.

Indexes to material shorter than book length. Short works are difficult to locate. They generally come in anthologies, and anthology titles do not necessarily indicate what specific works they contain. If you want to find a poem, short story, play, or essay, you may find the relevant anthology or anthologies by using an index or by asking other people on a BBS who share your interest.

For poetry:
> *Granger's Index to Poetry* (Poems are listed by author, first line, title, and subject.)

For short stories:
> *Short Story Index* (Short stories are indexed by author, title, and subject. Some periodicals are included, as well as anthologies.)

For essays:
> *Essays and General Literature Index* (Essays and literary criticism are indexed by author and subject.)

For plays:
> *Ottemiller's Index to Plays in Collections, 1900–1975* (Plays are indexed by author and title.)
>
> *Play Index* (Organized by year; each volume covers three to four years.)

Bibliographies. You can locate many bibliographies indirectly through the card catalog. When you find a book on a subject you are investigating, that book may have a bibliography. No bibliography in a book will be more up-to-date than the book itself, so note the publication date. The following are more general sources that will help you find bibliographies:

> *Bibliography of Bibliographies* (Lists many bibliographies.)
>
> *Bibliographic Index* (Also a bibliography of bibliographies.)
>
> *Subject Guide to Books in Print* (List of American books still in print. The list is arranged by subject and may prove useful as a means of finding titles of books on a particular subject.)
>
> *Cumulative Books Index* (Lists English-language books by subject, author, and title.)

If one or more of these books isn't available in your library, you may be able to find it by searching the holdings of other libraries on the Internet.

There are also many special-subject lists of books. A few examples are:

The Reader's Advisor
Sources of Information in the Social Sciences
Harvard Guide to American History
Science and Engineering Reference Sources

Guides to finding books. It is unreasonable to expect any library to carry all the books on every subject. You may have compiled a good bibliography, but then you may not find the books in your library. What do you do?

✔ Find out if your library participates in an interlibrary loan program. If so, there may be a catalog of the books available from another library.

✔ Look it up in *Books in Print* to find out if it can be purchased by you or by the library.

✔ Try *Paperbound Books in Print*. If you choose to buy the books yourself, you may find paperbacks more economical.

✔ Check the *Guide to U.S. Government Publications*. It provides a list of books available from the U.S. Government Printing Office.

✔ Electronically search the catalogs of other libraries, or check an up-to-date listing of titles available on CD–ROM.

BEYOND THE PUBLIC LIBRARY

The good researcher knows to go beyond the public library for many kinds of research. Here are some other sources of information, many of them accessible through computer networks.

Other kinds of libraries

Company libraries or reference rooms are more likely than a large library to have material on subjects of particular interest to that company's work. If your company does not have at least a reference shelf, it should begin to develop one. At times, you may be able to arrange to use other companies' libraries.

Museum libraries may have highly specialized materials that are helpful. Even a small museum may have a library that is complete in the field of that museum's specialization.

Private libraries may be general or specialized. They may belong to business associations, unions, or professional groups. Terms of use differ from one private library to another.

College and university libraries are often for the specific use of faculty and students. Sometimes, however, arrangements can be made by firms or individuals to use these libraries on a regular or temporary basis.

Many of these repositories are now accessible to you via any of the electronic sources discussed in the section "Papers and Reports."

Specialized collections of maps, costumes, recordings, pictures, and similar materials may be available in your area.

Government and public institutions

Try the offices of the city, town, county, or state government. There are often many maps, records, and special information bulletins available.

Government agencies of all levels have a wealth of information. It is up to you to locate the agency and to call or write for the information you need. If the topic in which you're interested is one of the subjects covered in the *ALA Guide*, you will find addresses, phone numbers, and E-mail addresses of the government agencies you want to contact.

Chambers of commerce are often glad to supply material and answer questions about their area. They will often direct you to other people or organizations who can supply what they cannot supply.

The federal government's Government Printing Office publishes a large number of pamphlets and books on a great variety of subjects. You can get their Subject Bibliography price list (describing all the Office's publications) or a price list on a specific subject by writing to:

> Superintendent of Documents
> Government Printing Office
> Washington, DC 20402

The following publications, many of them now available through a vendor or document delivery service, are sources of information about the federal government:

✔ *Congressional Record.* A daily record of the activities of Congress, including indexes giving the names, subjects, and history of all bills.

✔ *Federal Register.* A daily record of the activities of executive branch departments and agencies such as the Food and Drug Administration and Internal Revenue Service, including regulations, policy proposals, and public comments.

- ✔ *Official Congressional Directory.* Published by the Government Printing Office, a list of the names and addresses of everyone connected with the federal government, maps of Congressional Districts, and short biographies of members of Congress (published annually).
- ✔ *Official Register of the U.S. Government.* A list, by agency, of the name, title, salary, and address of all supervisory and administrative personnel of the federal government (published annually).

Private companies and agencies

Private companies can supply annual reports — a source of a great deal of economic information. Some libraries have collections of annual reports, but you can also obtain them by writing to the companies or, if they make such information available electronically, request that documents be faxed to you.

Private companies are often willing to supply other information about the industry or industries at large. Large companies often have pamphlets available about basic industrial techniques or products. Some of the material must be evaluated because the companies are trying to maintain a good public image and may not be presenting opposing views.

Private organizations often exist for the purpose of encouraging or discouraging certain practices. They are willing to supply information presenting their point of view. Again, this material must be carefully evaluated because it often presents only one viewpoint.

Private agencies and business organizations may have printed information available. For example, the New York Stock Exchange has a great deal of material on the operations of the stock market. Often, such agencies and organizations will answer questions, as well.

Trade magazines

Most industries are serviced by trade magazines. Trade magazines have useful articles. They usually produce yearly directories of the companies in a specific industry, and they may have indexes of articles published during the year.

They may also issue specialized handbooks of interest only to that trade. Most of these trade magazines would not be in a small public library. They may be available on the shelves of businesses in that field, and often back copies can be obtained from the publisher. Occasionally the staff members of trade magazines will answer questions or direct you to people who can answer them.

Interviews

Do not ignore the possibility of interviewing people, but keep in mind that some informants may be more reliable than others. You will have to evaluate the information received in interviews by checking it against what you have learned from other sources.

GUIDE TO BASIC REFERENCE WORKS

The Reference Department of a library can be one of the most valuable resources a researcher has. The librarians in this department help users make the most effective use of the library's resources. Reference books are the core of any reference department. Some of the multi-volume texts found in a reference department are now available on CD–ROM.

Encyclopedias

Encyclopedias provide good background material. They are a fine place to begin research on many topics. Often, an encyclopedia provides a short bibliography as well.

There are two kinds of encyclopedias — general and special purpose. Either kind may be organized alphabetically or by subject. Here are some examples of general encyclopedias:

> *Collier's Encyclopedia*
> *Compton's Encyclopedia and Fact Index*
> *Encyclopaedia Britannica*
> *Encyclopedia Americana*
> *Facts on File Encyclopedia of the Twentieth Century*
> *New Columbia Encyclopedia* — a good one-volume reference work

When it comes to special-purpose reference books, it can be hard to draw the line between encyclopedias and dictionaries. Both should be consulted (see the next section) if both exist in a special field. Here are some examples of special-purpose encyclopedias:

> *Encyclopedia of Computer Science and Engineering*
> *The Encyclopedia of Philosophy*
> *The International Cyclopedia of Music and Musicians*

> *McGraw-Hill Encyclopedia of Science and Technology*
> *The Oxford Companion to World Sports and Games*
> *Walker's Mammals of the World*

Dictionaries and word books

Dictionaries. General dictionaries contain information such as definitions, pronunciations, synonyms, and word histories. Here are some examples of useful general dictionaries:

> *The American Heritage® Dictionary of the English Language, Third Edition*
> *The American Heritage® College Dictionary, Third Edition*
> *The Random House Webster's College Dictionary*
> *Webster's New World Dictionary of the American Language*
> *Webster's Tenth New Collegiate Dictionary*
> *Webster's Third New International Dictionary,* unabridged

Word books. Specialized books are available for checking categories of words and word usage.

For slang:
> *Dictionary of American Slang* by Harold Wentworth and Stuart Berg Flexner
> *A Dictionary of Slang and Unconventional English* by Eric Partridge

For pronunciations:
> *A Pronouncing Dictionary of American English* by John S. Kenyon and Thomas A. Knott

For synonyms:
> *The Random House Thesaurus,* College Edition
> *Roget's II: The New Thesaurus*
> *Webster's Collegiate Thesaurus*
> *Webster's New Dictionary of Synonyms*
> *Webster's New World Thesaurus*

For word division and spelling:
> *The Legal Word Book,* Third Edition
> *The Medical & Health Sciences Word Book,* Third Edition
> *Word Check*

For word background and historical usages:

>*A Dictionary of American English on Historical Principles* by Craigie and Hulbert

>*A Dictionary of Americanisms on Historical Principles* by M. M. Mathews

>*An Etymological Dictionary of the English Language* by Walter William Skeat

>*Morris Dictionary of Word and Phrase Origins* by William Morris and Mary Morris

>*Origins* (for etymologies) by Eric Partridge

>*The Oxford English Dictionary* (often called the OED)

Concordances to the Bible, to Shakespeare, and to other works will help you find specific uses of words within the works. A concordance is a book that lists all the words used in a particular book and indicates exactly where each word is used each time it is used.

Special-purpose dictionaries. Note that it is often hard to draw the line between encyclopedias and dictionaries when it comes to special-purpose items. The following are a few examples of special-purpose dictionaries:

>*Academic Press Dictionary of Science and Technology*
>*The American Heritage Dictionary of Science*
>*The American Political Dictionary*
>*Black's Law Dictionary*
>*A Comprehensive Dictionary of Psychological and Psychoanalytic Terms*
>*Dictionary of American History*
>*Dictionary of Architectural Science*
>*Dictionary of the Bible*
>*A Dictionary of Classical Antiquities*
>*A Dictionary of Comparative Religion*
>*Dictionary of Education*
>*A Dictionary of the Social Sciences*
>*Dorland's Illustrated Medical Dictionary*

The Harvard Dictionary of Music
McGraw-Hill Dictionary of Scientific and Technical Terms
The New Grove's Dictionary of Music and Musicians
The American Heritage Stedman's Medical Dictionary
Webster's Sports Dictionary

English usage

There are many books available on grammar and writing. The following are among the best:

The American Heritage Book of English Usage

The Careful Writer by Theodore M. Bernstein

A Dictionary of Contemporary American Usage by Bergen Evans and Cornelia Evans

A Dictionary of Modern English Usage by H. W. Fowler

The Elements of Style by Strunk and White

Harper Dictionary of Contemporary Usage by William Morris and Mary Morris

Modern American Usage by Wilson Follet

Webster's Dictionary of English Usage

Editing and printing

Consult the following for information on editing, copy-editing, preparing manuscripts, book publication, and similar topics:

The Chicago Manual of Style, The University of Chicago Press
The New York Times Manual of Style and Usage, Times Books
Style Manual of the United States Government Printing Office
Words into Type, Prentice-Hall

Almanacs and yearbooks

For up-to-date facts, figures, and general information, almanacs and yearbooks are excellent. These almanacs are good sources of current data:

Information Please Almanac
Statesman's Year-Book
The World Almanac and Book of Facts

Several publishers issue yearbooks to add new data to and to update the information in their encyclopedias. There are also yearbooks issued for many different industries or fields of interest.

Biography books

There are many reference books that contain brief, condensed facts and dates about people. If you are not sure correct biography book to look at, try one from the following list:

Biography Almanac
Biography and Genealogy Master-Index
Biography Index

Below are some of the more popular biographical reference books:

Chambers Biographical Dictionary
Current Biography
Dictionary of American Biography
Dictionary of National Biography (for British history)
The International Who's Who
The McGraw-Hill Encyclopedia of World Biography
Twentieth Century Authors
Webster's Biographical Dictionary
Who's Who
Who's Who in America
Who's Who in Finance & Industry
Who Was Who in America

In addition, there are many specialized *Who's Who* books that are regional, professional, and even ethnic or religious in scope. There are also books of biographies of authors, scientists, and other types of professionals — for example, *Asimov's Biographical Encyclopedia of Science and Technology*. Short biographies can also be found in encyclopedias and in dictionaries of specialized fields.

Geography books

There are two basic kinds of geography books: atlases and gazetteers. Atlases may contain maps of the modern world, of the world during particular historical periods, or of extraterrestrial locations. Gazetteers generally contain facts and figures (population and area, for example) about places. Because the shapes and names of countries often change, current geographical information is best obtained by using the most recent edition of atlas or gazetteer you consult.

For current map information:

    Goode's World Atlas
    Hammond World Atlas
    National Geographic Atlas of the World
    The New International Atlas
    Rand McNally Cosmopolitan World Atlas
    The Times Atlas of the World

For historical information:

    Atlas of American History
    Atlas of the Classical World
    Atlas of World History
    Historical Atlas

For nonmap information:

    The Columbia Lippincott Gazetteer of the World
    Geo-Data: The World Almanac Gazetteer
    Political Handbook of the World
    The Stateman's Year Book World Gazetteer
    Webster's New Geographical Dictionary

Maps. There are a variety of sources from which you can obtain maps: The Automobile Association of America makes maps available to members, the National Geographic Society prepares both contemporary maps and historical maps, and

Rand McNally Co. puts out books of maps as well as individual maps. In addition, travel agencies, foreign consultants, chambers of commerce, and other organizations may offer maps.

Business directories

Check these publications for information about companies, industries, and other for-profit concerns:

> *Dun and Bradstreet's Million Dollar Directory*
> *Encyclopedia of Business Information Services*, edited by James Woy

Moody's puts out a series of directories on special subjects:

> *Standard & Poor's Register of Corporations, Directors and Executives*
>
> *Thomas Register of American Manufacturers* — many volumes under headings "Products & Services," "Company Profiles" (with brand name Index), "Catalog File."

Many industries issue handbooks. They are often called Red Books, Blue Books, or Year Books. Many are published annually and contain the names and addresses of companies and their main officers. Many trade magazines produce annual directories. Most major companies will provide free copies of their annual reports by written request to the corporate secretary.

Business and secretarial handbooks

Information about office procedures and skills can be found in these books:

> *Complete Secretary's Handbook* by Lillian Doris and Besse May Miller, revised by Mary A. DeVries
>
> *The Gregg Reference Manual* by William A. Sabin
>
> *The Professional Secretary's Handbook,* Houghton Mifflin
>
> *The Secretary's Handbook* by Sarah Augusta Taintor and Kate M. Monro

Standard Handbook for Secretaries by Lois Hutchinson

Webster's New World Secretarial Handbook, Simon & Schuster

Parliamentary procedure

For rules governing parliamentary procedure, consult the following:

Barnes & Noble Book of Modern Parliamentary Procedure by Ray E. Keesey

Robert's Rules of Order

Sturgis Standard Code of Parliamentary Procedure by Alice F. Sturgis

Computers and word processors

Books on computers and word processors are appearing on bookstore shelves almost as quickly as computers and word processors are appearing in offices and homes throughout the world. Because the field of computing changes daily, published information may be out of date before the book appears in print. Nevertheless, some of the following books may be useful to you:

The Business Guide to Small Computers by Lawrence Calmus

CompuServe Information Manager: The Complete Sourcebook by Charles Bowen and David Peyton

Computer Dictionary by Charles J. Sippl

The Computer Industry Almanac by Egil Juliussen and Karen Juliussen

Dictionary of Computer Words, revised edition, Houghton Mifflin

The Internet Direct Connect Kit by Peter John Harrison

Introduction to Word Processing by Hal Glatzer

Small Business Computer Primer by Robert B. McCaleb

Small Business Computing Made Easy: Everything You Need to Know to Get Started With a Computer by Linda Rohrbough

The Word Processing Book by Peter A. McWilliams

Statistics

Statistics may be found in almanacs, yearbooks, and various other reference books:

> *Statesman's Year-Book*
> *Statistical Abstract of the United States*
> *Statistical Yearbook United Nations*
> *Statistics Sources*

In addition, the U.S. Bureau of the Census puts out statistics on many subjects.

Document anthologies

If you need to find the text of the Magna Carta or Washington's Farewell Address, look in a book of documents. These go by many names, including documents, readings, and anthologies:

> *Documents of American History*
> *The World of Mathematics* (4 volumes)

Guides to miscellaneous information

Often you will need to find some odd bit of information. There are many books available that provide such information and those below are among the most useful:

> *The Book of Lists*
> *The Dictionary of Cultural Literacy*
> *Famous First Facts* by Joseph N. Kane
> *Guinness Book of World Records*
> *The People's Almanac* (three independent volumes)

Guides to audiovisual material

There are an increasing number of books available that will lead you to filmstrips, records, audiotapes and videotapes, and films of various speeds. Ask your librarian to help you locate these.

Books of quotations

Some books offer well-known quotations:

> *Contemporary Quotations* by James B. Simpson (after 1950)
> *Dictionary of Quotations* by Bergen Evans
> *Familiar Quotations*, Sixteenth Edition, by John Bartlett
> *Home Book of Quotations* by Burton E. Stevenson
> *Hoyt's New Cyclopedia of Practical Quotations*
> *The International Thesaurus of Quotations* by Rhoda T. Tripp

Many libraries now have an additional source for research on current issues called the *Social Issues Resources Series* (SIRS), which consists of loose-leaf volumes covering 32 social issues, including volumes on *Alcohol, Energy, Sexuality, The AIDS Crisis,* and *The Atmosphere Crisis.* Each volume in the series contains reprints of articles from newspapers, magazines, government documents, and journals representing a wide spectrum of opinions and written for specific reading levels. SIRS is available in print, microfiche, and CD–ROM formats.

ABBREVIATIONS

A

a 1. *also* **a.** are (measurement). 2. *Physics.* atto-.

A 1. *also* **a.** acre. 2. ampere. 3. area.

a. 1. about. 2. acceleration. 3. acreage. 4. *also* **A.** amateur. 5. *Lat.* anno (in the year). 6. *Lat.* annus (year). 7. anonymous. 8. *also* **A.** answer. 9. *Lat.* ante (before). 10. anterior.

A. 1. academician; academy. 2. alto. 3. America; American.

Å angstrom.

AA Alcoholics Anonymous.

A.A. Associate in Arts.

AAA Agricultural Adjustment Administration.

A and M ancient and modern.

A and R artists and repertory.

AARL Army Aeromedical Research Laboratory.

A.A.S. Associate in Applied Sciences.

AATC automatic air traffic control.

AB Alberta.

ab. about.

A.B. *Lat.* Artium Baccalaureus (Bachelor of Arts).

abbr. *or* **abbrev.** abbreviation.

ABCD accelerated business collection and delivery.

ABD all but dissertation.

abl. ablative.

ABM antiballistic missile.

abn airborne.

abor. abortion.

abr. abridged; abridgment.

abs. 1. absence; absent. 2. absolute; absolutely. 3. abstract.

abstr. abstract; abstracted.

abt. about.

ac 1. acre. 2. air-cooled. 3. *or* **AC** alternating current.

a.c. 1. *or* **a/c** air conditioning. 2. *Lat.* ante cibum (*Med.* before meals).

A.C. 1. air corps. 2. *Lat.* ante Christum (before Christ).

a/c account; account current.

acad. academic; academy.

accel. *Mus.* accelerando.

acct. account; accountant.

ACCTID account identifier.

ack. acknowledge; acknowledgment.

ACLS advanced cardiac life support system.

acpt. acceptance.

ACT American College Test.

A.C.T. Australian Capital Territory.

actg. acting.

ACTH adrenocorticotropic hormone.

acv actual cash value.

ACV air-cushion vehicle.

ad. adapter.

A.D. *Lat.* anno Domini (in the year of the Lord). — Usu. used in small capitals <A.D.>

ADC Aid to Dependent Children.

add. addendum.

ADDDS automatic direct-distance dialing system.

addn. addition.

adf automatic direction finder.

ADH antidiuretic hormone.

ad int. *Lat.* ad interim (in the meantime).

adj. **1.** adjective. **2.** adjunct. **3.** adjustment. **4.** *also* **Adj.** adjutant.

ad loc. *Lat.* ad locum (to *or* at the place).

adm. administrative; administrator.

admin. administration; administrator.

adv. **1.** adverb; adverbial. **2.** *Lat.* adversus (against). **3.** advertisement. **4.** advisory.

AEC Atomic Energy Commission.

AeEng aeronautical engineer.

AEIC advanced earned income credit.

AF *also* **A.F.** audio frequency.

AFB air force base.

AFDC Aid to Families with Dependent Children.

aff affirmative.

afft. affidavit.

Afg. Afghanistan.

AFL-CIO American Federation of Labor and Congress of Industrial Organizations.

Afr. Africa; African.

aft. afternoon.

A.G. *also* **AG** attorney general.

AGC advanced graduate certificate.

agcy. agency.

agr. agricultural; agriculture.

agric. agriculture; agriculturist.

agst. against.

agt. **1.** agent. **2.** agreement.

AH artificial heart.

A.H. *Lat.* **1.** anno Hebraico (in the Hebrew year). **2.** anno Hegirae (in the year of the Hegira). — Often used in small capitals. <A.H.>

AHF antihemophilic factor.

AI artificial intelligence.

a.i. *Lat.* ad interim (in the meantime).

AIDS acquired immune deficiency syndrome.

AK Alaska.

a.k.a. also known as.

AL **1.** American League. **2.** Alabama.

A.L.A. Associate in Liberal Arts.

Alb. Albania; Albanian.

alc. alcohol; alcoholic.

Ald. alderman.

alg. algebra.

Alg. Algeria.

allo. *Mus.* allegro.

alpha alphabetical.

a.l.s. *or* **A.L.S.** autograph letter signed.

alt. 1. alternate. 2. altimeter. 3. altitude.

ALU arithmetic logic unit.

am *or* **AM** amplitude modulation.

Am. America; American.

A.M. 1. airmail. 2. *Lat.* anno mundi (in the year of the world). — Usu. used in small capitals <A.M.> 3. *also* **a.m.** *Lat.* ante meridiem (before noon). — Usu. used in small capitals <A.M.> 4. *Lat.* Artium Magister (Master of Arts).

amb. *also* **Amb.** ambassador.

AMC automatic message counting.

amdt. amendment.

Amer. America; American.

Amex American Stock Exchange.

AMI acute myocardial infarction.

AML acute myoblastic leukemia.

amp hr. ampere-hour.

amt. amount.

amu *Physics.* atomic mass unit.

an. *Lat.* 1. anno (in the year). 2. ante (before).

anal. 1. analogous; analogy. 2. analysis; analytic.

anat. anatomist; anatomy.

ANC African National Congress.

anc. ancient.

and. *Mus.* andante.

And. Andorra.

Ang. Angola.

anim. *Mus.* animato.

ann. 1. annals. 2. annual. 3. annuity.

anon. anonymous.

ANS autonomic nervous system.

ans. answer.

ant. 1. antenna. 2. antiquarian; antiquity. 3. antonym.

Ant. Antarctica.

anthrop. anthropologic; anthropology.

antiq. 1. antiquarian; antiquary. 2. antiquities. 3. antiquity.

a/o account of.

AP 1. airplane. 2. air police. 3. American plan. 4. antipersonnel. 5. applied physics. 6. *or* **A.P.** Associated Press.

ap. apothecary.

a.p. 1. additional premium. 2. author's proof.

A/P accounts payable.

APB all points bulletin.

APL Adult Performance Level.

APO *or* **A.P.O.** Army Post Office.

app. 1. apparatus. 2. appendix. 3. applied. 4. appoint; appointed. 5. apprentice.

appl. applied.

appmt. appointment.

approx. approximate; approximately.

appt. appoint; appointment.

APR annual percentage rate.

Apr. April.

apt. 1. apartment. 2. aptitude.

AR 1. *also* **A/R** accounts receivable. 2. Arkansas.

ar. arrival; arrive.

A.R. *also* **AR** 1. Airman Recruit. 2. army regulation.

Arab. *or* **Ar.** 1. Arabia; Arabian. 2. Arabic.

ARC American Red Cross.

arch. 1. archaic; archaism. 2. archery. 3. archipelago.

archit. architecture.

archt. architect.

ARD acute respiratory disease.

Arg. Argentina; Argentine.

ARM automated route management.

Arm. Armenia; Armenian.

arr. 1. arranged. 2. arrival; arrive; arrived.

AS 1. American Samoa. 2. *also* **A.S.** Anglo-Saxon.

As. Asia; Asian.

a/s air speed.

ASAP as soon as possible.

ASBC American Standard Building Code.

ASE American Stock Exchange.

ASEAN Association of South East Asian Nations.

asgd. assigned.

asgmt. assignment.

ASL American Sign Language.

ASM assembler.

asm. assembly.

ASR air-sea rescue.

assn. association.

assoc. associate; association.

asst. assistant.

asstd. 1. assisted. 2. assorted.

assy. assembly.

Assyr. Assyrian.

astrol. astrologer; astrologic; astrology.

astron. astronomer; astronomical; astronomy.

at. 1. airtight. 2. atomic.

atc around the clock.

athl. athlete; athletic; athletics.

Atl. Atlantic.

atm *Physics.* atmosphere.

at. no. *also* **at no** atomic number.

ATP *Biochem.* adenosine triphosphate.

ATR audio tape recording.

att. 1. attached. 2. attorney.

attn. attention.

attrib. attribute; attributive.

atty. attorney.

Atty. Gen. attorney general.

ATV all-terrain vehicle.

at wt atomic weight.

a.u. *or* **A.u.** angstrom unit.

A.U. astronomical unit.

aud. audit; auditor.

aug. augmentative.

Aug. August.

Aus. *or* **Aust.** 1. Australia. 2. Austria.

auth. 1. authentic. 2. author. 3. authority. 4. authorized.

auto. 1. automatic. 2. automotive.

aux. auxiliary.

AV or **A.V. 1.** atrioventricular. **2.** audio-visual.

av. 1. or **Av.** avenue. **2.** average.

a.v. or **a/v** *Lat.* ad valorem (in proportion to the value).

AVC automatic volume control.

avdp. avoirdupois.

ave. or **Ave.** avenue.

AVF antiviral factor.

avg. average.

avn. aviation.

a.w. all water (transportation).

A/W actual weight.

AWAC airborne warning and control system.

ax. 1. axiom. **2.** axis.

AYH American Youth Hostels.

AZ Arizona.

az, 1. azimuth. **2.** azure.

Azo. Azores.

B

B *also* **b.** or **B. 1.** base. **2.** *Mus.* basso. **3.** bay. **4.** bolivar. **5.** book. **6.** born. **7.** breadth. **8.** brother.

B. 1. bachelor. **2.** bacillus. **3.** Baumé scale. **4.** Bible. **5.** British. **6.** brotherhood.

Ba. Bahamas.

B.A. *Lat.* Baccalaureus Artium (Bachelor of Arts).

BABS blind approach beacon system.

BAC blood alcohol concentration.

bact. bacteria; bacterial.

bacteriol. bacteriology.

B.A.E. 1. Bachelor of Agricultural Engineering. **2.** Bachelor of Architectural Engineering. **3.** Bachelor of Art Education.

B.A.Ed. Bachelor of Arts in Education.

B.Ae.E. Bachelor of Aeronautical Engineering.

B.A.M. 1. Bachelor of Applied Mathematics. **2.** Bachelor of Arts in Music.

B and B bed-and-breakfast.

B and E breaking and entering.

bankr. bankruptcy.

bar. barometer; barometric.

Barb. Barbados.

B.Arch. Bachelor of Architecture.

B.A.S. or **B.A.Sc. 1.** Bachelor of Agricultural Science. **2.** Bachelor of Applied Science.

bb *also* **b.b.** ball bearing.

BB B'nai B'rith.

B.B.A. Bachelor of Business Administration.

bbl or **bbl.** barrel.

BBS *Computer Sci.* bulletin board system.

BBT basal body temperature.

B.C. 1. Bachelor of Chemistry. **2.** Bachelor of Commerce. **3.** before Christ. — Usu. used in small capitals <B.C.> **4.** or **BC** British Columbia.

bcd or **BCD** *Computer Sci.* binary coded decimal.

B.C.E. 1. Bachelor of Civil Engineering. 2. before the Common Era. — Often used in small capitals <B.C.E.>

BCG bacillus Calmette-Guérin (tuberculosis vaccine).

B.Ch.E. Bachelor of Chemical Engineering.

B.C.S. 1. Bachelor of Chemical Science. 2. Bachelor of Commercial Science.

BCSE Board of Civil Service Examiners.

BD 1. bank draft. 2. *also* **b/d** bills discounted. 3. bomb disposal.

bd. 1. board. 2. bound.

b/d barrels per day.

bd. ft. board foot.

bdl *or* **bdle.** bundle.

bdrm. bedroom.

bds. bound in boards.

B.D.S. Bachelor of Dental Surgery.

B.E. 1. Bachelor of Education. 2. Bachelor of Engineering.

B/E 1. bill of entry. 2. bill of exchange.

BEC Bureau of Employees' Compensation.

B.Ed. Bachelor of Education.

bef. before.

Bel *or* **Belg.** Belgian; Belgium.

B.E.M. Bachelor of Engineering of Mines.

B.Eng. Bachelor of Engineering.

B.Eng.Sci. Bachelor of Engineering Science.

bet. between.

bf 1. board foot. 2. *also* **b.f.** *or* **bf.** boldface.

b.f. *or* **B/F** brought forward.

B.F.A. Bachelor of Fine Arts.

bhd. bulkhead.

BHE Bureau of Higher Education.

bhp *or* **b.hp.** brake horsepower.

Bhu. Bhutan.

BIA Bureau of Indian Affairs.

bibliog. bibliographer; bibliography.

b.i.d. *Lat.* bis in die (*Med.* twice a day).

biog. biographer; biographical; biography.

biol. biological; biologist; biology.

bk. 1. bank. 2. book.

bkcy. bankruptcy.

bkg. banking.

bkgd. background.

bkpg. bookkeeping.

bkpt. bankrupt.

bks. 1. barracks. 2. books.

bl. 1. black. 2. blue.

B.L. 1. Bachelor of Laws. 2. Bachelor of Letters; Bachelor of Literature.

B/L bill of lading.

B.L.A. Bachelor of Liberal Arts.

bld. 1. blood. 2. boldface.

bldg. building.

bldr. builder.

B.Lit. *or* **B.Litt.** *Lat.* Baccalaureus Litterarum (Bachelor of Literature).

blk. 1. black. 2. block. 3. bulk.

BLS Bureau of Labor Statistics.

B.L.S. Bachelor of Library Science.
blvd. boulevard.
BM basal metabolism.
b.m. 1. board measure. 2. bowel movement.
B.M. 1. Bachelor of Medicine. 2. Bachelor of Music.
B.M.E. 1. Bachelor of Mechanical Engineering. 2. Bachelor of Mining Engineering. 3. Bachelor of Music Education.
BMR basal metabolic rate.
B.M.S. Bachelor of Marine Science.
B.Mus. Bachelor of Music.
bn. *or* **Bn.** 1. baron. 2. battalion.
Bngl. Bangladesh.
B.O.D. biochemical oxygen demand.
Boh. Bohemia; Bohemian.
Bol. Bolivia.
bor. borough.
bot. 1. botanical; botanist; botany. 2. bottle. 3. bottom.
Bots. Botswana.
bp boiling point.
BP blood pressure.
B.P. 1. Bachelor of Pharmacy. 2. Bachelor of Philosophy.
bpd barrels per day.
B.P.E. Bachelor of Physical Education.
B.Ph. Bachelor of Philosophy.
bpi *Computer Sci.* bits per inch; bytes per inch.
bpl. birthplace.
bps *Computer Sci.* bits per second.

br. 1. branch. 2. brief. 3. bronze. 4. brother. 5. brown.
Br. 1. Breton. 2. Britain; British.
B/R bills receivable.
Braz. Brazil; Brazilian.
brev. brevet.
Br. Gu. British Guiana.
Br. Hond. British Honduras.
Brit. Britain; British.
bro. brother.
Bru. Brunei.
B.S. 1. Bachelor of Science. 2. balance sheet. 3. bill of sale.
BSA Boy Scouts of America.
B.S.A. Bachelor of Science in Agriculture.
B.S.A.A. Bachelor of Science in Applied Arts.
B.S.Arch. Bachelor of Science in Architecture.
B.S.Ec. Bachelor of Science in Economics.
B.S.Ed. Bachelor of Science in Education.
B.S.E.E. Bachelor of Science in Electrical Engineering.
B.S.F.S. Bachelor of Science in Foreign Service.
bsh. bushel.
bsk. basket.
B.S.N. Bachelor of Science in Nursing.
B.S.Ph. Bachelor of Science in Pharmacy.
B.S.P.H. Bachelor of Science in Public Health.
B.Th. Bachelor of Theology.

btry. battery.
Btu British thermal unit.
bu. 1. bureau. 2. *or* **bu** bushel.
bul. bulletin.
Bul. *or* **Bulg.** Bulgaria; Bulgarian.
bull. bulletin.
BUN blood urea nitrogen.
bur. bureau.
Bur. Burma; Burmese.
bus. business.
bvt. brevet; brevetted.
BW 1. biological warfare. 2. *also* **b/w** black and white.
bx. box.
b.y. billion years.
BYO bring your own.

C

c 1. *Physics.* candle. 2. carat. 3. centi-. 4. *or* **C** *Math.* constant. 5. cubic.
C 1. *Elect.* capacitance. 2. Celsius. 3. centigrade. 4. *Physics.* charge conjugation. 5. coulomb. **c.** *or* **C.** 1. capacity. 2. carton. 3. case. 4. cent. 5. centime. 6. century. 7. chapter. 8. church. 9. circa. 10. *Lat.* congius (*Med.* gallon). 11. consul. 12. copy. 13. copyright.
C. 1. Catholic. 2. Celtic. 3. chancellor. 4. chief. 5. city. 6. companion. 7. Congress. 8. court.
Ca cancer.
CA 1. California. 2. *also* **C.A.** chronological age.

C.A. 1. Central America. 2. *or* **c.a.** chartered accountant.
c/a current account.
CAA *or* **C.A.A.** Civil Aeronautics Authority.
CAB Civil Aeronautics Board.
CAD/CAM computer-aided design/computer-aided manufacturing.
C.A.F. cost and freight.
C.A.G.S. Certificate of Advanced Graduate Study.
CAI computer-aided instruction.
cal calorie (small).
Cal calorie (large).
calc. 1. calculation. 2. calculus.
Cam. Cameroon.
Camb. Cambodia.
Can. *also* **Canad.** Canada; Canadian.
canc. canceled; cancellation.
C & W country and western.
Can. Is. Canary Islands.
Cant. Cantonese.
CAP 1. *or* **C.A.P.** Civil Air Patrol. 2. computer-aided production.
cap. 1. capacity. 2. capital (city). 3. capital letter.
CAPCOM *Aerospace.* capsule communicator.
caps. 1. capitals (letters). 2. capsule.
car. carat.
CARE Cooperative for American Relief to Everywhere.
CAT 1. clear-air turbulence. 2. computerized axial tomography.

cat. catalogue.

cath. 1. cathedral. 2. cathode.

CATV community antenna television.

caus. causative.

cav. cavity.

CB *or* **C.B.** citizens band.

CBC complete blood count.

C.B.D. cash before delivery.

CBI Cumulative Book Index.

CBW chemical and biological warfare.

cc 1. carbon copy. 2. cubic centimeter.

CCC Commodity Credit Corporation.

CCF *or* **C.C.F.** Cooperative Commonwealth Federation of Canada.

cckw. counterclockwise.

CCTV closed circuit television.

CCU coronary care unit.

ccw. counterclockwise.

CD 1. *also* **C/D** certificate of deposit. 2. *also* **C.D.** civil defense. 3. compact disk.

cd. cord.

c.d. cash discount.

CDC Centers for Disease Control and Prevention.

CDT Central Daylight Time.

C.E. 1. chemical engineer. 2. civil engineer. 3. Common Era. 4. customer engineer.

CEA Council of Economic Advisers.

CED Committee for Economic Development.

CEEB College Entry Examination Board.

Cen. Afr. Rep. Central African Republic.

cent. *Lat.* centum (hundred).

CENTO Central Treaty Organizations.

CEO chief executive officer.

cert. certification; certified.

certif. certificate.

CETA Comprehensive Employment and Training Act.

cet. par. *Lat.* ceteris paribus (other things being equal).

CF cystic fibrosis.

cf. *Lat.* confer (compare).

c.f. 1. *Baseball.* center field; center fielder. 2. *or* **C.F.** cost and freight.

C/F carried forward.

CFA *also* **C.F.A.** chartered financial analyst.

c.f.i. *or* **C.F.I.** cost, freight, and insurance.

cfm *or* **c.f.m.** cubic feet per minute.

CFO chief financial officer.

cfs *or* **c.f.s.** cubic feet per second.

cg centigram.

c.g. 1. center of gravity. 2. *or* **C.G.** consul general.

cgs *or* **CGS** centimeter-gram-second (system of units).

ch chain (measurement).

ch. 1. chapter. 2. check. 3. *or* **Ch.** chief. 4. child; children.

Ch. China; Chinese.

c.h. *or* **C.H.** 1. clearing-house. 2. courthouse. 3. customhouse.

chan. channel.

Chanc. 1. chancellor. 2. chancery.

chap. chapter.

char. charter.

chem. chemical; chemist; chemistry.

chg. 1. change. 2. charge.

Chin. Chinese.

chm. 1. chairman. 2. checkmate.

chron. 1. chronicle. 2. chronological; chronology.

chronol. chronology.

CI cost and insurance.

CIA Central Intelligence Agency.

CID *also* **C.I.D.** Criminal Investigation Department.

c.i.f. *or* **C.I.F.** cost, insurance, and freight.

circ. circulation.

circum. circumference.

CIS Commonwealth of Independent States.

cit. 1. citation. 2. cited. 3. citizen.

civ. civil; civilian.

C.J. chief justice.

ck. 1. cask. 2. check. 3. cook.

cl centiliter.

cl. 1. class; classification. 2. clause. 3. clearance. 4. cloth.

c.l. 1. carload. 2. center line. 3. *or* **C.L.** civil law. 4. common law.

C.L.A. certified laboratory assistant.

class. 1. classic; classical. 2. classification; classified; classify.

clk. clerk.

clm. column.

clr. clear.

CLU *also* **C.L.U.** chartered life underwriter.

cm centimeter.

CMA *also* **C.M.A.** certified medical assistant.

cml. commercial.

cmm cubic millimeter.

C/N credit note.

CNS central nervous system.

CO 1. Colorado. 2. *or* **C.O.** conscientious objector.

co. 1. company. 2. county.

c.o. 1. carried over. 2. cash order.

c/o *also* **c.o.** care of.

COD *or* **C.O.D.** 1. cash on delivery. 2. collect on delivery.

coef. coefficient.

C. of C. chamber of commerce.

cog. cognate.

col. 1. collect; collected; collector. 2. college; collegiate. 3. colonial; colony. 4. color. 5. column.

Col. Colombia.

COLA cost-of-living adjustment.

coll. 1. collateral. 2. collect; collection; collector. 3. college; collegiate. 4. colloquial; colloquialism.

collat. collateral.

Colo. Colorado.

COM computer-output microfilm; computer-output microfilmer.

com. 1. comedy; comic. 2. comma. 3. commentary. 4. commerce; commercial. 5. common. 6. commune. 7. communication. 8. community.

comb. 1. combination. 2. combining. 3. combustion.

coml. commercial.

comm. 1. commerce. 2. commission; commissioner. 3. *also* **Comm.** committee. 4. communication.

comp. 1. comparative; comparison. 2. compensation. 3. compilation; compiled; compiler. 4. complete. 5. compose; composer. 6. composite; composition; compositor. 7. comprehensive. 8. comprising.

compar. comparative.

compd. compound.

compt. compartment.

Comr. commissioner.

con. 1. concerto. 2. *Law.* conclusion. 3. *Lat.* conjunx (wife). 4. connection. 5. consolidate; consolidated. 6. continued.

Con. Congo.

conc. 1. concentrate. 2. concrete.

cond. 1. condition. 2. conductivity. 3. conductor.

conf. 1. conference. 2. confidential.

confed. confederation.

cong. *Lat.* congius (*Med.* gallon).

Cong. Congress; Congressional.

conj. 1. conjugation. 2. conjunction. 3. conjunctive.

cons. 1. consigned; consignment. 2. consonant. 3. constitution; constitutional. 4. construction.

Cons. consul.

consol. consolidated.

const. 1. constant. 2. *or* **Const.** constitution. 3. construction.

cont. 1. containing. 2. contents. 3. continent. 4. continue; continued. 5. contract. 6. contraction. 7. control.

contemp. contemporary.

contr. 1. contract. 2. contraction. 3. contralto. 4. control.

contrib. contribution; contributor.

CONUS Continental United States.

conv. 1. convention. 2. convertible.

COO chief operating officer.

coop. cooperative.

cor. 1. corner. 2. cornet. 3. coroner. 4. corpus. 5. correction. 6. correspondence; correspondent; corresponding.

CORE Congress of Racial Equality.

corol. *or* **coroll.** corollary.

corp. corporation.

corr. 1. correction. 2. correspondence; correspondent.

correl. correlative.

C.O.R.T. certified operating room technician.

cos cosine.

COS *or* **C.O.S.** cash on shipment.

cot cotangent.

coth hyperbolic cotangent.

covers versed cosine.

cp *Physics.* candlepower.

CP 1. chemically pure. 2. Communist Party.

cp. compare.

C.P. Cape Province.

CPA *also* **C.P.A.** certified public accountant.

cpd. compound.

CPFF cost plus fixed fee.

cpi characters per inch.

CPI consumer price index.

cpm 1. copies per minute. 2. cycles per minute.

CPR cardiopulmonary resuscitation.

cps 1. *also* **CPS** characters per second. 2. cycles per second.

CPS *also* **C.P.S.** certified professional secretary.

CPSC Consumer Product Safety Commission.

CPU central processing unit.

CR *Psychol.* conditioned reflex; conditioned response.

cr. 1. credit; creditor. 2. creek. 3. crescendo. 4. crown.

C.R. Costa Rica.

crit. critic; critical; criticism.

CRT cathode-ray tube.

C.R.T.T. certified respiratory therapy technician.

CS 1. capital stock. 2. chief of staff. 3. civil service. 4. conditioned stimulus.

cs. case.

csc cosecant.

CSC civil service commission.

CSF cerebrospinal fluid.

csk. 1. cask. 2. countersink.

CSS College Scholarship Service.

CST 1.Central Standard Time. 2. convulsive shock treatment.

CT 1. Central Time. 2. Connecticut.

ct. 1. cent. 2. certificate. 3. court.

ctf. certificate.

ctg. *or* **ctge.** cartage.

ctn cotangent.

ctn. carton.

CTOL *Aerospace.* conventional takeoff and landing.

ctr. 1. center. 2. counter.

CTS carpal tunnel syndrome.

cu. *or* **cu** cubic.

cum. cumulative.

cur. 1. currency. 2. current.

CV cardiovascular.

C.V. Cape Verde.

CVA Columbia Valley Authority.

cvt. convertible.

cw *or* **CW** continuous wave.

cw. clockwise.

c.w.o. cash with order.

cwt. hundredweight.

CY calendar year.

cyl. cylinder.

CYO Catholic Youth Organization.

Czech. Czechoslovakia; Czechoslovakian.

D

d 1. day. 2. deci-. 3. dextro-.

D 1. *or* **D.** democrat; democratic. 2. deuterium.

d. 1. dam. 2. date. 3. daughter. 4. *or* **D.** deputy. 5. died. 6. *or* **D.** dose. 7. *or* **D.** drachma.

D. 1. December. 2. department. 3. Dutch.

DA 1. delayed action. 2. deposit account. 3. developmental age. 4. *also* **D.A.** don't answer.

Da. Danish.

D.A. 1. *also* **DA** district attorney. 2. Doctor of Arts.

DAC Department of the Army Civilian.

Dan. Danish.

D & C dilatation and curettage.

DAR damage assessment routine.

dB decibel.

DB *or* **D.B.** daybook.

d.b.a. doing business as.

D.B.A. Doctor of Business Administration.

d.b.h. diameter at breast height.

dbl. double.

dc *or* **DC** direct current.

DC District of Columbia.

D.C. 1. *Mus.* da capo. 2. Doctor of Chiropractic.

D.Ch.E. Doctor of Chemical Engineering.

DCI Director of Central Intelligence.

D.C.L. 1. Doctor of Canon Law. 2. Doctor of Civil Law.

DCM *also* **D.C.M.** Distinguished Conduct Medal.

dd. delivered.

D.D. 1. demand draft. 2. dishonorable discharge. 3. *Lat.* Divinitatis Doctor (Doctor of Divinity).

D.D.S. 1. Doctor of Dental Science. 2. Doctor of Dental Surgery.

DE Delaware.

deb. debenture.

dec. 1. deceased. 2. declaration. 3. declination. 4. decrease.

Dec. December.

decd. deceased.

decl. declension.

D.Ed. Doctor of Education.

def. 1. defective. 2. defendant. 3. defense. 4. deferred. 5. define. 6. definite. 7. definition.

deg *or* **deg.** degree.

del. 1. delegate. 2. delete.

dem. demurrage.

Dem. Democrat; Democratic.

demon. *Gram.* demonstrative.

Den. Denmark.

denom. denomination.

dent. dental; dentist; dentistry.

dep. 1. depart; departure. 2. department. 3. deponent. 4. deposed. 5. deposit. 6. depot.

Dep. dependency.

dept. 1. department. 2. deputy.

deriv. derivation; derivative.

Des. desert.

det. 1. detach. 2. detachment. 3. detail.

dev. deviation.

DEW distant early warning.

D.F.A. Doctor of Fine Arts.

dft. draft.

dg decigram.

DH designated hitter.

D.H. Doctor of Humanities.

D.H.A. Doctor of Hospital Administration.

diag. 1. diagonal. 2. diagram.

dial. 1. dialect; dialectal. 2. dialectic; dialectical. 3. dialogue.

diam diameter.

dict. 1. dictation. 2. dictionary.

dif. *or* **diff.** difference; different.

dig. digest.

dil. dilute.

dim. dimension.

dimin. 1. *Mus.* diminuendo. 2. diminutive.

dipl. diplomat; diplomatic.

dir. director.

disc. discount.

disp. dispensary.

diss. dissertation.

dissd. dissolved.

dist. 1. distance; distant. 2. district.

distr. distribution; distributor.

div. 1. divergence. 2. diversion. 3. divided; division. 4. dividend. 5. divorced.

DJ disc jockey.

D.J. 1. district judge. 2. *Lat.* Doctor Juris (Doctor of Law).

DJIA Dow-Jones Industrial Average.

dkg dekagram.

dkl dekaliter.

dkm dekameter.

dl deciliter.

D/L demand loan.

D.Lit. *or* **D.Litt.** *Lat.* Doctor Litterarum (Doctor of Letters; Doctor of Literature).

DLO dead letter office.

dlr. dealer.

D.L.S. Doctor of Library Science.

dlvy. delivery.

dm decimeter.

DM 1. data management. 2. Deutsche mark.

D.M.A. Doctor of Musical Arts.

D.M.D. *Lat.* Dentariae Medicinae Doctor (Doctor of Dental Medicine).

D.M.L. Doctor of Modern Languages.

DMSO dimethylsulfoxide.

dn. down.

DNR do not resuscitate.

D.O. 1. Doctor of Optometry. 2. Doctor of Osteopathy.

DOA *Med.* dead on arrival.

DOB date of birth.

DOC Department of Commerce.

doc. document.

DOD Department of Defense.

DOE Department of Energy.

dol. 1. *Mus.* dolce. 2. dollar.

dom. 1. domestic. 2. dominant. 3. dominion.

Dom. Dominican.

Dom. Rep. Dominican Republic.

DOS Department of State.

DOT Department of Transportation.

doz. dozen.

DP 1. data processing. 2. dew point. 3. *also* **D.P.** displaced person. 4. *Baseball.* double play.

DPH 1. Department of Public Health. 2. *also* **D.P.H.** Doctor of Public Health.

D.Ph. Doctor of Philosophy.

dpi dots per inch.

DPT *Med.* diphtheria, pertussis, tetanus (vaccine).

dpt. department.

DPW Department of Public Works.

dr dram.

dr. 1. debit. 2. debtor.

Dr. 1. doctor. 2. drive (in street names).

dr ap apothecaries' dram.

dr avdp avoirdupois dram.

dr t troy dram.

d.s. 1. *or* **D.S.** *Mus.* dal segno. 2. document signed.

DSC *also* **D.S.C.** Distinguished Service Cross.

DSM *also* **D.S.M.** Distinguished Service Medal.

DSO *or* **D.S.O.** Distinguished Service Order.

d.s.p. *Lat.* decessit sine prole (died without issue).

DSS Department of Social Services.

DST daylight-saving time.

DT *or* **D.T.** daylight time.

d.t. double time.

D.T. Doctor of Theology.

D.T.'s delirium tremens.

dup. duplicate.

D.V.M. Doctor of Veterinary Medicine.

D.V.S. Doctor of Veterinary Surgery.

DW 1. dead weight. 2. distilled water.

D/W dock warrant.

DWI driving while intoxicated.

dwt. pennyweight.

dyn *Physics.* dyne.

E

e 1. electron. 2. *or* **e.** *Baseball.* error.

E 1. Earth. 2. *or* **e** east. 3. *or* **E.** English. 4. excellent.

e. *or* **E.** engineer; engineering.

EA educational age.

ea. each.

E and OE errors and omissions excepted.

EbN east by north.

EbS east by south.

EC European Community (Common Market).

Ec. Ecuador.

ECCS emergency core cooling system.

ECG electrocardiogram.

ECM European Common Market.

ecol. ecological; ecology.

econ. economics; economy.

ed. 1. editor. 2. education.

E.D. election district.

edit. edition.

Ed.M. *Lat.* Educationis Magister (Master of Education).

EDP electronic data processing.

EDT Eastern Daylight Time.

educ. education; educational.

e.e. errors excepted.

E.E. electrical engineer; electrical engineering.

EEC European Economic Community.

EEG electroencephalogram; electroencephalograph.

EENT or **E.E.N.T.** eye, ear, nose, and throat.

EEO equal employment opportunity.

EEOC Equal Employment Opportunity Commission.

eff. efficiency.

EFL English as a foreign language.

EFTS electronic funds transfer system.

Eg. Egypt; Egyptian.

e.g. *Lat.* exempli gratia (for example).

EHF extremely high frequency.

EHV extra high voltage.

EKG electrocardiogram; electrocardiograph.

elec. electric; electrical; electrician; electricity.

elem. elementary.

elev. elevation.

ELF extremely low frequency.

ELSS extravehicular life support system.

EM electromagnetic.

E.M. Engineer of Mines.

emf or **EMF** electromotive force.

EMT 1. emergency medical technician. 2. end of magnetic tape.

emu electromagnetic unit.

enc. or **encl.** enclosed; enclosure.

ency. or **encycl.** encyclopedia.

ENE east-northeast.

eng. 1. engine. 2. engineer.

Eng. England; English.

engin. engineering.

engr. 1. engineer. 2. engraver.

enl. 1. enlarged. 2. enlisted.

ENT ear, nose, and throat.

EO executive order.

e.o. *Lat.* ex officio (by virtue of office).

e.o.m. end of month.

EP 1. European plan. 2. extended play.

EPA Environmental Protection Agency.

eq. 1. equal. 2. equation. 3. equivalent.

E.Q. educational quotient.

Equat. Gui. Equatorial Guinea.

equip. equipment.

equiv. equivalency; equivalent.

ER emergency room.

ERA 1. *Baseball.* earned run average. 2. Equal Rights Amendment.

ESE east-southeast.

Esk. Eskimo.

ESL English as a second language.

ESOP employee stock ownership plan.

ESP extrasensory perception.

esp. especially.

Esq. Esquire (title).

ESR electron spin resonance.

EST Eastern Standard Time.

est. 1. established. 2. *Law.* estate. 3. estimate.

esu electrostatic unit.

ET 1. Eastern Time. 2. elapsed time.

ETA estimated time of arrival.

et al. *Lat.* et alii (and others).

etc. *Lat.* et cetera (and so forth).

ETD estimated time of departure.

Eth. Ethiopia.

ETV educational television.

Eur. Europe; European.

EURATOM European Atomic Energy Community.

eV electron volt.

evg. evening.

ex. 1. examination. 2. example. 3. except; excepted; exception. 4. exchange. 5. executive. 6. express. 7. extra.

exam. examination.

exc. 1. excellent. 2. except; exception.

exch. exchange.

excl. 1. exclamation. 2. exclusive.

exec. 1. executive. 2. executor.

exp *Math.* exponential.

exp. 1. expenses. 2. experiment. 3. expiration; expired. 4. export; exporter. 5. express.

exptl. experimental.

exr. executor.

exrx. executrix.

ext. 1. extension. 2. external. 3. extinct. 4. extra. 5. extract.

F

f 1. *Physics.* femto-. 2. focal length. 3. *or* **F.** *Mus.* forte. 4. function.

F 1. Fahrenheit. 2. farad. 3. *or* **F.** fellow (as of a university).

f. 1. *or* **F** *also* **f.** *or* **F.** female. 2. *or* **F.** *Gram.* feminine. 3. *or* **F.** *Metallurgy.* fine. 4. *or* **F.** folio. 5. following.

F. 1. French. 2. Friday.

f/ relative aperture of a lens.

FA 1. fine art. 2. football association.

f.a. fire alarm.

FAA Federal Aviation Administration.

f.a.a. *or* **F.A.A.** free of all average.

fac. 1. facsimile. 2. faculty.

FACA Fellow of the American College of Anesthesiologists.

FACC Fellow of the American College of Cardiologists.

FACD Fellow of the American College of Dentists.

FACOG Fellow of the American College of Obstetricians and Gynecologists.

FACP Fellow of the American College of Physicians.

FACR Fellow of the American College of Radiologists.

FACS Fellow of the American College of Surgeons.

FAD flavin adenine dinucleotide.

FAIA Fellow of the American Institute of Architects.

Falk. Is. Falkland Islands.

fam. family.

FAO Food and Agriculture Organization.

FAQ fair average quality.

FAS Foreign Agricultural Service.

f.a.s. free alongside ship.

fasc. fascicle.

F.B. 1. foreign body. 2. freight bill.

FBI also **F.B.I.** Federal Bureau of Investigation.

f.c. 1. follow copy. 2. font change.

FCA Farm Credit Administration.

fcap. or **fcp.** foolscap.

FCC Federal Communications Commission.

FCPS Fellow of the College of Physicians and Surgeons.

fcy. fancy.

FD 1. fatal dose. 2. fire department. 3. focal distance.

FDA Food and Drug Administration.

FDIC Federal Deposit Insurance Corporation.

fdn. foundation.

fdry. foundry.

Feb. February.

fed. federal; federated; federation.

fem. female; feminine.

FEPC Fair Employment Practices Commission.

FERC Federal Energy Regulatory Commission.

FET 1. federal excise tax. 2. field effect transistor.

ff *Mus.* fortissimo.

ff. 1. folios. 2. following.

FG fine grain.

fgn. foreign.

fgt. freight.

FHA Federal Housing Administration.

FHLBB Federal Home Loan Bank Board.

FICA Federal Insurance Contributions Act.

fict. 1. fiction. 2. fictitious.

fid. fidelity.

fig. figure.

fin. 1. finance; financial. 2. finish.

Fin. Finland; Finnish.

fl fluid.

FL 1. Florida. 2. focal length. 3. foreign languages.

fl. 1. floor. 2. florin. 3. *Lat.* floruit (flourished). 4. fluid. 5. flute.

fl dr fluid dram.

fl oz fluid ounce.

FM 1. field manual. 2. *or* **fm** frequency modulation.

fm. 1. fathom. 2. from.

FMB Federal Maritime Board.

FMCS Federal Mediation and Conciliation Service.

FMN flavin mononucleotide.

fn. footnote.

FNMA Federal National Mortgage Association.

FO 1. finance officer. 2. *or* **F/O** flight officer. 3. *or* **F.O.** Foreign Office.

f.o.b. *also* **F.O.B.** free on board.

fol. 1. folio. 2. following.

for. 1. foreign. 2. forest; forestry.

fort. fortification.

4WD four-wheel drive.

fp 1. foot-pound. 2. freezing point.

FP flash point.

fp. foolscap.

FPC Federal Power Commission.

fpm *or* **f.p.m.** feet per minute.

FPO fleet post office.

fprf. fireproof.

fps *or* **f.p.s.** 1. feet per second. 2. frames per second.

fr. 1. franc. 2. from.

Fr. 1. France; French. 2. Friday.

f.r. *Lat.* folio recto (right-hand page).

FRB Federal Reserve Board.

freq. 1. frequency. 2. frequentative. 3. frequently.

F.R.G. Federal Republic of Germany.

FRGS *or* **F.R.G.S.** Fellow of the Royal Geographical Society.

Fr. Gu. French Guiana.

Fri. Friday.

Fris. Frisian.

front. frontispiece.

FRS Federal Reserve System.

frt. freight.

frwy. freeway.

FS 1. Foreign Service. 2. Forest Service.

FSA Federal Security Agency.

FSH follicle-stimulating hormone.

FSLIC Federal Savings and Loan Insurance Corporation.

ft foot.

ft. fort; fortification.

FTC Federal Trade Commission.

furn. furnished.

fut. future (in grammar).

f.v. *Lat.* folio verso (on the back of the page).

FWA Federal Works Agency.

FWD front-wheel drive.

fwd. forward.

FX foreign exchange.

FY fiscal year.

FYI for your information.

G

g 1. acceleration of gravity. 2. gram.

G 1. *Physics.* gauss. 2. giga-. 3. gigabyte. 4. *or* **G.** good. 5. *Physics.* gravitation constant.

g. 1. gender. 2. genitive. 3. *or* **G.** gourde. 4. *or* **G.** guilder. 5. *or* **G.** guinea (money). 6. *or* **G.** gulf.

ga gauge.

GA 1. general agent. 2. *also* **G.A.** general assembly. 3. Georgia.

G.A. general average.

gal. gallon.

galv. galvanized.

Gam. Gambia.

GAO General Accounting Office.

GATT General Agreement on Tariffs and Trade.

GAW guaranteed annual wage.

gaz. gazette; gazetteer.

GB gigabyte.

G.B. Great Britain.

GC gigacycle.

GCA ground control approach.

gcd *or* **g.c.d.** greatest common divisor.

gcf *or* **g.c.f.** greatest common factor.

GCI ground control intercept.

GCM Good Conduct Medal.

GCT *or* **G.c.t.** Greenwich civil time.

gd. good.

G.D. grand duchy.

gde. gourde.

gds. goods.

GED general equivalency diploma.

GEM ground-effect machine.

gen. 1. gender. 2. general; generally. 3. generator. 4. generic. 5. genitive. 6. genus.

genit. genitive.

genl. general.

geog. geographer; geographic; geography.

geol. geologic; geologist; geology.

geom. geometric; geometry.

ger. gerund.

Ger. German; Germany.

GHQ general headquarters.

GI 1. gastrointestinal. 2. general issue. 3. Government Issue.

Gib. Gibraltar.

GIGO *Computer Sci.* garbage in, garbage out.

Gk. Greek.

gl. gloss.

gloss. glossary.

gm gram.

GM 1. general manager. 2. grand master.

GMAT 1. Graduate Management Admissions Test. 2. *or* **G.m.a.t.** Greenwich mean astronomical time.

GMT *or* **G.m.t.** Greenwich mean time.

GNI gross national income.

GNP gross national product.

GO general order.

GOP *or* **G.O.P.** Grand Old Party.

Goth. Gothic.

gov. 1. government. 2. *or* **Gov.** governor.

Gov. Gen. governor general.

govt. government.

G.P. *or* **GP** general practitioner.

GPA grade-point average.

g.p.h. gallons per hour.

GPO 1. general post office. 2. Government Printing Office.

g.p.s. gallons per second.

gr. 1. grade. 2. grain. 3. gross. 4. group.

Gr. Greece; Greek.

gram. grammar.

GRAS generally recognized as safe.

Grc. Greece.

GRE Graduate Record Examination.

Grnld. Greenland.

gro. gross.

gr. wt. gross weight.

GSA 1. General Services Administration. 2. Girl Scouts of America.

GSL guaranteed student loan.

GST *or* **G.s.t.** Greenwich sidereal time.

GSV guided space vehicle.

gt. 1. gilt. 2. great. 3. *Med.* gutta.

Gt. Brit. Great Britain.

G.T.C. good till canceled.

gtd. guaranteed.

GTS gas turbine ship.

gtt. *Med.* guttae.

GU 1. genitourinary. 2. Guam.

Guad. Guadaloupe.

guar. guaranteed.

Guat. Guatemala.

Guin. Guinea.

Guy. Guyana.

gyn. gynecologist; gynecology.

H

h 1. hecto-. 2. *or* **h.** hit. 3. hour. 4. *Physics.* Planck's constant.

H humidity.

h. 1. *or* **H.** harbor. 2. *or* **H.** hard; hardness. 3. *or* **H.** height. 4. *or* **H.** high. 5. *or* **H.** *Mus.* horn. 6. hundred. 7. *or* **H.** husband.

ha 1. hectare. 2. hour angle.

h.a. *Lat.* hoc anno (this year).

hab. corp. habeas corpus.

Hai. Haiti.

Hb hemoglobin.

H.B.M. Her *or* His Britannic Majesty.

HBO Home Box Office.

H.C. hard copy.

hcf highest common factor.

HD heavy-duty.

hd. head.

hdbk. handbook.

HDL high-density lipoprotein.

hdqrs. headquarters.

hdwe. hardware.

HE high explosive.

H.E. 1. His Eminence. 2. Her *or* His Excellency.

Heb. Hebrew.

hex. hexagon; hexagonal.

hf high frequency.

HF height finding.

hf. half.

hg 1. hectogram. 2. heliogram.

HG *also* **H.G.** High German.

hgb. hemoglobin.

HGH human growth hormone.

hgt. height.

hgwy. highway.

H.H. 1. Her *or* His Highness. 2. His Holiness.

hhd hogshead.

HHFA Housing and Home Finance Agency.

HHS Department of Health and Human Services.

HI Hawaii.

H.I. Hawaiian Islands.

HIAA Health Insurance Association of America.

HID *Med.* headache, insomnia, depression.

H.I.H. Her *or* His Imperial Highness.

HII Health Insurance Institute.

H.I.M. Her *or* His Imperial Majesty.

hist. historian; historical; history.

HIV human immunodeficiency virus.

hld. hold.

hlt. halt.

H.M. Her *or* His Majesty.

HMS *or* **H.M.S.** Her *or* His Majesty's Ship.

HO head office; home office.

Hon. 1. Honorable (title). 2. *or* **hon.** honorary.

Hond. Honduras.

HOP high oxygen pressure.

HOPE Health Opportunity for People Everywhere.

hor. horizontal.

hort. horticultural; horticulture.

hosp. hospital.

hp horsepower.

HP high pressure.

HPF highest possible frequency.

HQ *or* **h.q.** headquarters.

hr hour.

h.r. home run.

H.R. 1. home rule. 2. House of Representatives.

H.R.E. Holy Roman Emperor; Holy Roman Empire.

H. Rept. House report.

H. Res. House resolution.

H.R.H. Her *or* His Royal Highness.

hrs hours.

HS *or* **H.S.** high school.

HSGT high-speed ground transit.

H.S.H. Her *or* His Serene Highness.

HSL high-speed launch.

HST 1. Hawaiian Standard Time. 2. hypersonic transport.

ht height.

HT 1. halftone. 2. Hawaiian Time.

Hts. Heights.

HUD *or* **H.U.D.** Housing and Urban Development.

Hun. *or* **Hung.** Hungarian; Hungary.

HV 1. high velocity. 2. high-voltage.

hvy. heavy.

HW 1. high water. 2. hot water.

HWM high-water mark.

hwy. highway.

hyp. 1. hypotenuse. 2. hypothesis.

Hz hertz.

I

i 1. current. 2. interest. 3. intransitive. 4. *or* **I.** island; isle.

IA Iowa.

i.a. *Lat.* in absentia (in absence).

IADB Inter-American Defense Board.

IAEA International Atomic Energy Agency.

IAP international airport.

IATA International Air Transport Association.

ib. *or* **ibid.** *Lat.* ibidem (in the same place).

IBY International Biological Year.

IC integrated circuit.

ICA International Cooperation Administration.

ICAO International Civil Aviation Organization.

ICBM intercontinental ballistic missile.

ICC 1. Indian Claims Commission. 2. Interstate Commerce Commission.

Ice. *or* **Icel.** Iceland; Icelandic.

ICJ International Court of Justice.

ICU intensive care unit.

ID 1. Idaho. 2. *also* **I.D.** identification. 3. intradermal.

i.d. inside diameter.

IDA International Development Association.

IDP 1. integrated data processing. 2. international driving permit.

IE industrial engineering.

i.e. *Lat.* id est (that is).

IFC International Finance Corporation.

IFF identification, friend or foe.

IFO identified flying object.

Ig immunoglobulin.

IG *or* **I.G.** inspector general.

ign. ignition.

IGY International Geophysical Year.

IL Illinois.

ill. illustrated; illustration.

illus. illustrated; illustration.

ILP Independent Labour Party.

ILS instrument landing system.

IM intramuscular.

IMF International Monetary Fund.

imit. imitate; imitation.

immun. immunization.

imp. 1. imperative. 2. imperfect. 3. import; imported. 4. important. 5. imprimatur.

in *or* **in.** inch.

IN Indiana.

inbd. inboard.

inc. 1. income. 2. incomplete. 3. *also* **Inc.** incorporated. 4. increase.

incl. including; inclusive.

incog. incognito.

incr. 1. increase; 2. incremental.

IND investigational new drug.

ind. 1. independent. 2. index. 3. indigo. 4. industry.

Ind. 1. India. 2. Indian. 3. Indies.

indef. indefinite.

indic. 1. indicative (in grammar). 2. indicator.

indiv. individual.

indn. indication.

Indon. Indonesia; Indonesian.

indus. industrial; industry.

inf. 1. inferior. 2. infinitive. 3. information.

infin. infinitive.

infl. influence; influenced.

inj. injection.

INP International News Photo.

inq. inquiry.

INS Immigration and Naturalization Service.

ins. 1. inspector. 2. insulated; insulation. 3. insurance.

insp. inspected; inspector.

inst. 1. instant. 2. *or* **Inst.** institute; institution.

instr. 1. instructor. 2. instrument.

int. 1. interest. 2. interior. 3. internal. 4. interval.

inter. intermediate.

interj. interjection.

interp. interpreter.

interrog. interrogative.

intl. international.

intr. intransitive.

intro. introduction; introductory.

inv. 1. invented; invention; inventor. 2. invoice.

I/O input/output.

IP 1. installment paid. 2. intraperitoneal.

IPA International Phonetic Alphabet.

ips *or* **i.p.s.** inches per second.

IQ *or* **I.Q.** intelligence quotient.

IR 1. information retrieval. 2. infrared.

Ir. Irish.

IRA 1. Individual Retirement Account. 2. *also* **I.R.A.** Irish Republican Army.

IRBM intermediate range ballistic missile.

Ire. Ireland.

irid. iridescent.

IRO International Refugee Organization.

irreg. irregular; irregularly.

IRS Internal Revenue Service.

is. *or* **Is.** island.

ISBN International Standard Book Number.

ISC interstate commerce.

Isr. Israel; Israeli.

ISSN International Standard Serial Number.

isth. isthmus.

It. Italian; Italy.

I.T. inhalation therapist.

ITA Initial Teaching Alphabet.

ital. italic.

Ital. Italian; Italy.
ITV instructional television.
IU international unit.
IUD intrauterine device.
IV intravenous; intravenously.
i.w. inside width.

J

J 1. current density. 2. joule.
J. 1. journal. 2. judge. 3. justice.
JA 1. joint account. 2. *also* **J.A.**
  judge advocate.
JAG *also* **J.A.G.** Judge Advocate
  General.
Jam. Jamaica.
Jan. January.
Jav. Javanese.
JC junior college.
JCS *or* **J.C.S.** Joint Chiefs of
  Staff.
jct. junction.
JD 1. Justice Department. 2. *also*
  J.D. juvenile delinquent.
J.D. *Lat.* Jurum Doctor (Doctor of
  Laws).
JIT job instruction training.
JJ 1. judges. 2. justices.
jnr. junior.
jour. 1. journal; journalist. 2.
  journeyman.
JP *or* **J.P.** justice of the peace.
jr. *or* **Jr.** junior.
J.S.D. *Lat.* Juris Scientiae Doctor
  (Doctor of Juristic Science).
jt. joint.

jun. *or* **Jun.** junior.
junc. junction.
juv. juvenile.
JV junior varsity.
jwlr. jeweler.

K

k *or* **K** 1. karat. 2. kilo-.
K 1. kelvin (temperature unit). 2.
  Kelvin (temperature scale). 3.
  kilobyte. 4. kindergarten.
k. *or* **K.** 1. king. 2. knight.
Kbyte kilobyte.
kc kilocycle.
kcal kilocalorie.
kcs *or* **kc/s** kilocycles per second.
kg kilogram.
kg. keg.
KGB *or* **K.G.B.** *Russian.* Komitèt
  Gosudarstvénnoi Bezopasnost'i
  (Committee of State Security).
Kg-cal kilogram-calorie.
kHz kilohertz.
KIA killed in action.
KKK *or* **K.K.K.** Ku Klux Klan.
km kilometer.
K of C Knights of Columbus.
Kor. Korea; Korean.
KS Kansas.
kt. karat.
Kuw. Kuwait.
kV kilovolt.
kW kilowatt.
kWh kilowatt-hour.
KY Kentucky.

L

l liter.

L 1. lambert. 2. *also* **L.** large.

l. 1. *also* **L.** lake. 2. land. 3. late. 4. left. 5. length. 6. line. 7. lira.

L. 1. Latin. 2. licentiate (in titles). 3. Linnaean. 4. lodge (society).

LA Louisiana.

L.A. 1. Legislative Assembly. 2. local agent. 3. *also* **LA** Los Angeles.

Lab. Labrador.

lam. laminated.

lang. language.

lat. latitude.

Lat. 1. Latin. 2. Latvia; Latvian.

lav. lavatory.

LB Labrador.

lb *Lat.* libra (pound).

lc *also* **l.c.** lower case.

LC *or* **L.C.** Library of Congress.

L/C letter of credit.

LCD liquid crystal display.

LCL less-than-carload lot.

LCT local civil time.

LD 1. learning-disabled. 2. *Med.* lethal dose.

ld. 1. lead (in printing). 2. load.

Ld. 1. limited. 2. lord (title).

LDC less-developed country.

ldg. landing.

LDL low-density lipoprotein.

Leb. Lebanese; Lebanon.

lectr. lecturer.

LED light-emitting diode.

leg. 1. legal. 2. legate. 3. *Mus.* legato. 4. legislation; legislature.

legis. legislation; legislative; legislature.

LEM lunar excursion module.

Leso. Lesotho.

lex. lexicon.

lf 1. *also* **l.f.** *or* **lf.** lightface. 2. low frequency.

LG *also* **L.G.** Low German.

lg. *or* **lge.** large.

LH luteinizing hormone.

l.h. *also* **LH** left hand.

L.I. Long Island.

lib. 1. liberal. 2. librarian; library.

Lib. Liberia; Liberian.

Liech. Liechtenstein.

LIFO last in, first out.

lim. limit.

lin. 1. lineal. 2. linear.

ling. linguistics.

liq. 1. liquid. 2. liquor.

lit. 1. liter. 2. literal; literally. 3. literary. 4. literature.

Lit.B. *or* **Litt.B.** *Lat.* Litterarum Baccalaureus (Bachelor of Letters; Bachelor of Literature).

Lit.D. *or* **Litt.D.** *Lat.* Litterarum Doctor (Doctor of Letters; Doctor of Literature).

lith. lithograph; lithography.

Lith. Lithuania; Lithuanian.

litho. *or* **lithog.** lithograph; lithography.

ll *or* **ll.** lines.

LL.D. *Lat.* Legum Doctor (Doctor of Laws).

lm lumen.

LM lunar module.

LMP last menstrual period.

LMT local mean time.

ln natural logarithm.

LNG liquefied natural gas.

loc. cit. *Lat.* loco citato (in the place cited).

long. longitude.

loq. *Lat.* loquitur (speaks).

LPG liquefied petroleum gas.

LPM *or* **lpm** lines per minute.

LPN *or* **L.P.N.** licensed practical nurse.

LRV lunar roving vehicle.

L.S. *Lat.* locus sigilli (the place of the seal).

LSAT Law School Admissions Test.

LSD 1. least significant digit. 2. lysergic acid diethylamide.

LSS lifesaving service.

lt. light.

l.t. *or* **LT** local time.

ltd. *or* **Ltd.** limited.

Lt. Gov. lieutenant governor.

LTS 1. launch telemetry station. 2. launch tracking station.

Lux. Luxembourg.

lv. 1. leave. 2. livre.

LW low water.

LWM low-water mark.

lx lux.

lyr. lyric.

LZ landing zone.

M

m 1. *or* **M a.** em (printing measure). **b.** pica em. 2. *Physics.* mass. 3. meter (measure). 4. milli-. 5. *or* **M** *Physics.* modulus.

M mega-.

m. 1. *or* **M.** male. 2. manual. 3. married. 4. *or* **M.** masculine. 5. *or* **M.** medium. 6. *or* **M.** meridian. 7. *or* **M.** *Lat.* meridies (noon). 8. mile. 9. month. 10. morning.

M. 1. majesty. 2. mark (currency). 3. Monday. 4. Monsieur.

mA milliampere.

MA 1. Maritime Administration. 2. Massachusetts. 3. *also* **M.A.** mental age.

M.A. *Lat.* Magister Artium (Master of Arts).

MAC Municipal Assistance Corporation.

Maced. Macedonia; Macedonian.

mach. machine; machinery; machinist.

MACV Military Assistance Command, Vietnam.

MAD mutual assured destruction.

Mad. *or* **Madag.** Madagascar.

M.A.E. 1. Master of Aeronautical Engineering. 2. Master of Art Education. 3. Master of Arts in Education.

M.A.Ed. Master of Arts in Education.

mag. 1. magazine. 2. magnetism. 3. magneto. 4. magnitude.

M.Agr. Master of Agriculture.

Mal. Malay; Malayan.

Mala. Malaysia.

M.A.L.S. Master of Arts in Library Science.

man. manual.

manuf. *or* **manufac.** manufacture.

MAP modified American plan.

mar. 1. maritime. 2. married.

Mar. March.

marg. margin.

MARS Military Affiliate Radio System.

Mart. Martinique.

masc. masculine.

MASH Mobile Army Surgical Hospital.

mat. matinee.

M.A.T. Master of Arts in Teaching.

math. mathematical; mathematician; mathematics.

max. maximum.

mb millibar.

MB 1. Manitoba. 2. megabyte.

M.B.A. Master of Business Administration.

MBO management by objectives.

MC 1. Medical Corps. 2. *or* **M.C.** Member of Congress.

M.C. *or* **m.c.** master of ceremonies.

MCAT Medical College Admissions Test.

mcf thousand cubic feet.

M.C.L. Master of Civil Law.

M.C.S. Master of Computer Science.

MD 1. Maryland. 2. medical department. 3. muscular dystrophy.

M.D. *Lat.* Medicinae Doctor (Doctor of Medicine).

m/d months after date.

Mdm. Madam.

M.D.S. Master of Dental Surgery.

mdse. merchandise.

MDT Mountain Daylight Time.

ME 1. Maine. 2. *also* **M.E.** Middle English.

M.E. 1. mechanical engineer. 2. medical examiner. 3. military engineer. 4. mining engineer.

meas. measurable; measure.

mech. 1. mechanical; mechanics. 2. mechanism.

med. 1. medical; medicine. 2. medieval. 3. medium.

M.Ed. Master of Education.

Med. Lat. Medieval Latin.

meg megabyte.

mem. 1. member. 2. memoir. 3. memorandum. 4. memorial.

meq. milliequivalent.

mer. meridian.

met. 1. metaphor. 2. metaphysics. 3. meteorology. 4. metropolitan.

metal. *or* **metall.** metallurgic; metallurgy.

metaph. 1. metaphor; metaphoric. 2. metaphysics.

meteor. *or* **meteorol.** meteorological; meteorology.

METO Middle East Treaty Organization.

Mex. Mexican; Mexico.

mf medium frequency.

m.f. *Mus.* mezzo-forte.

M.F.A. Master of Fine Arts.

mfd. manufactured.

mfg. manufacture; manufacturing.

MFN most-favored nation.

mfr. manufacture; manufacturer.

mg milligram.

Mgr. 1. *or* **mgr.** manager. 2. Monseigneur; Monsignor.

mgt. management.

MH 1. Medal of Honor. 2. mental health.

M.H.A. Master of Hospital Administration.

mHg millimeters of mercury.

M.H.L. Master of Hebrew Literature.

MHW mean high water.

MHz megahertz.

MI 1. Michigan. 2. military intelligence.

mi. mile.

MIA missing in action.

mid. middle.

mil. military; militia.

min. 1. mineralogical; mineralogy. 2. minimum. 3. mining. 4. minor. 5. *or* **min** minute.

MIPS million instructions per second.

misc. miscellaneous.

mk. 1. mark. 2. markka.

mks meter-kilogram-second (system of units).

mksA meter-kilogram-second-ampere (system of units).

mkt. market.

mktg. marketing.

ml milliliter.

ML *also* **M.L.** Medieval Latin.

MLD minimum lethal dose.

Mlle. Mademoiselle.

M.L.S. Master of Library Science.

M.L.T. Medical Laboratory Technician.

MLW mean low water.

mm millimeter.

MM. Messieurs.

m.m. *Lat.* mutatis mutandis (with the necessary changes having been made).

Mme. Madame.

MMPI Minnesota Multiphasic Personality Inventory.

MN 1. magnetic north. 2. Minnesota.

M.N. Master of Nursing.

mngr. manager.

MO Missouri.

mo. month.

m.o. *or* **M.O.** 1. mail order. 2. medical officer. 3. modus operandi. 4. *also* **MO** money order.

mod *Math.* modulus.

mod. 1. moderate. 2. *Mus.* moderato. 3. modern.

modif. modification.

MOL Manned Orbital Laboratory.

mol. molecular; molecule.

mol wt molecular weight.

m.o.m. middle of month.

Mon. Monday.

Mong. Mongolia; Mongolian.

MOR middle-of-the-road.

Mor. Moroccan; Morocco.

morph. morphology.

mos. months.

Moz. Mozambique.

mp *or* **m.p.** 1. melting point. 2. *Mus.* mezzo-piano.

MP *or* **M.P.** military police.

M.P.A. 1. Master of Public Accounting. 2. Master of Public Administration.

M.P.E. Master of Physical Education.

mpg *or* **m.p.g.** miles per gallon.

mph *or* **m.p.h.** miles per hour.

M.P.H. Master of Public Health.

MR map reference.

Mr. Mister.

MRI magnetic resonance imaging.

mRNA messenger RNA.

ms millisecond.

MS 1. Mississippi. 2. multiple sclerosis.

ms. *or* **MS.** *or* **ms** manuscript.

M.S. *or* **M.Sc. Lat.** Magister Scientiae (Master of Science).

msec millisecond.

MSG monosodium glutamate.

msg. message.

Msgr. Monseigneur; Monsignor.

MSH melanocyte-stimulating hormone.

M.S. in L.S. Master of Science in Library Science.

mss. *or* **MSS.** *or* **mss** manuscripts.

MST Mountain Standard Time.

M.S.W. 1. Master of Social Welfare. 2. Master of Social Work.

MT 1. *or* **M.T.** medical technologist. 2. Montana. 3. Mountain Time.

mt. *or* **Mt.** mount; mountain.

m.t. *or* **M.T.** metric ton.

mtg. 1. meeting. 2. mortgage.

mtge. mortgage.

mtn. mountain.

mts. *or* **Mts.** mountains.

mun. *or* **munic.** municipal; municipality.

mus. 1. museum. 2. music.

Mus.B. *Lat.* Musicae Baccalaureus (Bachelor of Music).

Mus.D. *or* **Mus.Dr.** *Lat.* Musicae Doctor (Doctor of Music).

Mus.M. *Lat.* Magister Musicae (Master of Music).

MV 1. market value. 2. mean variation. 3. megavolt.

MVA Missouri Valley Authority.

MVD *Russian.* Ministeyrstvo Vnutreynnikh Deyl (Ministry of Internal Affairs).

MVP most valuable player.

mW milliwatt.

MW megawatt.

mxd. mixed.

m.y. million years.

myc. *or* **mycol.** mycology.

myth. *or* **mythol.** mythology.

N

n 1. *or* **N** en (printing measure). 2. nano-. 3. neutron. 4. *also* **N** *or* **n-** *Chem.* normal.

N 1. Avogadro number. 2. *also* **N.** *or* **n** *or* **n.** north; northern.

n. 1. *Lat.* natus (born). 2. net. 3. *or* **N.** noon. 4. note. 5. noun. 6. number.

N.A. 1. Narcotics Anonymous. 2. National Academician; National Academy. 3. North America. 4. not applicable. 5. not available.

NAACP *or* **N.A.A.C.P.** National Association for the Advancement of Colored People.

NAD nicotinamide-adenine dinucleotide.

NADP nicotinamide-adenine dinucleotide phosphate.

NARU Naval Air Reserve Unit.

NASA National Aeronautics and Space Administration.

NASCAR National Association for Stock Car Auto Racing.

NASDAQ National Association of Securities Dealers Automated Quotations.

nat. 1. native. 2. natural.

natl. national.

NATO North Atlantic Treaty Organization.

NATS Naval Air Transport Service.

naut. nautical.

nav. 1. naval. 2. navigable. 3. navigation.

NB 1. narrow band. 2. New Brunswick.

n.b. *or* **N.B.** nota bene.

NBA 1. National Basketball Association. 2. *also* **N.B.A.** narrowband allocation.

NbE north by east.

NBS National Bureau of Standards.

NbW north by west.

NC 1. no charge. 2. North Carolina. 3. Nurse Corps.

NCAA National Collegiate Athletic Association.

N.Cal. New Caledonia.

NCI noncoded information.

NCUA National Credit Union Administration.

NCV no commercial value.

ND North Dakota.

n.d. *or* **N.D.** no date.

NDEA National Defense Education Act.

NE 1. Nebraska. 2. *or* **N.E.** New England. 3. northeast.

NEATO Northeast Asian Treaty Organization.

NEbE northeast by east.

NEbN northeast by north.

NED *or* **N.E.D.** New English Dictionary (Oxford).

neg. negative.

n.e.i. not elsewhere included; not elsewhere indicated.

n.e.m. not elsewhere mentioned.

NEP New Economic Policy.

Nep. Nepal.

n.e.s. not elsewhere specified.
NET National Educational Television.
Neth. Netherlands.
neur. *or* **neurol.** neurology.
neut. 1. neuter. 2. neutral.
New Hebr. New Hebrides.
NF 1. National Formulary. 2. Newfoundland. 3. nonfiler.
n/f no funds.
NFL National Football League.
NFS not for sale.
ng nanogram.
NG *also* **N.G.** 1. National Guard. 2. no good.
NGr *or* **NGr.** New Greek.
NH New Hampshire.
N.Heb. New Hebrides.
NHL National Hockey League.
Nic. Nicaragua.
Nig. Nigeria.
NIH National Institutes of Health.
N.Ire. Northern Ireland.
NIT National Intelligence Test.
NJ New Jersey.
NKVD *or* **N.K.V.D.** *Russian.* Narodny Kommissariat Vnutrennikh Del (People's Commissariat for Internal Affairs).
NL 1. National League. 2. New Latin. 3. *also* **n.l.** new line.
n.l. *Lat.* non licet (not permitted).
N.L. *Lat.* non liquet (not clear).
NLF National Liberation Front.
NLRB *also* **N.L.R.B.** National Labor Relations Board.

nm 1. nanometer. 2. *or* **n.m.** nautical mile.
NM New Mexico.
NMR nuclear magnetic resonance.
NNE north-northeast.
NNW north-northwest.
no. *or* **No.** 1. north; northern. 2. number.
n.o.p. not otherwise provided (for).
Nor. 1. Norman. 2. Norway.
NORAD North American Air Defense Command.
norm. normal.
Norm. Norman.
Norw. Norway; Norwegian.
n.o.s. not otherwise specified.
Nov. November.
NOW 1. National Organization for Women. 2. negotiable order of withdrawal.
n.p. no place.
N.P. 1. notary public. 2. nurse practitioner.
n.p.d. *Lat.* nihil per os (*Med.* nothing by mouth).
n.p.t. normal pressure and temperature.
nr near.
NR no remittance.
NRC 1. National Research Council. 2. Nuclear Regulatory Commission.
ns *or* **nsec** nanosecond.
NS 1. *or* **N.S.** Nova Scotia. 2. nuclear ship.

n.s. 1. new series. 2. not specified.
N.S. New Style.
n/s not sufficient.
NSC National Security Council.
NSE National Stock Exchange.
NSF National Science Foundation.
n.s.f. or **N.S.F.** not sufficient funds.
N.S.W. New South Wales.
NT 1. net tax. 2. Northwest Territories. 3. nurse technicians.
n.t.p. or **N.T.P.** normal temperature and pressure.
NTSB National Transportation Safety Board.
nt. wt. net weight.
n.u. name unknown.
num. 1. number. 2. numeral.
numis. or **numism.** numismatics.
NV Nevada.
NW northwest.
n.wt. net weight.
N.W.T. Northwest Territories.
NY New York.
NYC New York City.
NYP not yet published.
NYSE New York Stock Exchange.
N.Z. New Zealand.

O

O or **O.** 1. ocean. 2. order.
o. 1. *Lat.* octarius (pint). 2. or **O.** octavo.
o/a on or about.

OAS Organization of American States.
OAU Organization for African Unity.
OB obstetrics.
ob. 1. *Lat.* obiit (she or he died). 2. obstetric.
obj. 1. object; objective (in grammar). 2. objection.
obl. 1. oblique. 2. oblong.
obs. 1. obscure. 2. observation. 3. or **Obs.** observatory. 4. obsolete. 5. obstetrician; obstetrics.
obstet. obstetric; obstetrics.
obv. obverse.
OC Office of Censorship.
oc. or **Oc.** ocean.
o.c. *Lat.* opere citato (in the work cited).
o/c overcharge.
OCA Office of Consumer Affairs.
OCAS Organization of Central American States.
occ. 1. occident; occidental. 2. occupation.
occas. occasional; occasionally.
OCD Office of Civil Defense.
OCR optical character recognition.
OCS Officer Candidate School.
oct. octavo.
Oct. October.
OD overdose.
o.d. 1. *Lat.* oculus dexter (right eye). 2. olive drab. 3. *Lat.* omni die (*Med.* every day). 4. on demand. 5. outside diameter.

O.D. 1. Doctor of Optometry. 2. *also* **o/d** overdraft. 3. overdrawn.

OE *also* **O.E.** Old English.

OECD Organization for Economic Cooperation and Development.

OED *also* **O.E.D.** Oxford English Dictionary.

OEM original equipment manufacturer.

OEO Office of Economic Opportunity.

off. office; officer; official.

O.F.S. Orange Free State.

OG *or* **O.G.** 1. officer of the guard. 2. original gum.

OGPU *or* **O.G.P.U.** *Russian.* Ob'edinyonnoye Gosudarstvennoye Politicheskoye Upravlenie (Unified Government Political Administration).

OH Ohio.

OIT Office of International Trade.

OK Oklahoma.

Om. Oman.

OMB Office of Management and Budget.

ON 1. *also* **O.N.** Old Norse. 2. Ontario.

ONI Office of Naval Intelligence.

ONR Office of Naval Research.

op *or* **OP** *or* **op.** *or* **o.p.** out of print.

op. 1. *also* **Op.** operation. 2. opposite. 3. *also* **Op.** opus.

op. cit. *Lat.* opere citato (in the work cited).

OPEC Organization of Petroleum Exporting Countries.

opp. opposite.

opt. 1. optative. 2. optician; optics. 3. optimum. 4. optional.

OR Oregon.

o.r. owner's risk.

O.R. *or* **OR** operating room.

orch. orchestra.

ord. 1. order. 2. ordinal. 3. ordinance.

ordn. ordnance.

org. 1. organic. 2. organization; organized.

orig. original; originally.

ornith. ornithologic; ornithology.

orth. orthopedic; orthopedics.

o.s. 1. *Lat.* oculus sinister (left eye). 2. old series. 3. *or* **o/s** out of stock.

O.S. 1. Old Style. 2. ordinary seaman.

OSHA U.S. Occupational Safety and Health Administration.

OSS Office of Strategic Services.

o.t. *or* **O.T.** 1. occupational therapy. 2. overtime.

OTB off-track betting.

OTC *also* **O.T.C.** over-the-counter.

otol. otology.

OTS *also* **O.T.S.** Officers' Training School.

OV *Aerospace.* orbiter vehicle.

Ox. *or* **Oxf.** Oxford.

oz *also* **oz.** ounce.

oz ap apothecaries' ounce.

oz av *or* **oz avdp** avoirdupois ounce.

oz t troy ounce.

P

p 1. momentum. 2. *or* **p.** *Mus.* piano (direction). 3. *Physics.* pico-. 4. *symbol for* proton.

P 1. parental generation. 2. *Physics.* parity. 3. petite. 4. *Physics.* pressure.

p. 1. page. 2. part. 3. participle. 4. past. 5. penny. 6. per. 7. peseta. 8. peso. 9. pint. 10. pipe. 11. pole. 12. population. 13. *or* **P.** president. 14. purl.

PA 1. Pennsylvania. 2. public-address system.

p.a. *Lat.* per annum (by the year).

P.A. 1. physician's assistant. 2. *or* **P/A** power of attorney. 3. press agent. 4. prosecuting attorney.

PABX *also* **P.A.B.X.** Private Automatic Branch Exchange.

Pac. *or* **Pacif.** Pacific.

Pak. Pakistan.

Pal. Palestine.

pam. pamphlet.

Pan. Panama.

P and L profit and loss.

par. 1. paragraph. 2. parallel. 3. parenthesis. 4. parish.

Par. *or* **Para.** Paraguay.

paren. parenthesis.

parl. parliamentary.

part. 1. participle. 2. particular.

pass. 1. passage. 2. passenger. 3. passive.

pat. patent.

patd. patented.

path. *or* **pathol.** pathological; pathology.

PATO Pacific-Asian Treaty Organization.

PAU *or* **P.A.U.** Pan American Union.

PAYE *or* **P.A.Y.E.** 1. pay as you earn. 2. pay as you enter.

payt. payment.

P.B. passbook.

PBGC Pension Benefit Guaranty Corporation.

PBS Public Broadcasting Service.

PBX *also* **P.B.X.** Private Branch Exchange.

PC 1. personal computer. 2. politically correct.

p.c. 1. per cent. 2. *also* **p/c** *or* **P/C** petty cash. 3. postcard. 4. *Lat.* post cibum (after meals).

p/c *or* **P/C** prices current.

PCB printed circuit board.

PCP phencyclidine.

pct. percent.

PD interpupillary distance.

p.d. *or* **P.D.** per diem.

P.D. 1. Police Department. 2. postal district. 3. potential difference.

PDT Pacific Daylight Time.

pe *also* **p.e.** printer's error.

PE Prince Edward Island.

P.E. 1. physical education. 2. *Statistics.* probable error. 3. professional engineer.

P/E price/earnings.

P.E.I. Prince Edward Island.

pen. *or* **Pen.** peninsula.

per. 1. period. 2. person.

perf. 1. perfect. 2. perforated.

perm. permanent.

perp. perpendicular.

pers. 1. person. 2. personal.

Pers. Persia; Persian.

PERT program evaluation and review technique.

pert. pertaining.

pet. petroleum.

petrog. petrography.

petrol. petrology.

Pfc *or* **Pfc.** *or* **PFC** private first class.

pfd. preferred.

pg. page.

Pg. Portugal; Portuguese.

P.G. 1. paying guest. 2. postgraduate.

PGA Professional Golfers' Association.

pH hydrogen ion concentration.

PH *also* **P.H.** 1. Public Health. 2. Purple Heart.

ph. phase.

PHA Public Housing Administration.

Phar.B. *Lat.* Pharmaciae Baccalaureus (Bachelor of Pharmacy).

Phar.D. *Lat.* Pharmaciae Doctor (Doctor of Pharmacy).

pharm. *or* **Pharm.** pharmaceutical; pharmacist; pharmacopoeia; pharmacy.

Phar.M. *Lat.* Pharmaciae Magister (Master of Pharmacy).

Ph.B. *Lat.* Philosophiae Baccalaureus (Bachelor of Philosophy).

Ph.D. *Lat.* Philosophiae Doctor (Doctor of Philosophy).

phil. philosopher; philosophical; philosophy.

Phil. Philippines.

Phil. I. *or* **Phil. Is.** Philippine Islands.

philol. philology.

philos. philosopher; philosophical; philosophy.

Ph.M. *Lat.* Philosophiae Magister (Master of Philosophy).

PHN public health nurse.

phon. 1. phonetic; phonetics. 2. phonology.

photog. photography.

phr. phrase.

PHS Public Health Service.

phys. 1. physical. 2. physician. 3. physicist. 4. physiology.

physiol. physiological; physiology.

PIN personal identification number.

pizz. *Mus.* pizzicato.

PK psychokinesis.

pk. 1. pack. 2. park. 3. peak. 4. *or* **pk** peck.

pkg. *or* **pkge.** package.

pkt. packet.

PKU phenylketonuria.

pkwy. parkway.

pl. 1. *or* **Pl.** place. 2. plural.

plat. 1. plateau. 2. platform. 3. platoon.

plf. plaintiff.

pln. plain.

PLO Palestine Liberation Organization.

PLSS portable life support system.

PM *or* **P.M.** 1. postmaster. 2. provost marshal.

pm. premium.

p.m. *also* **P.M.** post mortem.

P.M. 1. *also* **p.m.** post meridiem. — Usu. used in small capitals <P.M.> 2. Prime Minister.

P.M.G. postmaster general.

pmk. postmark.

PMS premenstrual syndrome.

pmt. payment.

p.n. *or* **P/N** promissory note.

pneum. pneumatic; pneumatics.

p.n.g. persona non grata.

PO *or* **P.O.** 1. Personnel Officer. 2. postal order. 3. post office.

POE *or* **P.O.E.** 1. port of embarkation. 2. port of entry.

poet. poetic; poetical; poetry.

Pol. Poland; Polish.

polit. political; politics.

pop. 1. popular. 2. population.

Port. Portugal; Portuguese.

POS point-of-sale.

pos. 1. position. 2. positive.

poss. 1. possession. 2. possessive. 3. possible; possibly.

pot. potential.

POW *or* **P.O.W.** prisoner of war.

pp *or* **pp.** *Mus.* pianissimo.

pp. 1. pages. 2. past participle.

p.p. *or* **P.P.** 1. parcel post. 2. past participle. 3. postpaid.

ppb parts per billion.

PPC plain paper copier.

ppd. 1. postpaid. 2. prepaid.

pph. pamphlet.

ppm 1. pages per minute. 2. parts per million.

P.P.S. *also* **p.p.s.** *Lat.* post postscriptum (additional postscript).

ppt 1. parts per thousand. 2. parts per trillion.

ppt. precipitate.

pptn. precipitation.

p.q. previous question.

P.Q. *or* **PQ** Province of Quebec.

PR *or* **P.R.** 1. public relations. 2. Puerto Rico.

pr. 1. pair. 2. present. 3. price. 4. printing. 5. pronoun.

pred. predicate.

pref. 1. preface; prefatory. 2. preference; preferred. 3. prefix.

prem. premium.

prep. 1. preparation; preparatory; prepare. 2. preposition.

prepd. prepared.

prepn. preparation.

pres. 1. present. 2. president.

Pres. President.

PRF 1. pulse recurrence frequency. 2. pulse repetition frequency.

prf. proof.

prim. 1. primary. 2. primitive.

prin. 1. principal. 2. principle.

print. printing.

priv. 1. private. 2. privative.

p.r.n. *Lat.* pro re nata (*Med.* as the situation demands).

PRO *also* **P.R.O.** public relations officer.

prob. 1. probable; probably. 2. problem.

proc. 1. proceedings. 2. process.

prod. 1. produce. 2. produced. 3. product; production.

prof. 1. professional. 2. *also* **Prof.** professor.

prom. promontory.

pron. 1. pronominal; pronoun. 2. pronounced; pronunciation.

prop. 1. proper. 2. property. 3. proposition. 4. proprietary.

propr. proprietor.

pros. prosody.

Pros. Atty. prosecuting attorney.

protec. protectorate.

prov. 1. province; provincial. 2. provisional. 3. provost.

Prov. 1. Provençal.

P.S. 1. permanent secretary. 2. Police Sergeant. 3. *also* **p.s.** postscript. 4. public school.

PSAT Preliminary Scholastic Aptitude Test.

pseud. pseudonym.

psf pounds per square foot.

psi pounds per square inch.

PSRO Professional Standards Review Organization.

PST Pacific Standard Time.

psych. *or* **psychol.** psychological; psychologist; psychology.

pt. 1. part. 2. payment. 3. pint. 4. point. 5. port. 6. preterit.

p.t. *Lat.* pro tempore (temporarily).

P.T. 1. *also* **PT** Pacific Time. 2. physical therapy. 3. physical training. 4. postal telegraph.

PTA Parent Teacher Association.

ptg. printing.

PTO 1. Parent Teacher Organization. 2. Patent and Trademark Office.

p.t.o. *or* **PTO** please turn over.

PTV 1. pay television. 2. public television.

pty. proprietary.

pub. 1. public. 2. publication. 3. published; publisher.

PV polyvinyl.

PWA *also* **P.W.A.** Public Works Administration.

pwr. power.

pwt. pennyweight.

pxt. *Lat.* pinxit (he *or* she painted this).

pyro. pyrotechnics.

Q

q. 1. quart. 2. quarter. 3. quarterly. 4. query. 5. question. 6. quire.

Q.B. Queen's Bench.

QC 1. quality control. 2. quartermaster corps.

Q.E.D. *Lat.* quod erat demonstrandum (which was to be demonstrated).

Q.E.F. *Lat.* quod erat faciendum (which was to be done).

QF quick-firing.

q.i.d. *Lat.* quater in die (*Med.* four times a day).

ql. quintal.

Qld. Queensland.

qlty. quality.

Q.M. *Lat.* quaque mane (every morning).

qn. question.

q.p. *or* **q.pl.** *Lat.* quantum placet (as much as you please).

qq. questions.

qq.v. *Lat.* quae vide (which [things] see).

qr. 1. quarter. 2. quarterly. 3. quire.

q.s. *Lat.* quantum sufficit (as much as suffices).

QSO *Astron.* quasi-stellar object.

QSRS *Astron.* quasi-stellar radio source.

QSTOL quiet short takeoff and landing.

qt *or* **qt.** quart.

qt. quantity.

qto. quarto.

qty. quantity.

quad. 1. quadrangle. 2. quadrant.

qual. qualitative.

quant. quantitative.

quar. 1. quarter. 2. quarterly.

Que. Quebec.

ques. question.

quot. quotation.

q.v. *Lat.* quod vide (which see).

qy. query.

R

r 1. *or* **R** radius. 2. *or* **R** *Elect.* resistance.

R roentgen (unit of radiation).

r. 1. *or* **R.** railroad; railway. 2. range. 3. rare. 4. retired. 5. *or* **R.** right. 6. *or* **R.** river. 7. *or* **R.** road. 8. rod (unit of length).

R. Republican.

R.A. 1. *or* **RA** Regular Army. 2. *Astron.* right ascension.

rad. 1. radical. 2. radio. 3. radius. 4. radix.

RADM rear admiral.

RAM *Computer Sci.* random-access memory.

R & B rhythm and blues.

R & D research and development.

R and R rest and recreation.

RBC *or* **rbc** red blood cell; red blood (cell) count.

RBE *Physics.* relative biological effectiveness.

rbi *also* **r.b.i.** run batted in.

RC Red Cross.

RCAF *also* **R.C.A.F.** Royal Canadian Air Force.

RCMP *also* **R.C.M.P.** Royal Canadian Mounted Police.

rcpt. receipt.

rct. recruit.

rd rod (unit of length).

RD 1. registered dietician. **2.** rural delivery.

rd. 1. *or* **Rd.** road. **2.** round.

RDA recommended daily allowance.

RDF radio direction finder.

R.E. *or* **RE** real estate.

rec. 1. receipt. **2.** record; recording. **3.** recreation.

recd. *or* **rec'd.** received.

recip. reciprocal; reciprocity.

rect. 1. receipt. **2.** rectangle; rectangular. **3.** rectified.

red. reduced; reduction.

ref. 1. referee. **2.** reference. **3.** referred. **4.** refining. **5.** reformation; reformed. **6.** refunding.

refl. 1. reflection; reflective. **2.** reflex; reflexive.

reg. 1. regent. **2.** regiment. **3.** region. **4.** register; registered. **5.** registrar. **6.** registry. **7.** regular; regularly. **8.** regulation. **9.** regulator.

regd. registered.

rel. 1. relating. **2.** relative. **3.** released. **4.** religion; religious.

rem. remittance.

rep. 1. repair. **2.** repetition. **3.** report. **4.** reporter. **5.** *or* **Rep.** representative. **6.** reprint. **7.** *or* **Rep.** republic.

Rep. Republican.

r.e.p. roentgen equivalent, physical.

repl. replace; replacement.

repr. representing.

rept. report.

req. 1. require; required. **2.** requisition.

RES reticuloendothelial system.

res. 1. research. **2.** reserve. **3.** residence; resident; resides. **4.** resolution.

Res. 1. Reservation. **2.** Reservoir.

resp. 1. respective; respectively. **2.** respiration.

ret. 1. retain. **2.** retired. **3.** return.

rev. 1. revenue. **2.** reverse; reversed. **3.** review; reviewed. **4.** revise; revision. **5.** *or* **Rev.** revolution.

RF radio frequency.

rf. 1. reef. **2.** refund.

r.f. right field; right fielder.

RFD *also* **R.F.D.** rural free delivery.

RGB red-green-blue.

r.h. 1. relative humidity. **2.** *also* **RH** right hand.

rhbdr. rhombohedron.

rheo. rheostat.

rhet. rhetoric.

R.H.I.P. rank has its privileges.

rhomb. rhombic.

rhp *or* **r.hp.** rated horsepower.

RI Rhode Island.

R.I.P. *Lat.* requiescat in pace (may she *or* he rest in peace).

rit. *Mus.* ritardando.

riv. river.

RJ road junction.

R.L.T. registered laboratory technologist.

rm. 1. ream. 2. room.

rms root mean square.

RMS Railway Mail Service.

RN *or* **R.N.** registered nurse.

RNA ribonucleic acid.

rnd. round.

ro. rood (measure).

ROG receipt of goods.

rom *also* **rom.** roman (type).

ROM *Computer Sci.* read-only memory.

Rom. 1. Roman. 2. Romance (language). 3. Romania; Romanian.

rot. rotating; rotation.

ROTC Reserve Officers' Training Corps.

R.Ph. registered pharmacist.

rpm *or* **r.p.m.** revolutions per minute.

R.P.O. Railway Post Office.

RPQ request for price quotation.

rps *or* **r.p.s.** revolutions per second.

rpt. 1. repeat. 2. report.

R.Q. respiratory quotient.

RR *also* **R.R.** 1. railroad. 2. rural route.

R.R.A. registered records administrator.

RRB Railroad Retirement Board.

rRNA ribosomal RNA.

RS 1. recording secretary. 2. right side.

R.S.V.P. *or* **r.s.v.p.** *French.* répondez s'il vous plaît (please reply).

RT 1. radio telephone. 2. room temperature.

rt. right.

RTC Resolution Trust Corporation.

rte. route.

Rus. *or* **Russ.** Russia; Russian.

RV *or* **R.V.** 1. recreational vehicle. 2. *Aerospace.* reentry vehicle.

Rw. Rwanda.

rwy. *or* **ry.** railway.

S

s 1. second (unit of time). 2. second of arc. 3. stere.

S 1. *Bible.* Samuel. 2. siemens. 3. *also* **S.** *or* **s** *or* **s.** south; southern. 4. specialist.

s. 1. *or* **S.** school. 2. *or* **S.** sea. 3. see. 4. semi-. 5. shilling. 6. singular. 7. sire. 8. sister. 9. small. 10. *or* **S.** society. 11. solo. 12. son. 13. *or* **S.** soprano. 14. sou. 15. stock. 16. substantive. 17. surplus.

S. 1. Saturday. 2. Saxon. 3. September. 4. *Med.* signature. 5. signor; signore. 6. Sunday.

SA Salvation Army.

s.a. *Lat.* sine anno (without date).

S.A. 1. South Africa. 2. South America.

Sab. Sabbath.

SAC Strategic Air Command.

SACEUR Supreme Allied Commander, Europe.

S.Afr. South Africa.

Sal. El Salvador.

SALT Strategic Arms Limitations Talks.

SAM 1. sequential-access method. 2. surface-to-air-missile.

s. ap. apothecaries' scruple.

SASE self-addressed stamped envelope.

sat. saturate; saturation.

Sat. Saturday.

satd. saturated.

Sau. Ar. Saudi Arabia.

Sax. Saxon; Saxony.

SB simultaneous broadcast.

sb. substantive.

S.B. *Lat.* Scientiae Baccalaureus (Bachelor of Science).

SBA Small Business Administration.

SBN Standard Book Number.

SC 1. Security Council. 2. South Carolina.

sc. 1. scale. 2. scene. 3. science. 4. *Lat.* scilicet (namely). 5. scruple (weight).

Sc. Scotch; Scottish.

s.c. *also* **sc** small capitals.

S.C. Supreme Court.

Scand. Scandinavia; Scandinavian.

SCAP Supreme Commander for the Allied Powers.

SCC storage connecting circuit.

sch. school.

sci. science; scientific.

SCORE Service Corps of Retired Executives.

Scot. Scotch; Scotland; Scottish.

scr. scruple (unit of weight).

sct. scout.

sctd. scattered.

sculp. 1. *or* **sculpt** *Lat.* sculpsit (she *or* he sculptured [it]). 2. sculptor; sculptress; sculpture.

SD 1. sight draft. 2. South Dakota. 3. special delivery. 4. standard deviation.

sd. sound.

s.d. *Lat.* sine die (indefinitely).

SE 1. southeast; southeastern. 2. standard English. 3. stock exchange. 4. systems engineer.

SEATO Southeast Asia Treaty Organization.

sec 1. secant. 2. second. 3. secondary.

SEC Securities and Exchange Commission.

sec. 1. secretary. 2. sector. 3. *Lat.* secundum (according to).

sect. section.

secy. secretary.

sed. sediment.

sed rate erythrocyte sedimentation rate.

sel. select; selected.

SEM scanning electron microscope.

sen. or **Sen. 1.** senate; senator. **2.** senior.

sep. separate; separation.

Sep. September.

sepd. separated.

Sept. September.

seq. 1. sequel. **2.** *Lat.* sequens (the following).

seqq. *Lat.* sequentia (the following [things]).

ser. 1. serial. **2.** series. **3.** sermon.

Serb. Serbia; Serbian.

serv. 1. servant. **2.** service.

SES socioeconomic status.

sess. session.

SF science fiction.

sfz. *Mus.* sforzando.

sg specific gravity.

SG surgeon general.

S.G. or **SG** solicitor general.

sgd. signed.

sh. 1. share. **2.** sheet.

Shak. Shakespeare.

SHAPE Supreme Headquarters Allied Powers, Europe.

shf or **SHF** superhigh frequency.

shpt. shipment.

shr. share.

shtg. shortage.

SI *French.* Système Internationale d'Unités (International System of Units).

Sib. Siberia; Siberian.

Sic. Sicilian; Sicily.

SIDS sudden infant death syndrome.

sig. 1. signal. **2.** signature. **3.** or **Sig.** signor; signore.

sing. singular.

SINS ships inertial navigational system.

SJC supreme judicial court.

S.J.D. *Lat.* Scientiae Juridicae Doctor (Doctor of Juridical Science).

SK Saskatchewan.

sk. sack.

Skr. or **Skt.** Sanskrit.

SL 1. sea level **2.** south latitude.

sl. slightly.

S.L. Sierra Leone.

s.l.a.n. *Lat.* sine loco, anno, vel nomine (without place, year, or name).

Slav. Slavic.

SLBM submarine-launched ballistic missile.

sld. 1. sailed. **2.** sealed. **3.** sold.

SLIP symmetric list processor.

SLV standard launch vehicle.

sm. small.

S.M. Scientiae Major (Master of Science).

s.n. *Lat.* sine nomine (without name).

SNG synthetic natural gas.

so. or **So.** south; southern.

s.o. 1. seller's option. **2.** strikeout.

soc. 1. social. **2.** socialist. **3.** society.

SOF sound on film.

sol. 1. solicitor. **2.** soluble.

Sol. Is. Solomon Islands.

soln. solution.

Som. Somalia.

SOP standard operating procedure.

sop. soprano.

soph. sophomore.

sou. *or* **Sou.** south; southern.

SP self-propelled.

sp. 1. special. 2. specialist. 3. species. 4. specific. 5. spelling.

Sp. Spain; Spanish.

s.p. *Lat.* sine prole (without issue).

SPCA Society for the Prevention of Cruelty to Animals.

SPCC Society for the Prevention of Cruelty to Children.

spec. 1. special. 2. specification. 3. speculation.

specif. specifically.

SPF sun protection factor.

sp gr specific gravity.

sp ht specific heat.

SPOT satellite positioning and tracking.

spp. species (plural).

SPQR small profits, quick returns.

S.P.Q.R. *Lat.* Senatus Populusque Romanus (the Senate and the People of Rome).

spr. spring.

s.p.s. *Lat.* sine prole supersite (without surviving issue).

spt. seaport.

sq. square.

Sr. 1. *or* **sr.** senior. 2. señor.

SRO 1. single-room occupancy. 2. standing room only.

Srta. señorita.

ss. *Lat.* 1. *or* **ss** scilicet (namely). 2. semis (one half).

S.S. 1. *or* **SS** steamship. 2. sworn statement.

s/s same size.

SSA Social Security Administration.

SSE south-southeast.

SSI Supplemental Security Income.

ssp. subspecies.

SSS Selective Service System.

SST supersonic transport.

SSW south-southwest.

ST standard time.

st. 1. stanza. 2. start. 3. state. 4. *or* **St.** statute. 5. stet. 6. stitch. 7. stone. 8. *or* **St.** strait. 9. *or* **St.** street. 10. strophe.

s.t. short ton.

sta. 1. station. 2. stationary.

stat. 1. *Lat.* statim (immediately). 2. stationary. 3. statistics. 4. statute.

stbd. starboard.

STD sexually transmitted disease.

std. standard.

Ste. *French.* sainte (feminine form of saint).

steno *or* **stenog.** *also* **sten.** stenographer; stenography.

St. Ex. stock exchange.

stge. storage.

stip. 1. stipend. 2. stipulation.
stk. stock.
STOL short takeoff and landing.
STP standard temperature and pressure.
STR synchronous transmitter receiver.
str. 1. steamer. 2. *or* **Str.** strait.
stud. student.
sub. 1. subaltern. 2. substitute.
subj. 1. subject. 2. subjective. 3. subjunctive.
subs. subscription.
subst. substantive.
Sud. Sudan.
suf. *or* **suff.** 1. sufficient. 2. suffix.
Sun. Sunday.
sup. 1. superior. 2. superlative (in grammar). 3. supine (in Latin). 4. supplement. 5. supply. 6. *Lat.* supra (above).
super. 1. superintendent.
supp. *or* **suppl.** supplement; supplementary.
supt. *or* **Supt.** superintendent.
supvr. supervisor.
sur. 1. surface. 2. surplus.
Sur. Surinam.
surg. surgeon; surgery; surgical.
surr. surrender.
s.v. 1. *also* **SV** sailing vessel. 2. *Lat.* sub verbo; sub voce ([look] under the word).
svgs. savings.
sw short wave.
SW southwest.
Sw. Sweden; Swedish.

SWAT *also* **S.W.A.T.** Special Weapons and Tactics Team.
Swaz. Swaziland.
swbd *or* **swbd.** switchboard.
Swe. *or* **Swed.** Sweden; Swedish.
Switz. Switzerland.
sym. 1. symbol. 2. symmetric. 3. symphony.
syn. synonym; synonymy.
synd. syndicate.
Syr. 1. Syria; Syrian. 2. Syriac.

T

t 1. ton. 2. troy (system of weights).
T 1. surface tension. 2. temperature. 3. *Physics.* tera-. 4. tesla.
t. 1. tare (weight). 2. teaspoonful; teaspoons. 3. tempo. 4. *Lat.* tempore (in the time of). 5. *or* **T.** *Mus.* tenor. 6. *Gram.* tense. 7. terminal. 8. *or* **T.** territory. 9. *or* **T.** time. 10. *or* **T.** town. 11. transit. 12. *Gram.* transitive.
T. 1. tablespoon; tablespoonful. 2. Tuesday.
TA teaching assistant.
tab. table.
TAC Tactical Air Command.
tan tangent.
Tan. Tanzania.
TAS 1. telephone answering system. 2. true air speed.
Tas. *or* **Tasm.** Tasmania; Tasmanian.

TAT Thematic Apperception Test.

TB *also* **T.B.** tuberculosis.

t.b. trial balance.

TBA *or* **tba** to be announced.

tbs. *or* **tbsp.** tablespoon; tablespoonful.

tchr. teacher.

TD 1. *also* **td** touchdown. 2. *also* **T.D.** treasury department.

TDN total digestible nutrients.

tech. technical.

technol. technology.

TEFL teaching English as a foreign language.

tel. 1. telegram. 2. telegraph; telegraphic. 3. telephone.

teleg. 1. telegram. 2. telegraph; telegraphic; telegraphy.

temp. 1. temperance. 2. temperature. 3. template. 4. temporary. 5. *Lat.* tempore (in the time of).

ten. 1. tenor. 2. *Mus.* tenuto.

term. 1. terminal. 2. termination.

terr. 1. terrace. 2. territory.

TESL teaching English as a second language.

TESOL teachers of English to speakers of other languages.

test. 1. testator. 2. testatrix. 3. testimony.

Teut. Teuton; Teutonic.

tfr. transfer.

TG transformational grammar.

t.g. type genus.

TGIF thank God it's Friday.

Th. Thursday.

Thai. Thailand.

THC tetrahydrocannabinol.

Th.D. *Lat.* Theologiae Doctor (Doctor of Theology).

theat. theater.

theol. theologian; theology.

therap. therapeutic; therapeutics.

THF tremendously high frequency.

Th.M. *Lat.* Theologiae Magister (Master of Theology).

thp *or* **t.hp.** thrust horsepower.

Thurs. *also* **Thur.** Thursday.

t.i.d. *Lat.* ter in die (*Med.* three times a day).

tit. title.

tk. truck.

TKO technical knockout.

tkt. ticket.

t.l. *or* **t/l** total loss.

TLC tender loving care.

t.l.o. total loss only.

tlr. tailor.

TM 1. trademark. 2. transcendental meditation.

t.m. true mean.

TMJ temporomandibular joint.

TMV tobacco mosaic virus.

TN Tennessee.

tn. 1. ton. 2. town. 3. train.

tng. training.

TNT trinitrotoluene.

t.o. turn over.

topog. topographic; topography.

tp. township.

t.p. title page.

TPI *Computer Sci.* tracks per inch.

tpk. turnpike.

TQC total quality control.

TR or **T-R** transmit-receive.

tr 1. *Gram.* transitive. 2. translated; translation; translator. 3. transpose; transposition. 4. treasurer. 5. *Law.* trust; trustee.

trans. 1. transaction. 2. *Gram.* transitive. 3. transportation. 4. transpose; transposition. 5. transverse.

transl. translated; translation.

transp. transportation.

trav. traveler; travels.

treas. treasurer; treasury.

trib. tributary.

trig. *also* **trigon.** trigonometry.

tripl. triplicate.

tRNA transfer RNA.

trop. tropic; tropical.

TSH thyroid-stimulating hormone.

tsp. teaspoon; teaspoonful.

TSS toxic shock syndrome.

TT 1. telegraphic transfer. 2. teletypewriter. 3. transit time. 4. tuberculin tested.

Tu. Tuesday.

T.U. trade union.

Tues. Tuesday.

Tun. Tunisia; Tunisian.

Tur. or **Turk.** Turkey; Turkish.

TVA Tennessee Valley Authority.

twp. township.

TX Texas.

txn. taxation.

typ. typographer; typography.

typo. or **typog.** typographer; typographical; typography.

typw. typewriter; typewritten.

U

U *Math.* union.

u. 1. *or* **U.** uncle. 2. unit. 3. *or* **U.** upper.

U.A.E. United Arab Emirates.

U.A.R. United Arab Republic.

u.c. *also* **UC** upper case.

UCMJ Uniform Code of Military Justice.

UCS universal character set.

UDC universal decimal classification.

Ug. Uganda.

UGT urgent (telegram).

uhf or **UHF** ultrahigh frequency.

U.K. United Kingdom.

ULF ultra low frequency.

ult. 1. ultimate; ultimately. 2. ultimo.

UN *or* **U.N.** United Nations.

unan. unanimous.

unb. *or* **unbd.** unbound.

UNESCO United Nations Educational, Scientific, and Cultural Organization.

UNICEF United Nations International Children's Emergency Fund.

univ. 1. universal. 2. *or* **Univ.** university.

unm. unmarried.

unp. unpaged.

UNRRA United Nations Relief and Rehabilitation Administration.

UNRWA United Nations Relief and Works Agency.

UPC Universal Product Code.

UPI *or* **U.P.I.** United Press International.

UPU Universal Postal Union.

Ur. Uruguay.

URA Urban Renewal Administration.

US *or* **U.S.** United States.

u.s. *Lat.* 1. ubi supra (where [mentioned] above). 2. ut supra (as above).

U.S. 1. Uncle Sam. 2. Uniform System (of lens aperture).

USA 1. United States Army. 2. United States of America.

USAF United States Air Force.

USAFA United States Air Force Academy.

USAFI United States Armed Forces Institute.

USAR United States Army Reserve.

USAREUR United States Army, Europe.

USASCII United States of America Standard Code for Information Interchange.

U.S.C. United States Code.

USCG United States Coast Guard.

USCGA United States Coast Guard Academy.

USDA United States Department of Agriculture.

USES United States Employment Service.

USIA United States Information Agency.

USITC United States International Trade Commission.

U.S.M. United States Mail.

USMA United States Military Academy.

USMC United States Marine Corps.

USN United States Navy.

USNA United States Naval Academy.

USNR United States Naval Reserve.

USO United Service Organizations.

U.S.P. United States Pharmacopoeia.

USPO United States Post Office.

USPS United States Postal Service.

U.S.S. 1. United States Senate. 2. *also* **USS** United States Ship.

USSR *or* **U.S.S.R.** Union of Soviet Socialist Republics.

usu. usually.

usw. *German.* und so weiter (and so forth).

UT 1. Universal time. 2. Utah.

ut dict. *Lat.* ut dictum (*Med.* as directed).

UV ultraviolet.

UW underwriter.

ux. *Lat.* uxor (wife).

V

V 1. *Physics.* velocity. 2. victory. 3. *Elect.* volt. 4. volume.

v. 1. verb. 2. verse. 3. version. 4. verso. 5. versus. 6. vide. 7. *or* **V.** village. 8. violin. 9. voice. 10. volume (book). 11. vowel.

V. 1. venerable (in titles). 2. viscount; viscountess.

VA Virginia.

VA Veterans' Administration.

VAB voice answer back.

vac. vacuum.

val. 1. valley. 2. valuation; value.

VAR visual-aural range.

var. 1. variable. 2. variant. 3. variation. 4. variety. 5. various.

VAT value-added tax.

V.C. 1. vice chairman. 2. vice chancellor. 3. vice consul.

VD *also* **V.D.** venereal disease.

v.d. 1. vapor density. 2. various dates.

VDT 1. video display terminal. 2. visual display terminal.

VDU visual display unit.

veg. vegetable.

vel. 1. vellum. 2. velocity.

Venez. Venezuela.

ver. 1. verse. 2. version.

vert. vertical.

vet. 1. veteran. 2. veterinarian.

veter. veterinary.

V.F. *also* **VF** 1. video frequency. 2. visual field.

VFD volunteer fire department.

VFR visual flight rules.

VGA Video Graphics Array.

vhf *or* **VHF** very high frequency.

VI *or* **V.I.** Virgin Islands.

v.i. *Lat.* vide infra (see below).

V.I. volume indicator.

vic. vicinity.

Viet. Vietnam; Vietnamese.

VIN vehicle identification number.

vis. 1. visibility. 2. visual.

VISTA Volunteers in Service to America.

viz. *Lat.* videlicet (namely).

vlf *or* **VLF** very low frequency.

V.M.D. *Lat.* Veterinariae Medicinae Doctor (Doctor of Veterinary Medicine).

VN visiting nurse.

VNR video news release.

VO verbal order.

vo. verso.

VOA Voice of America.

voc. vocative.

vocab. vocabulary.

vol. 1. volcano. 2. volume. 3. volunteer.

VOR 1. very-high-frequency omnidirectional radio range. 2. voice-operated relay.

vou. voucher.

VP 1. variable pitch. 2. verb phrase. 3. *or* **V.P.** vice president.

vs. versus.

v.s. *Lat.* vide supra (see above).

V.S. veterinary surgeon.

vss. 1. verses. 2. versions.

VT 1. vacuum tube. 2. variable time. 3. Vermont.
VTR videotape recorder; videotape recording.
VU volume unit.
vulg. vulgar.
v.v. vice versa.

W

w *or* **W** *Physics.* work.
W 1. *Elect.* watt. 2. *also* **W.** *or* **w** *or* **w.** west; western.
w. 1. week. 2. weight. 3. wide. 4. width. 5. wife. 6. with.
W. 1. Wednesday. 2. Welsh.
WA 1. Washington. 2. with average.
W.A. Western Australia.
war. warrant.
WAT weight, altitude, and temperature.
WATS Wide-Area Telecommunications Service.
w.b. 1. water ballast. 2. *also* **W.B.** waybill. 3. westbound.
W.B. Weather Bureau.
WBC *or* **wbc** white blood cell; white blood (cell) count.
w.c. 1. water closet. 2. without charge.
wd. 1. wood. 2. word.
Wed. Wednesday.
WEE western equine encephalitis.
wf *or* **w.f.** wrong font.
w.g. wire gauge.

wh. 1. which. 2. white.
whf. wharf.
WHO World Health Organization.
W-hr watt-hour.
whs. warehouse.
whsle. wholesale.
WI Wisconsin.
w.i. when issued (financial stock).
W.I. West Indian; West Indies.
WIA wounded in action.
wid widow; widower.
wk. 1. weak. 2. week. 3. work.
wkly. weekly.
WL *or* **w.l.** 1. water line. 2. wavelength.
wmk. watermark.
WNW west-northwest.
w/o without.
w.o.c. without compensation.
WP 1. weather permitting. 2. word processing; word processor. 3. *or* **w/p** without prejudice.
WPA Work Projects Administration.
WPC watts per candle.
wpm *or* **w.p.m.** words per minute.
wpn. weapon.
WPS word processing secretary.
WR *or* **W.r.** Wassermann reaction.
WS working storage.
WSW west-southwest.
WT withholding tax.
wt. weight.
WV West Virginia.
WVS Women's Volunteer Service.

WW I *or* **W.W.I** World War I.
WW II *or* **W.W.II** World War II.
w/w wall-to-wall.
WY Wyoming.

XYZ

x 1. *Math.* abscissa. **2.** broken type. **3.** by. **4.** *or* **X** power of magnification. **5.** *or* **X** *Math.* **a.** Unknown number. **b.** algebraic variable.

X 1. Christ; Christian. **2.** extra. **3.** times (multiplied by). **4.** *also* **x** unknown. **5.** — Used to indicate location, as on a map.

x. ex.

XD *or* **x-div.** ex dividend.

XI *or* **x-int.** ex interest.

XL 1. extra large. **2.** extra long.

XS 1. extra short. **2.** extra small.

y *Math.* ordinate.

Y 1. *Elect.* admittance. **2. a.** YMCA **b.** YMHA **c.** YWCA **d.** YWHA.

y. year.

YA young adult.

YB yearbook.

yd yard (measurement).

yel. yellow.

Yem. Yemen.

yeo. yeoman; yeomanry.

YMCA Young Men's Christian Association.

YMHA Young Men's Hebrew Association.

YOB year of birth.

yr. 1. year. **2.** younger. **3.** your.

YT *or* **Y.T.** Yukon Territory.

Yugo. Yugoslavia; Yugoslavian.

YWCA Young Women's Christian Association.

YWHA Young Women's Hebrew Association.

Z atomic number.

z. 1. zero. **2.** zone.

z.B. *German.* zum Beispiel (for example).

zool. zoological; zoology.

ZPG zero population growth.

INDEX